WIPO
Patent Drafting
manual

Second edition

This work is licensed under the Creative Commons Attribution 4.0 International.

The user is allowed to reproduce, distribute, adapt, translate and publicly perform this publication, including for commercial purposes, without explicit permission, provided that the content is accompanied by an acknowledgement that WIPO is the source and that it is clearly indicated if changes were made to the original content.

Suggested citation: WIPO (2022), *WIPO Patent Drafting Manual, 2nd edition*. Geneva: WIPO.

Adaptation/translation/derivatives should not carry any official emblem or logo, unless they have been approved and validated by WIPO. Please contact us via the WIPO website to obtain permission.

For any derivative work, please include the following disclaimer: "The Secretariat of WIPO assumes no liability or responsibility with regard to the transformation or translation of the original content."

When content published by WIPO, such as images, graphics, trademarks or logos, is attributed to a third-party, the user of such content is solely responsible for clearing the rights with the right holder(s).

To view a copy of this license, please visit
https://creativecommons.org/licenses/by/4.0

Any dispute arising under this license that cannot be settled amicably shall be referred to arbitration in accordance with Arbitration Rules of the United Nations Commission on International Trade Law (UNCITRAL) then in force. The parties shall be bound by any arbitration award rendered as a result of such arbitration as the final adjudication of such a dispute.

The designations employed and the presentation of material throughout this publication do not imply the expression of any opinion whatsoever on the part of WIPO concerning the legal status of any country, territory or area or of its authorities, or concerning the delimitation of its frontiers or boundaries.

This publication is not intended to reflect the views of the Member States or the WIPO Secretariat.

© WIPO, 2022

First edition published 2007
Second edition published 2022

World Intellectual Property Organization
34, chemin des Colombettes, P.O. Box 18
CH-1211 Geneva 20, Switzerland

DOI: 10.34667/tind.44657
ISBN: 978-92-805-3264-7

 Attribution 4.0 International (CC BY 4.0)

Photo credits: Getty Images

Table of contents

Foreword	**6**
Acknowledgments	**7**

Module I
Intellectual property: an
introduction   **8**

1. Intellectual property types	**9**
2. More patent basics	**9**

Module II
Patents   **11**

1. Detailed overview of patents	**12**
1.1 What is a patent?	12
1.2 What can be the subject of a patent?	13
1.3 Why are patents important?	16
2. Legal requirements for patentability	**18**
2.1 Novelty	18
2.2 Inventive step/nonobviousness	19
2.3 Industrial application/utility	21
2.4 Patentable subject matter	22
2.5 Disclosure requirement	23

Module III
Patent application preparation   **27**

1. Preparing patent applications	**28**
1.1 Obtaining invention disclosures from inventors	30
1.2 Identifying patentable inventions	31
1.3 Understanding the invention (core inventive concept)	32
1.4 Inventorship	32
2. Typical parts of the patent application	**33**
2.1 Request	33
2.2 Description	33
2.3 Claims	33
2.4 Drawings	34
2.5 Abstract	34
2.6 Application format	34

Module IV
Fundamentals of claim drafting   **35**

1. Theory of the patent claim	**36**
1.1 Overview: inventions, embodiments and claims	36
1.2 Broad and narrow claims	37
1.3 Patent protection and infringement: all-elements rule	37
2. Patent claim format	**38**
2.1 Parts of a claim	38
2.2 Grammar of a claim and other detail	41
2.3 Two-part claims or improvement claims	44
2.4 Alternative elements and Markush claims	45
2.5 Functional elements and means-plus-function claims	47
3. Claim sets	**48**
3.1 Independent claims	48
3.2 Dependent claims	50
3.3 Multiple dependent claims	53
3.4 Claims referring to features of another claim	56
3.5 Claim sets based on set theory	57
3.6 Schematic example of drafting a set of claims	60

Module V
Types of claim   **66**

1. Basic types of claim	**67**
1.1 Product claims	67
1.2 Process (or method) claims	68
1.3 Preamble with the purposive expression "for"	68
2. Specific types of claim	**69**
2.1 Product-by-process claims	69
2.2 Parameter claims	70
2.3 General use claims	71
2.4 Medical indication claims	71
2.5 Composition claims	73
2.6 Biotechnology claims	73
2.7 Computer-implemented invention claims	74

Module VI
Patent claim design — 76

1. **Prepare the claims first** — 77

2. **Broad and narrow claims** — 77

3. **Clarity, claim word choice and inconsistencies** — 79
   3.1 Defining terms — 79
   3.2 Distinguishing elements — 80
   3.3 Relative terms — 80
   3.4 Uncertainty — 81
   3.5 "In" — 81
   3.6 Inconsistency — 82
   3.7 Putting this into practice — 82

4. **Claim variations and modifications of the invention** — 83

5. **Avoiding unnecessary limitations** — 84

6. **Negative limitations and disclaimers** — 84

7. **Claims and competing products** — 85

8. **Claims must overcome prior art** — 85

9. **Using multiple claim types for the same invention** — 85

10. **Ensuring that the description supports the claims** — 86

11. **Unity of invention** — 87

12. **Claim point of view** — 88

13. **Narrowing a patent claim during prosecution** — 91

14. **Exclusions from patentability** — 92

15. **Requirement for industrial applicability** — 93

16. **"Reading on" a patent claim** — 93

17. **Claim construction in the courts** — 93

Module VII
Drafting a description, drawings and an abstract — 96

1. **Key audiences of patent applications** — 97

2. **Order in which to draft a patent application** — 97

3. **Drafting parts of a description** — 98
   3.1 Title of invention — 98
   3.2 Technical field — 98
   3.3 Background art — 98
   3.4 Summary of invention — 100
   3.5 Brief description of drawings — 101
   3.6 Description of embodiments — 101

4. **Drafting drawings** — 105
   4.1 Types of drawing — 105
   4.2 Reference indicators — 105
   4.3 Level of detail — 106
   4.4 Drawings provided by the inventor — 106

5. **Drafting an abstract** — 106

Module VIII
Filing patent applications — 108

1. **Domestic/priority filings** — 110

2. **Foreign filings** — 110

3. **Patent office procedures and fees** — 112
   3.1 Patent office procedures — 112
   3.2 Fees and other cost considerations — 112

4. **Application filing procedures in specific jurisdictions** — 114
   4.1 Filing with the United States Patent and Trademark Office (USPTO) — 114
   4.2 Filing with the European Patent Office (EPO) — 115
   4.3 Filing under the Patent Cooperation Treaty (PCT) — 115

Module IX
Prosecuting patent
applications 120

1.	**Responding to office actions**	**121**
2.	**Drafting responses**	**122**
3.	**Amendments**	**123**
3.1	Principle and basic requirement	123
3.2	Determining original disclosure and new matter	123
3.3	Broadening claims and adding claims	124
4.	**Getting claims allowed**	**125**
4.1	Interview	125
4.2	Responding to a second office action	125
4.3	Final office action	126
4.4	Deadlines	126
4.5	Appeal	126
4.6	Divisional applications, continuation applications and continuation-in-part applications	127
5.	**Opposition proceedings**	**127**
6.	**Issuance of the patent**	**127**

Module X
Patent strategy 129

1.	**Offensive blocking patenting to mount attacks on competitors**	**131**
2.	**Defensive patenting to protect against infringement actions**	**132**
3.	**Design-around techniques**	**132**

Module XI
Organizing, educating and
motivating the technical team 134

1.	**Training management personnel and marketing personnel to understand the significance of patents and portfolio building**	**135**
2.	**Training scientists/technologists to understand what might be patentable and who might be a co-inventor, and to prepare invention disclosures**	**137**
3.	**Setting up an in-house patent review committee to periodically review invention disclosures and make patenting recommendations**	**138**
4.	**Inventor incentive programs to encourage inventors to invent and report**	**138**
5.	**Professional ethics**	**139**

Annexes 142

Annex A **Examples of databases**	**143**
Annex B **Example of an invention disclosure form**	**144**
Annex C **WIPO resources and tools**	**147**

Endnotes 148

Foreword

Innovation is a worldwide phenomenon, occurring in all parts of the globe and constantly improving our well-being and quality of life. Over the last decade, as shown in WIPO's *Global Innovation Index* (GII), innovation expenditures worldwide have been growing faster than GDP. In high-income countries, private sector funding drove much of this growth in innovation expenditure, while in middle- and low-income countries, the contribution of public funds in research and development expenditure, could be as high as 75 percent.

It is human nature to seek technical solutions whenever we encounter problems, whether in relation to daily life needs or a quest to explore outer space. Therefore, the growing number on filings of patent applications is an indicator of human inventiveness in very diverse technological fields.

The patent system offers inventors recognition for their creativity and the possibility of material reward for their inventions. At the same time, the obligatory publication of patents and patent applications facilitates the spread of new technical knowledge and the acceleration of innovation activities in society as a whole.

In reality, however, the potential benefits offered by the patent system have not been fully enjoyed by innovators in all parts of the world. While there may be many reasons for this, the opportunity to obtain the special skill set needed to draft a patent application that fully captures the potential of a new invention is a challenge in many countries.

Innovators need well-drafted patent applications if they want to secure the best possible protection for their inventions and reduce the risk of rejection of applications. For third parties, well-drafted patents are just as important: they are not only a valuable source of new knowledge, they show the clear demarcation of the scope of the patent protection, helping to avoid the inadvertent infringement of patent rights or to support a challenge to the validity of a patent. For patent offices, receiving applications that are well drafted enables more efficient handling of patent prosecution.

The first edition of the *WIPO Patent Drafting Manual* was published in 2007. It was designed to help inventors and their advisors to acquire the technical skills needed to prepare and file well-drafted patent applications. Since then, it has been valuable background reading material, supporting the successful delivery of training activities organized by WIPO. In addition, the manual has been widely used by other national and regional institutions in their patent drafting training activities.

WIPO offers training programs with different content and of varying lengths, catering to the needs of the targeted country and trainees. This extensive training experience has shown that patent drafting requires a combination of both theoretical knowledge and practical drafting skills. When participants have access to comprehensive background material that covers all aspects of patent drafting theory, training workshops can focus on hands-on drafting exercises. It is also clear that while the ability to draft proper claims is a core skill in the preparation of a patent application, the drafting of other parts of the application is equally important for the protection and disclosure of inventions.

The general intellectual property capacities and technology bases of many developing countries have evolved rapidly, so patent drafters need knowledge and skills suited to technical complexities and the demands of local innovators. There have also been important changes in national patent laws and practices in some countries in recent years.

This second edition of the *WIPO Patent Drafting Manual* has drawn from the lessons learned and has been adapted to today's users and their needs. In this new edition, the drafting of both claims and descriptions are explained in detail. Additional explanations and examples of claim formats that are typically used for chemical inventions (for example, Markush claims) or computer-implemented inventions are also included in the new edition. In order to improve the manual's readability, diagrams and charts that visualize the concept of patent claims have been added. In addition, since patent drafters often find it necessary to amend their applications during the patent examination phase, a new section dedicated to amendments of patent applications has been included. The order of the modules has also been rearranged so that the manual follows the process of preparing, drafting, filing and prosecuting patent applications in chronological order.

We trust that the second edition of the *WIPO Patent Drafting Manual* will be an effective tool for those studying or teaching patent drafting. It is hoped that the new edition will continue to assist Member States that wish to enhance, refine and expand their capacity to assist inventors in protecting their intellectual property through carefully drafted patent applications.

Marco M. Alemán
Assistant Director General
World Intellectual Property Organization

Acknowledgments

WIPO would like to express its great appreciation to Pascual Segura (Spain) and Kay Konishi (Japan), who thoroughly reviewed the first edition of the WIPO Patent Drafting Manual, identifiec and suggested areas for improvement, and made contributions to the text to update and supplement the contents of the first edition. As an experienced patent attorney and a qualified tutor for teaching patent drafting, the expertise they provided to trainees from different backgrounds was indispensable in the successful completion of the second edition. Valuable contributions and suggestions were also made by Anton Blijlevens (New Zealand), Pablo Paz (Argentira), Karl Rackette (Germany), Robert Sayre (United States of America). Thanks are due to the various WIPO officials who peer reviewed the draft content, in particular to Tomoko Miyamoto for the hard work and coordination which were key for this work to be finished successfully.

Since the second edition of the WIPO Patent Drafting Manual is largely based on its first edition, the contribution of Thomas Ewing (United States of America), who was the principal author of the first edition, is fully acknowledged. Equally, WIPO acknowledges the valuable contributions made by the following experts and institutions throughout the preparation of the first edition: Markus Engelhard (Germany), Takashi Fujita (Japan), Valérie Gallois (France), Wendy Herby (United States of America), Albert Jacobs (United States of America), Karuna Jain (India), Emmanuel Jelsch (Switzerland), Samuel Le Cacheux (France), Carlos Olarte (Colombia), Karl Rackette (Germany), Sorin Schneiter (Switzerland), Kanika Radhakrishnan (India and United States of America), Douglas Weinstein (United States of America) and the Geneva International Academic Network.

Module I
Intellectual property: an introduction

1.	**Intellectual property types**	9
2.	**More patent basics**	9

1. Intellectual property types

Intellectual property (IP) is the name given to patents, trademarks, copyrights, industrial designs and other types of intangible property that arise from creations of the mind and which, in their broadest sense, have no physical form.

Figure 1: Various types of properties and their values and results

Property
- Real
- Personal
- Capital
- Intellectual

Value creation activity
- Product creation
- Investment
- Improvement
- Sale
- Rent or licensing

Results
- Revenues/profits
- Employment
- Appreciation
- Solution of needs

Like all types of property, IP is often the result of investment, is owned and may generate income. For this reason, IP is considered an asset. Intellectual property differs from tangible property because it has no physical form and comes into being because of human intelligence, creativity and imagination.

Each type of IP has its own unique laws. It is sometimes divided into two general categories: industrial property and copyright.

Industrial property refers to assets created primarily for the advancement of technology, industry and trade, such as patents (inventions), industrial designs, trademarks, service marks and geographical indications.[1]

Patents
A patent is a legal document granting its holder the exclusive right to control the use of an invention, as defined in the patent's claims, within a limited geographical area and time by stopping others from, among other things, making, using or selling the invention without authorization. For example, patents could be granted for a battery that efficiently stores solar energy, a vaccine to protect against malaria or a new compound for transforming fish bones into agricultural fertilizer.

Industrial designs
Industrial design protection allows its owner to control the exploitation of the ornamental shapes associated with products, such as the stylish shape of a new sports car, the distinctive plastic casing of a certain type of computer or the shape of a soft drink bottle.

Trademarks
A trademark allows its owner to assure the public of the origin of the goods. Examples of trademarks include the distinctive names of products, such as Nando's® or Coca Cola®, or a logo, such as the Mercedes Benz® triad symbol.

Service marks
A service mark is a form of trademark that allows its owner to assure the public of the origin of a service, such as "Cheques for Two®."

Copyright refers to original expressions and "works of authorship." The person who creates a copyrighted work is called an *author*. Examples of copyrighted works include paintings, photographs, music, dance, poetry, literature, etc. Copyright also applies to original expressions associated with technology, such as computer software, technical specifications and related documentation.

One difference between copyright and industrial property is that, generally, copyright does not need to be registered with a government authority to be effective as protection against unauthorized use. Industrial property rights, however, must be expressly granted by and registered with a government authority if they are to be recognized and enforced.

In theory, anyone can draft a patent application for this purpose. In practice, however, professional patent attorneys and technical professionals known as *patent agents* or *patent engineers* usually write patent applications and file them with the relevant government authorities, because such applications can be technically and procedurally complex.

2. More patent basics

Patents may be granted to protect inventions in all fields of technology that are new, involve an inventive step and are capable of industrial application.[2] The patent has to be for an invention that works or – as some countries define it – is capable of being "reduced to practice." In general, a patent application must disclose the invention sufficiently clearly and completely that a person skilled in the art can carry out the invention. Thus a clever notion that cannot presently be put into actual practice (e.g., a time machine) cannot be patented.

Different countries may use different definitions of patentable "inventions." For example, inventions must generally be technical in nature, but not all jurisdictions share the same definition of what is "technical" and what is not.

In many countries, the term for which a patent is available is 20 years from the date on which the application was filed. In principle, a patent gives its owner the right to exclude others from making, using, offering for sale or selling the invention or importing the patented invention into a country where the patent has been granted. In other words, a patent provides a property right that allows the owner to say who *cannot* use the invention protected by the patent. Although there are certain exceptions and limitations to patent rights, in general, anyone who is neither the patent owner nor licensed by the patent owner and who nonetheless manufactures, uses, imports, offers for sale or sells a product or performs a process covered by the patent is known as an *infringer*. An infringer can be sued in court to force them to stop the infringement and to pay the owner damages.

Patents are *territorial* – that is, they have effect only in countries where they have been applied for and granted. Each country has the sovereign right to grant or refuse to grant a patent. In some regions, a group of nations have agreed by treaty to provide for common filing and examination of patent applications. For example, in Europe, the European Patent Convention established the European Patent Office (EPO), which examines European patent applications and grants European patents, while the African Intellectual Property Organization (OAPI) grants regional patents that are enforceable in all OAPI member states.

Module VIII provides more information about patent filing procedures.

This manual explores how patents are applied for and registered. The objective of this manual is to help you to develop a general understanding of the skills needed to draft a patent application, file it and work with patent authorities to have it issued. Since national/regional laws and practices may vary significantly, you must also seek out and understand the specific requirements for the jurisdiction(s) to which you and your client(s) are subject.

Note that, in this manual, the term *patent drafter* is used not in the legal and technical sense of a professional certified by national authorities to represent patent applicants in defined circumstances but rather as a generic term to mean anyone who drafts a patent application (including an inventor, a patent agent and a patent attorney).

Key words

- Intellectual property
- industrial property
- patent
- industrial design
- trademark
- service mark
- copyright
- invention
- territorial
- infringement

Self-Test

☐ What is intellectual property (IP)?

☐ Why is IP an asset?

☐ What is the difference between industrial property and copyright?

☐ Give an example of each type of IP that you can see in the room where you are now.

☐ Can a software code be protected by copyright?

☐ A patent generally gives its owner the right to exclude others from making, using or selling the invention defined in the patent's claims. True or false?

☐ Once a patent has been issued in one country, it is entitled to recognition all over the world. True or false?

☐ Who are patent infringers?

Module II
Patents

1.	**Detailed overview of patents**	**12**
1.1	What is a patent?	12
1.2	What can be the subject of a patent?	13
1.3	Why are patents important?	16
2.	**Legal requirements for patentability**	**18**
2.1	Novelty	18
2.2	Inventive step/nonobviousness	19
2.3	Industrial application/utility	21
2.4	Patentable subject matter	22
2.5	Disclosure requirement	23

1. Detailed overview of patents

A patent confers a limited exclusive right granted by a government for an invention. In the past, rulers awarded patents for almost any good or service whether or not an invention was involved. For example, a king might bestow a patent on salt to a trusted ally. In modern times, governments have reduced the scope of patents to protect inventions only. The Republic of Venice created one of the first patent systems of the modern era. The original term for a patent was set at 14 years – twice the length of the average apprenticeship. The term was later extended to 17 years following the grant of the patent. At present, the term of patent protection available in most countries is set at 20 years from the date of the application's filing, in principle.

1.1 What is a patent?

A patent generally grants the patent owner the exclusive right to control who makes, uses, sells, offers for sale and/or imports any product or process defined by the patent's claims. *Patent claims* are sets of sentences that define the invention being protected. To obtain a patent, claims must typically be for an invention that is new (novel), involves inventive step (is nonobvious) in view of the "prior art" and is industrially applicable (useful). *Prior art* is a technical term that generally refers to all the knowledge available to the public at the time of filing of the patent application.

Professional tip

You must file a patent application before publicly disclosing any important research results that may lead to a valuable product or technology. This caution applies especially to research institutions, where earliest publication of academic works is considered of utmost importance.

To ensure that publication in a review journal or presentation at a conference will not destroy the novelty of a patent application in countries where patent protection is sought, academic research institutions may set up an internal publication clearance procedure that reviews researchers' journal and conference submissions.

There are numerous other requirements that must also be met to obtain a patent. For example, the subject matter of the invention must be patentable under the applicable law, and the patent application must disclose the invention sufficiently clearly and completely. We will explain these legal requirements for obtaining a patent in detail in section 2 of this module.

In many countries, patents are granted under *substantive examination systems* in which a patent application is thoroughly reviewed by a government-employed patent examiner. Among other things, the patent examiner will compare the related prior art against the application's claims to determine whether the claimed invention provides a legally sufficient advancement of that art.

Some countries have *registration systems* in which an applicant receives a patent once certain formalities have been completed but without any such substantive examination. In such systems, the validity of the patent in view of prior art is not assessed until or unless the patent is later challenged in court.

A patent is said to be *valid* once it has been granted, provided that it has not been successfully challenged in a court or before the relevant patent office. A patent is said to be *invalid* when it is rejected or cancelled because the invention is not new in view of the prior art or for other reasons. Some of the world's patent systems hold that patents are deemed to be valid unless proven otherwise. This is especially true in the substantive examination systems, where an impartial government official has examined a patent application and relevant prior art before granting a patent.

The world's patent laws typically recognize patent protection for different types of invention. Many patent systems aim to provide uniform treatment for all inventions, regardless of the type of invention. When people speak of patents, they usually mean "patents of invention," which are known as *utility patents* in the United States of America. These patents protect machines, processes, chemical compositions and the other kinds of invention that are valuable because of their usefulness.

Some countries offer protection for inventions by means of *utility model registrations*, which are also known as innovation patents, utility innovations or short-term patents. The requirements for the registration of utility models are typically less stringent than those for obtaining a patent of invention.

Since the knowledge and skills required for drafting utility model applications are similar to those for drafting patent applications, this manual is also relevant to utility model registrations.

This manual relates most directly to patents of invention or utility patents.[3]

In practice, protection for utility models is typically sought for innovations of an incremental nature that might not satisfy the criteria for patents of invention (e.g., they may not demonstrate the necessary inventive step). The term of protection for utility models is significantly shorter than that for patents. Some patent offices do not conduct substantive examination of utility model applications prior to their registration; consequently, the precise nature of the right granted will be in question until a dispute arises between the owner and another party. In some countries, utility model protection can be obtained only for certain fields of technology and only for products not processes.

1.2 What can be the subject of a patent?

Let us look at: U.S. Patent No. 6,434,955 B1, issued on August 20, 2002, bearing the title "Electro-Adsorption Chiller: A Miniaturized Cooling Cycle with Applications from Microelectronics to Conventional Air-Conditioning."

The abstract for this patent reads:

A novel modular and miniature chiller is proposed that symbiotically combines absorption and thermoelectric cooling devices. The seemingly low efficiency of each cycle individually is overcome by an amalgamation with the other. This electro-adsorption chiller incorporates solely existing technologies. It can attain large cooling densities at high efficiency, yet is free of moving parts and comprises harmless materials. The governing physical processes are primarily surface rather than bulk effects, or involve electron rather than fluid flow. This insensitivity to scale creates promising applications in areas ranging from cooling personal computers and other micro-electronic appliances, to automotive and room air-conditioning.

While the patent examiner assigned to review this application ultimately found it patentable, they nevertheless reviewed

nearly 15 pieces of prior art and used 2 pieces of this prior art in rejecting the claims of the application as originally filed. The issued patent has 19 claims in two sets, with one set of 11 device claims followed by a second set of 7 method claims (see Figure 2).

Let us look more closely at some categories of invention that are commonly patented.

Mechanical devices and articles of manufacture

Mechanical devices and articles of manufacture are the traditional inventions covered by patent law. Consequently, the publicly available prior art in these fields may be long established. For example, a modern patent applicant seeking to protect an invention related to specialized hockey skates should not be surprised to find that an issued patent from the 1860s has been cited by an examiner to show that at least one claim in the modern patent application "reads on" the prior art. When a claim *reads on* prior art, this means that there is prior art that discloses subject matter that anticipates the content of the claim.

Processes/methods

Inventions can be processes and methods. Many processes and methods are also related to a physical device. A patentee is not limited to seeking protection using only one type of claim; consequently, a patent application can include both apparatus and method claims. So, for example, an inventor can patent *both* their new apparatus for filtering and purifying plant extracts *and* the filtration method.

Chemical compositions or compounds

Inventors may seek patent protection for chemical compositions, such as those arising in the fields of pharmaceuticals, biotechnology, materials science and petrochemicals. For example, a patent was issued long ago on acetylsalicylic acid, a chemical compound that relieves headaches. Indeed, patents covering pharmaceuticals tend to be among the most individually profitable. Given that the patent application must be filed prior to public disclosure and given that rigorous testing must be conducted for new drugs, it is not uncommon for pharmaceutical companies to file many patent applications on a variety of compounds to protect them while they are still in the early stages of testing. Consequently, many of these applications are abandoned prior to issuance, because the manufacturer subsequently learns that the compound is either not effective or is unsafe.

Isolated and characterized molecules

In many countries, molecules that have been isolated and characterized according to their function and potential utility may be patented.

Figure 2: Example of a published patent

(12) **United States Patent**
Ng et al.

(10) Patent No.: **US 6,434,955 B1**
(45) Date of Patent: **Aug. 20, 2002**

(54) **ELECTRO-ADSORPTION CHILLER: A MINIATURIZED COOLING CYCLE WITH APPLICATIONS FROM MICROELECTRONICS TO CONVENTIONAL AIR-CONDITIONING**

(75) Inventors: **Kim Choon Ng**, Singapore (SG); **Jeffrey M. Gordon**, Sede Boqer (IL); **Hui Tong Chua**, Singapore (SG); **Anutosh Chakraborty**, Dhaka (BD)

(73) Assignee: **The National University of Singapore**, Singapore (SG)

(*) Notice: Subject to any disclaimer, the term of this patent is extended or adjusted under 35 U.S.C. 154(b) by 0 days.

(21) Appl. No.: **09/922,712**

(22) Filed: **Aug. 7, 2001**

(51) Int. Cl.[7] **F25B 17/00**; F25B 21/02
(52) U.S. Cl. **62/106**; 62/144; 62/480; 62/3.3
(58) Field of Search 62/101, 106, 109, 62/480, 3.2, 3.3, 141, 142, 144

(56) **References Cited**

U.S. PATENT DOCUMENTS

3,734,293 A	5/1973	Biskis
5,046,319 A	9/1991	Jones
5,157,938 A	10/1992	Bard et al.
5,463,879 A	11/1995	Jones

FOREIGN PATENT DOCUMENTS

JP	A6154593	3/1986
JP	06154543 A	* 6/1994
JP	10202041 A	* 8/1998
JP	A2000-39428	2/2000

OTHER PUBLICATIONS

Ramaswamy, et al, IEEE Transactions on Components and Packaging Technologies, pp. 1–7 (Mar. 2000).
Drost, et al, Aiche 1998 Spring National Meeting, New Orleans, 5 pgs. (Mar. 1998).
Uemura, Applications of Thermoelectric Cooling, pp. 622–631 (1998).
Viswanatham et al, Adsorption, vol. 4, pp. 299–311 (1998).
Boelman et al, Ashrae Transactions: Research, vol. 103, Part 1, pp. 139–148 (1997).
Cho et al, Energy, vol. 17, No. 9, pp. 829–839 (1992).
Chua et al, International Journal of Refrigeration, vol. 22, pp. 194–204 (1999).

* cited by examiner

Primary Examiner—Chen-Wen Jiang
(74) *Attorney, Agent, or Firm*—Birch, Stewart, Kolasch & Birch, LLP

(57) **ABSTRACT**

A novel modular and miniature chiller is proposed that symbiotically combines absorption and thermoelectric cooling devices. The seemingly low efficiency of each cycle individually is overcome by an amalgamation with the other. This electro-adsorption chiller incorporates solely existing technologies. It can attain large cooling densities at high efficiency, yet is free of moving parts and comprises harmless materials. The governing physical processes are primarily surface rather than bulk effects, or involve electron rather than fluid flow. This insensitivity to scale creates promising applications in areas ranging from cooling personal computers and other micro-electronic appliances, to automotive and room air-conditioning.

19 Claims, 7 Drawing Sheets

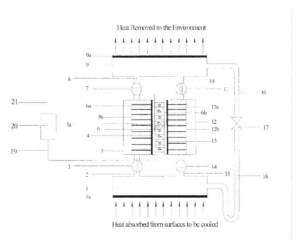

Genetic organisms/gene sequences

Some countries provide patent protection for genetic organisms. Where patentable, such inventions assign a functional purpose to a genetic sequence – but a mere nucleic acid sequence without an indication of a function is not a patentable invention. In cases in which a sequence or partial sequence of a gene is used to produce a protein or a part of a protein, it is necessary to specify which protein or part of a protein is produced and what function this protein or part of a protein performs.

The issue of the patentability of genetic materials is, however, contentious and, in some countries, these materials are not considered patentable subject matter. Any patent application in those countries claiming naturally occurring genetic sequences will be rejected on the ground that the sequence is part of nature.

Computer programs

There has been much debate about the extent to which computer programs should be patentable. Different countries have different rules on this subject. In many countries, while computer programs as such, written in a programming or machine language, are not patentable, a software-implemented invention is considered to be patentable subject matter. Such an invention may be a system, method and/or apparatus for achieving a certain end by running a computer program. In some countries, a computer program may also be patentable because it implements, through software instructions, a useful function in a new way (e.g., by making the computer program process data more efficiently and faster).

This manual will assume that software-implemented inventions are patentable but that a pure mathematical algorithm or equation is not.

Improvements

Most patents are for inventions that are themselves improvements on prior inventions. An *improvement patent*, however, is a new patent that covers an improved or enhanced effect as compared with the earlier patent.

Example

Inventor A holds a patent for an apparatus used to fill medicine bottles. Later, Inventor B receives a patent for a filling apparatus that represents an improvement on Inventor A's machine. Inventor B's invention fills the bottles more quickly and with less spillage, in a novel way.

Even though Inventor B in our example holds a patent on the improved machine, they may not be able to practice their patent B without consent from Inventor A if it is covered by the scope of patent A's claims. Typically, in this instance consent will be sought through a licensing negotiation in which both Inventor A and Inventor B recognize the commercial and financial advantages of cooperation. (Whether they ultimately reach agreement on licensing terms and on which party pays more for the license will depend upon their negotiating skills and the unique characteristics of their circumstances.)

Remember too, in relation to our example, that patents are "territorial." This means that if Inventor A obtains a patent in the United States only, Inventor B can produce and sell its improved machine in any other country (assuming that, apart from Inventor A's patent, there are no other patents in those countries that cover the scope of Inventor B's machine).

> **Professional tip**
>
> Many of the world's patent laws have prohibitions against patent protection for inventions associated with methods of treatment of the human body. You must therefore pay special attention to any such prohibitions when drafting claims for new uses of known pharmaceuticals and for methods of treating various conditions with novel compounds.

1.3 Why are patents important?

Patents can be significant corporate assets. For example, MPEG-4 is a technical standard for video and audio technology in various consumer products, such as smartphones or smart televisions. Manufacturers have to obtain a license from the patent holders of the MPEC-4 technology to use it in their products. Such license fees can generate substantive income for the patent holders.

Consider also that a company may start with a first-to-market advantage but that competitors may quickly learn how to make and market the same product successfully. At least one competitor will eventually learn how to make the product more cheaply than the original manufacturer. Unless the first-to-market company holds valuable patents, it may eventually see its revenue shrink as larger players enter the market. By exploiting its patents, however, the company can foreclose the ability of others to manufacture the product or it may enjoy licensing revenues that bear a healthy relationship with the size of its own profits, were it to sell the product.

Let us look at some of the most common patent exploitation models.

Revenue source
One such model is that of a sole inventor who obtains a patent on a key product and then enjoys royalties by licensing the patent to others and/or by using their patent to build an industry around the patent-protected product (e.g., Bell and the telephone). This still occurs, although the sole-inventor blockbuster patent has become somewhat rare. It is now more common for a successful company with sufficient resources to enforce its patent rights against others. While smaller companies can certainly derive significant revenues from licensing their patent rights, many large companies derive large revenues from licensing their patent portfolios (i.e., collections of patents relating to the same product or in the same field).

Generally, an inventor should have realistic (conservative) expectations of the income that they might derive from licensing their patent. In the first instance, many more patents exist nowadays than did in the past and today's entrepreneur may face hundreds – even thousands – of related patents, such that determining for which, if any, they need a license is complicated. In the second, patent litigation is expensive and many patentees simply cannot afford to enforce their rights against infringers, especially where infringement occurs across multiple countries.

Marketing benefit
A patent owner may indicate that a given product is protected by a patent (or patents). The patent laws of some countries include some sort of patent marking requirement, stipulating that products covered by the patent be marked with the patent number. The patent number can simply be stamped on some products, particularly those made of solid material, and its purpose is to provide notice (e.g., to the manufacturer's competitors) that the product cannot be freely copied because it is protected under law.

Over time, many companies have found that such marking also serves as an effective marketing tool, allowing them to assure the general public of the provenance of the product. Companies routinely refer to their "patented technology" in press releases and advertising materials. Some companies even provide information about their patent portfolios in their investment materials.

Bargaining chip
Patents have uses beyond litigation seeking injunctions prohibiting infringement and/or collecting licensing fees. Many companies and research institutions use their patent portfolios as tools to obtain a competitive or strategic advantage. For example, a patent holder might use its own patents to obtain cross-licenses on any competitor's patents of interest to the company. One patent owner might even use the strength of its own patent portfolio to convince a competitor that the two companies should cross-license each other's patent portfolios and hence eliminate the possibility of litigation between them – to the detriment of any third competitor, which would have to obtain licenses on the patent portfolios of *both* companies.

Industry control/influence
Most directly, a patent can be used to obtain an injunction against infringement by a competitor who makes, uses, sells, offers to sell or imports a product or service covered by the patent's claims. Under certain circumstances, this *blocking patent* gives its owner control of the related industry or product line. Of course, the claims of most patents are not so broad as to control the manufacture of all products in any given product category (e.g., a patent covering all computers). This is because claims that are too broad do not meet patentability requirements and so, if ever granted, they would be easily invalidated.

Similarly, an entire patent portfolio or a patent that is essential for implementation of an important technical standard could sometimes be so significant that it influences an entire industry. Such circumstances may lead to abuse of this dominant market position and hence here, in many countries, competition law or antitrust law steps in to mitigate the risk.

Defensive uses
The term *defensive patenting* – a term that has three possible meanings – is commonplace in the context of patent exploitation.

- In one sense, a patent (or patents) is used "defensively," for example, to prevent competitors from copying a

company's most important product or to create prior art that will prevent competitors from patenting their own concept.
– In another sense, patents are used to "defend" the company, should a competitor launch a hostile patent infringement lawsuit.
– In a third sense, "defensive patenting" refers to an inadequate or underfunded patent program.

A strategically defensive patenting program is likely to be no less expensive than an aggressive patenting program.

For a detailed discussion of defensive and offensive patent strategies, see Module X.

Self-Test

☐ What is generally the term of a patent available in most countries?

☐ Patent claims are sets of sentences, typically appearing at the end of the patent, that describe the invention in detail. True or false?

☐ What is the difference between examination systems and registration systems for a patent application?

☐ Which of the following types of patent is generally used to protect processes or chemical compositions?
a) Patents for invention (utility patents)
b) Design patents
c) Plant patents

☐ A patent application may include both apparatus and method (process) claims. True or false?

☐ List four reasons why patents are significant for many businesses.

☐ What is a blocking patent and why is it important?

Key words

- Patent right
- Claims
- Prior art
- Patent examination
- Utility model
- License
- Cross-license
- Patent exploitation models

2. Legal requirements for patentability

In this section of this module, we will expand on the basic facts about patents outlined in the first section to offer a more detailed understanding of patent laws and legal requirements.

To be patentable, an invention must fulfill several requirements. The main requirements may be broadly classified as novelty, inventive step (nonobviousness) *and* industrial applicability (utility). Furthermore, an invention may be patented only if it is subject matter eligible for protection under the relevant national/regional law.

Other legal issues relating to disclosure of the invention, such as the need to provide an enabling disclosure, are also among the fundamental requirements of patent law.

2.1 Novelty

Principle
Novelty generally requires that the *claimed* invention must not have been "made available to the public" before the filing date (or priority date[4]) of the invention. Whether the claimed invention is novel or not is determined in relation to the "prior art." The claimed invention is *not* novel if all of its elements (features) are found in a single prior art reference, such as an article in a technical journal or an earlier published patent. In other words, the claimed invention is novel as long as at least *one* feature or element is found in the claimed invention but *not* in the single prior art reference.

In patent prosecution, a lack of novelty is also known as *anticipation*. If a single anticipating reference contains all of the elements or features of a claimed invention, the invention as claimed is said to have "been anticipated by" the reference.

Example

A prior art reference discloses a chair with a seat and four legs, which may be made of wood or metal. Inventor A invents a rocking chair with a seat and four legs made of wood, and the inventor's pending claims refer only to a seat and four legs but make no mention of the rocker attachments for the chair.

Does the prior art reference anticipate this invention?

Yes, because all of the elements of the claimed invention are to be found in the prior art reference – that is, the reference anticipates the claimed invention. However, depending on what was already disclosed in the application as filed, the claims may be amended to recite an invention that avoids the prior art, such as by adding the rocker attachments to the claims.

Note too that all of the elements must be present in the single reference. A patent examiner may not combine multiple references to argue that the invention is not novel. As we will discuss in section 2.2 on nonobviousness and inventive step, however, several references may be combined to show that an invention is obvious and thus not patentable.

"Made available to the public"
The claimed invention has been "made available to the public" if knowledge of the claimed invention was shared with or accessible to any member of the public who is free to disclose the knowledge to others. It is not necessary to prove that any such person did in fact know of the claimed invention – that is, to be considered as a prior art reference, it does not matter whether any member of the public has actually read the reference (document).

Accordingly, concluding a nondisclosure agreement (NDA) with anyone with whom an inventor proposes to share (disclose) the invention before doing so will help to preserve its novelty.

Geographical scope and form of prior disclosure
Although the principle of novelty is universal, the scope of the prior art, which is a basis for determining the novelty, may vary slightly from jurisdiction to jurisdiction. In many countries, a public disclosure anywhere in the world represents valid prior art against a claimed invention. The prior art disclosure may take any form, such as oral disclosure, publication and use or display of the claimed invention, including at exhibitions, on social media and online more generally.

Prior-filed and later-published patent application
In addition to the prior art made available to the public before the filing (or priority) date, a patent application filed in the same country before the filing (or priority) date but published only thereafter – that is, a prior-filed and later-published patent application – also becomes part of the prior art in many jurisdictions. Because such patent publication is not yet in effect as of the filing date of the patent application to be examined, it is referred to as the *secret prior art* or *fictive prior art*.

The scope of prior art eligibility for such patent publication varies from jurisdiction to jurisdiction. For example, in Europe and Japan, the prior-filed, later-published patent application is taken into account only for examining novelty; in the United States, the prior-filed, later-published patent application is taken into account for examining both novelty and inventive step. In the United States and Japan, meanwhile, the prior-filed, later-published patent application is part of the prior art only if it is filed by a third party. In other words, any prior-filed, later-published patent application filed by the same inventor or applicant is excluded from the prior art. However, this is not the case in Europe and China.

Grace period (nonprejudicial disclosure)

In principle, the inventor's *own* public disclosure may also constitute prior art – that is, publication of the inventor's own research results before the filing of a patent application can destroy the novelty of their own invention. Thus, an applicant must file their patent application *before* making any public disclosure of the invention. There are exceptions to this rule, however, in the form of a *grace period* during which – for a limited time only – the inventor's own disclosure about their invention cannot become prior art against their patent application (i.e., is nonprejudicial).

The types of disclosure covered by the grace period and its duration vary from one country to another. For example, the United States and Japan have a comprehensive grace period. Any type of disclosure, including a commercial disclosure, made by the inventor or applicant within one year prior to the filing date is considered nonprejudicial and is not taken into consideration in determining novelty and inventive step. In contrast, in Europe, under the European Patent Convention (EPC), and in China, the grace period applies only exceptionally: in principle, the disclosure of the invention by the inventor or applicant destroys the novelty of the invention *except* in the case of disclosure at an international exhibition or similar. In Europe and China, publishing new and useful research (where this includes disclosing an invention) will preclude the inventor or applicant from obtaining a patent on the invention in an application filed at any later date.

In general, therefore, and particularly when they are seeking patent protection in more than one country, an inventor or applicant is well advised to file a patent application before they disclose their invention.

Example

Inventor A, who is based in the United States, presents a paper in Country X on April 30, 2020. They then return to the States and become preoccupied with other work. In November 2020, Inventor A remembers that they need to file a patent application on the invention. They rush to their patent drafter for advice.

Is it too late for Inventor A to seek patent protection?

In the United States and some other countries, *no*: a grace period of one year covers any form of disclosure by the inventor before patent filing. In this case, it has been less than a year since the initial disclosure, and therefore, it is considered nonprejudicial and the novelty requirement is satisfied.

In some other countries, where the grace period does not cover the inventor's prior public presentation (e.g., most European counties) or where a grace period is no longer

than six months, *yes*: Inventor A's own public presentation has destroyed the novelty of their invention.

Generic concept and specific example

When the invention claims generic concept A and the prior art reference discloses specific concept a1, which is included in generic concept A, the prior art reference destroys the novelty of the claimed invention. For example, when the claimed invention claims a "conductive material" and the prior art reference discloses a "copper material," the claimed invention is not novel.

When the claimed invention claims specific concept a1 and the prior art reference discloses a generic concept A that includes specific concept a1, however, the prior art reference does not necessarily destroy the novelty of the claimed invention. For example, when the claimed invention claims a "copper material" and the prior art reference discloses a "conductive material," the claimed invention may be novel if the claimed "copper" is proved to have a technical feature that can sufficiently distinguish it from other subsets of the "conductive material" such as "aluminum" and the like (e.g., if copper has a particular conductivity that distinguishes it from other kinds of conductive material).

2.2 Inventive step/nonobviousness

Principle

The second requirement for patentability is that the invention possesses an "inventive step" or is "nonobvious." *Inventive step/nonobviousness* requires that an invention must not have been obvious to a "person skilled in the art" (at which we will look in more depth shortly) or one "of ordinary skill in the art." At its most basic conceptual level, obviousness means that if any person of average skill in the scientific/technical field of the invention could put together different pieces of known information and arrive at the claimed invention, then that invention is not patentable.

Nonobviousness differs from novelty in the sense that an invention may be obvious even though it is not *precisely* disclosed in a single piece of prior art. Put another way, a patent examiner may find an invention to be obvious when several publications that each disclose a piece of the overall inventive picture can be combined. The purpose behind the nonobviousness requirement is that a patent should be granted only if an invention represents an appropriate level of improvement over the prior art and of contribution to technological development that benefits society.

When determining the inventive step, the claimed invention (i.e., the claimed subject matter) is taken into consideration as a whole – that is, it should not be considered piece by piece.

Example

A U.S. court invalidated a patent for Merck's blockbuster osteoporosis drug Fosamax (in once-weekly form) because of prior art that rendered the claimed invention obvious. About a year before Merck filed its patent application[5], two articles had been published in a pharmaceutical journal about osteoporosis. These articles suggested using a weekly dose of bisphosphonate to treat osteoporosis instead of a daily dose. The weekly dose alleviated some of the gastro-intestinal complications caused by taking the pills daily.

Merck attempted to patent this once-a-week dosage of the medicine that was seven times the daily dosage.

Since the articles had previously disclosed the concept of the weekly dosage, the patent – although initially granted – was subsequently found to be invalid because it was "obvious" in light of prior art.

"A person skilled in the art" – A *person skilled in the art* is a hypothetical person who is presumed to have access to all publicly available prior art information and have the capacity to understand all technical matters in the scientific or technical field relevant to the claimed invention, as well as the general knowledge and ordinary practical skills common to the field. This person will also have access to the normal means and capacity for routine experimentation to, for example, clarify ambiguities on known technology. The person skilled in the art does not, however, have inventive capabilities beyond the capacity to exercise the usual faculties of logic and reason to combine the knowledge. In other words, this person is not expected to exercise inventive imagination, to add knowledge to the prior art and to advance the technology.

Sometimes, this hypothetical "person" should be presumed to be a group of persons or a team of specialists, each of whom has a particular skill. For example, for an invention regarding a bioinformatic tool in the medical field, a team gathered from biotechnology, medicine and information technology might be presumed.

The level of skill and knowledge of a person skilled in the art may vary depending on the particular technological field involved. In general, the level of knowledge and skill of the person skilled in the art is not the average of a layperson (i.e., the minimum knowledge and skill) or a leading specialist's skill (i.e., the maximum knowledge and skill), but rather the skill expected of an ordinary, duly qualified practitioner in the relevant field.

Analysis for determining inventive step/nonobviousness

In some jurisdictions, such as the United States, the analysis of obviousness generally involves several steps aiming to determine:

– the scope and content of the prior art;
– the difference(s) between the prior art and the claimed invention; and
– the level of those skilled in the pertinent art.

In some other countries and, for example, at the European Patent Office (EPO), a slightly different approach, which is known as the *problem–solution approach*, is used for the analysis of inventive step. This approach involves:

– determining the closest prior art;
– establishing the distinguishing features between the claimed invention and the closest prior art;
– formulating the "objective technical problem" to be solved; and
– considering whether or not the claimed invention (the solution), starting from the closest prior art and the objective technical problem, would have been obvious to those skilled in the art.

Identifying the differences between the prior art and the invention requires carefully comparing the prior art and the *claimed* invention to detect the precise similarities and differences between the two. For example, if both the claimed invention and the prior art references disclose a method or process for manufacturing compound X, the patent examiner will compare the steps in the methods to determine whether the two are distinct. Likewise, if an invention is a chemical compound with a specific structure, the examiner will compare the chemical structure with other compounds in the prior art to determine how the individual components in the structure are different.

If the patent examiner finds that a prior art reference completely discloses the applicant's invention (as claimed), the patent examiner will find that the patent application's novelty has been destroyed.

If the patent examiner finds that this prior art reference disclosure is so close to the applicant's invention (as claimed) that a person skilled in the art could obviously arrive at the invention, the patent examiner may find that the claimed invention is "obvious." This may be especially so if the patent examiner finds other prior art references that, in combination with the first reference, disclose the entirety of the claimed invention.

See Module IX for a more detailed discussion of the mechanics of rejecting or allowing claims during patent prosecution.

Impermissible hindsight analysis (*ex post facto analysis*)

Once an inventor conceives an invention, the invention often seems to be obvious to others. This is because knowledge of the invention naturally and inevitably influences that determination. The patent examiner and the courts must take special care to avoid such "hindsight analysis" or "*ex post facto* analysis" when determining the obviousness of a claimed invention.

Teaching away

In determining nonobviousness, the patent examiner will compare all of the characteristics of the claimed invention with the prior art references. However, if a prior art reference explicitly excludes an element of the invention, this reference may not be used to show obviousness. This is called *teaching away*.

Example

Prior art reference X discloses a copper electroplating solution comprising:

(i) an alkaline solution of copper sulfate;
(ii) any concentrated acid of 30–50 grams per liter (*excluding sulfuric acid*); and
(iii) an aqueous solution of a pH-modifying substrate in an amount sufficient to adjust the pH to a value of 3.5–5.0.

Inventor A has come up with a similar invention of a copper electroplating solution comprising:

(i) an alkaline solution of copper sulfate;
(ii) *sulfuric acid* of 10–20 grams per liter; and
(iii) an aqueous solution of a pH-modifying substrate in an amount sufficient to adjust the pH to a value of 3.5–5.0.

Here, the invention may satisfy the nonobviousness requirement because the prior art explicitly "teaches away," or excludes, sulfuric acid from its description of the copper electroplating solution. Even though the prior art reference explicitly states that sulfuric acid will not work, the inventor came up with a new copper electroplating solution in which sulfuric acid *can* be used.

Secondary consideration

In addition to all of these factors, patent examiners – as well as the courts – may sometimes consider secondary factors when deciding the issue of nonobviousness. These secondary factors include whether the invention solves a long-standing problem, overcomes the failure of others or is a commercial success. The existence of any of these factors may be demonstrative of the nonobviousness of the claimed invention. Put another way, these secondary factors help to demonstrate that even though the invention seems obvious, it is in fact not so because other people failed in their attempts to solve the problem.

Also, in some jurisdictions, evidence that an invention is a commercial success helps to demonstrate that the invention was not obvious.

Note, however, that if the primary consideration holds an invention to be clearly obvious, secondary factors will usually not help to overcome the objection.

2.3 Industrial application/utility

To be patentable, an invention must be useful. In patent language, this is called "utility" in some jurisdictions; in others, "industrial application."[6] Although frequently conflated, these terms are not identical.

Typically, *utility* requires only that an invention performs the functions specified and achieves some minimally beneficial result; a patent will not be granted otherwise. This is based on the historical consideration that society receive a positive benefit from any exclusive right granted to an applicant. To comply, an invention does not need to demonstrate superiority to existing products or processes. One obvious class of "invention" that would be excluded under utility would be articles or processes alleged to operate in a manner clearly contrary to well-established physical laws (e.g., a perpetual motion machine).

In some jurisdictions, the patent applicant may have to show that their invention satisfies a requirement for *industrial application*, which generally means that an invention can be made or used in any kind of industry in the broad sense, including agriculture, fishery, services, etc. The word "industry" is usually understood to include any physical activity of "technical character" – that is, an activity that belongs to the useful or practical arts, as distinct from the aesthetic arts. "Industry" does not necessarily imply the use of a machine or the manufacture of an article, however, and could cover, for example, a process for dispersing fog or for converting energy from one form to another. The requirement for industrial application also denies the patentability of a perpetual motion machine.

An applicant does not typically need to demonstrate that an invention is commercially viable to satisfy the utility/industrial applicability requirement.

Example

Inventor A has discovered that the metal platinum has a unique property by which it prevents water from freezing into ice. The inventor then realizes that this property could be applied to the plumbing industry by means of an inventive process that lines water pipes with platinum to prevent them from bursting in freezing weather.

Even though the invention may be too expensive to implement commercially, this use of platinum in water pipes would nevertheless satisfy the utility/industrial applicability requirement.

Professional tip

When looking at research results and reflecting on whether they are patentable, ask the inventor: "Are the results *useful*?" If they *are* useful for solving a practical problem, even if the problem is small, you should take further steps to determine whether the invention meets the other requirements of patentability.

The utility/industrial applicability requirement is usually easily met for mechanical devices and processes, but can be more challenging for inventions in the field of chemistry or biotechnology. In the life sciences domain, for example, an inventor might discover a new compound or new process to make a compound without discovering a specific practical purpose to which it can be applied. The courts of some countries have found sufficient utility if a chemical compound produces effects in laboratory animals, such as reducing a tumor in laboratory mice or as an intermediate to produce other compounds of known utility. Similarly, an inventor might have isolated DNA fragments, but unless they can demonstrate a suitable use for such fragments, they will not be able to satisfy the industrial applicability/utility requirement (see also Module VI, section 15).

2.4 Patentable subject matter

Patentable subject matter – also referred to as *patent-eligible subject matter* – is one of the fundamental patentability requirements. Patent eligibility functions as a gatekeeper or threshold to further patentability questions such as novelty or inventive step (nonobviousness), because technically, neither is worth assessing unless the invention qualifies as patentable subject matter.

In some jurisdictions, patentable subject matter is positively defined in patent law. For example, in the United States, patentable subject matter is defined as "any new and useful process, machine, manufacture, or composition of matter"[7] – that is, a claimed invention is required to fall within any of those four categories. However, the United States does not statutorily define what *cannot* be patented Over the years, U.S. case law has instead established certain categories of creation that cannot be patented, including a "law of nature," "abstract ideas" and "natural phenomena." In Japan, patentable subject matter is statutorily defined as "a creation of a technical idea utilizing a law of nature."[8] Accordingly, creations utilizing laws other than laws of nature (e.g., economic principles) or mere mental activities are considered ineligible for patent protection.

There are, however, many other countries – including those that are party to the EPC – that do not offer a positive definition of patentable subject matter; instead, they provide a non-exhaustive list of *non*patentable inventions. The EPC lists examples of nonpatentable subject matter as:

– discoveries, scientific theories and mathematical methods;
– aesthetic creations;
– schemes, rules and methods for performing mental acts, playing games or doing business, and programs for computers; and
– presentations of information.[9]

Such nonpatentable subject matter is excluded from patentability only if claims are directed to this subject matter "as such."[10]

When interpreting "as such" to differentiate the nonpatentable subject matter from the patentable subject matter, in general, the "technical character" of an invention is tested. What is meant by "technical" is a complicated issue of legal interpretation, which has been developed in cases brought before the EPO's Boards of Appeal.

Patent eligibility is mostly questioned when the claimed invention relates to computer-implemented inventions (e.g., software-related invention), inventions implementing business methods or biotechnology-related inventions. In some jurisdictions, field-specific examination guidelines are made available to the public to define the boundaries peculiar to a given technical field.

Example 1

The discovery that radiation exists in a certain wavelength range (e.g., X-rays) as such is not patentable subject matter because such discovery falls within the laws of nature and hence X-rays as such are not patentable. Any method of *producing* such X-rays is patentable subject matter, however, and any apparatus *using* such X-rays, such as an X-ray machine for inspecting the structure of bodies, etc., is also patentable subject matter.

Example 2

The presentation of information as such (i.e., the "content") is not patentable subject matter. A novel and inventive *method* of presenting that information may be eligible – such as a method of generating an icon with a three-dimensional effect by arranging the colors and brightness of its outer boundary.

Some jurisdictions have laws in place to exclude certain inventions from patentability for other reasons. While the exact scope of these exclusions varies from one country to another, they generally include:

– where the prevention of the commercial exploitation of an invention is necessary to protect *order public* or morality, including to protect human, animal or plant life or health or to avoid serious prejudice to the environment;
– diagnostic, therapeutic and surgical methods for the treatment of humans or animals; and
– plants and animals (other than microorganisms) and essentially biological processes (other than microbiological processes).

The exclusion from patentability of methods for diagnostic, therapeutic and surgical treatments does not, however, apply to products designed for *use* in any of these treatments; hence patents may be obtained for medical products, apparatus and devices with which such methods of diagnosis, surgery or therapy may be carried out.

In the United States, where such methods of treatment are *not* excluded from patentability, if a patent is granted on such methods, a patentee cannot enforce the patent against a medical practitioner.

2.5 Disclosure requirement

In return for the grant of exclusive patent rights, patent holders are required to sufficiently disclose to the public information about the invention. It is through this disclosure requirement that the patent system facilitates the dissemination of, and access to, the technological information contained in patents. It allows third parties to learn about new inventions without "reinventing the wheel," and to avoid any duplicative efforts and investments in research and development (R&D). The disclosure requirement also ensures that patent rights are not extended to something that is withheld from the public: it would be difficult to justify a patent grant if a patent were granted on claimed subject matter that the patentee had neither "invented" before the filing date nor disclosed in the patent application as filed. Furthermore, the disclosure requirement also makes sure that the scope of the patent protection defined by the claims is clearly communicated to others, so that they can avoid infringement of, or bring a challenge to, the patent, as appropriate.

To meet these various objectives, the disclosure requirement in most jurisdictions comprises provisions such as:

– a support requirement (or, in the United States, a written description requirement);
– an enablement requirement; and
– a clarity requirement.

In addition, in some countries, a patent applicant must indicate in the specification the best mode known to the inventor for carrying out the invention (a best mode requirement).

Support requirement (or written description requirement)

The *support requirement*, which is comparable to the written description requirement in the United States, functions to balance the breadth of the claims (i.e., the scope of patent protection) with what is disclosed in the description and drawings.

The laws of many countries require claims to be supported by the description. In general, this means that there must be a basis in the description for the subject matter of every claim and that the scope of the claims must not be broader than is justified by the description and drawings. As a general rule, a claim is regarded as supported by the description unless there are well-founded reasons for believing that the person skilled in the art would be unable, on the basis of the

Professional tip

You will first need to assess carefully whether your invention is patent-eligible subject matter in the jurisdiction(s) for which patent protection is sought. If *not*, you will not be able to obtain a patent even if the invention is both novel and inventive/nonobvious.

Professional tip

The disclosure requirement is very important because, once a patent application is filed, you will not be able to add new subject matter to the disclosure as of the filing date (see Module IX, section 3, on amendments). In other words, if you have not properly drafted the patent application at the time of filing, you will find it difficult – sometimes impossible – to meet the disclosure requirement by amending the patent application at a later date.

information given in the application as filed, to extend the particular teaching of the description to the whole of the field claimed.

The law of the United States stipulates that the specification shall contain a written description of the invention. To satisfy the *written description requirement*, a patent specification must describe the claimed invention in sufficient detail that a person skilled in the art would reasonably conclude that the inventor had possession of the claimed invention at the time the application was filed.

Module VI, section 10, and Module VII offer more practical details about how to draft a patent application that meets the support requirement (or the written description requirement).

Enablement requirement

The patent laws of many countries require an applicant to disclose the invention sufficiently clearly and completely that a person skilled in the art could, based on the disclosure, make and use the claimed invention. This *enablement requirement* also functions to balance the breadth of the claims and the extent of the disclosure to the public of the invention in the description and drawings.

It follows from this requirement that, on the basis of the information disclosed in the application as filed and the common general knowledge in the art, a person skilled in the art can carry out the invention without undue burden (undue experimentation) or without any inventive effort. In other words, a detailed description of a well-known feature of the invention, plus the tools and processes that are commonly known to a person skilled in the art, are not necessarily required to be provided in a patent application – although the patent drafter should keep in mind that novel aspects (features) of the invention *are* required to be explicitly disclosed in detail in the enabling manner.

Various factors need to be considered in determining whether undue experimentation is needed by a person skilled in the art to carry out the claimed invention. For example, since a person skilled in the art must be able to deliver the entire scope of the claimed invention, if the claims become broader, more extensive disclosure may be necessary to meet the enablement requirement.

Similarly, in general, the more is known about the nature of the invention in the prior art and the more the art is predictable, the less information is needed in the application itself in order for a person skilled in the art to carry out the claimed invention. For example, if a new invention relates to an improvement of a well-known machine in the mechanical field, a person skilled in the art might be able to make and use the invention without lengthy and detailed explanations in the description. But if an invention is a new chemical compound, comparatively speaking, more information about, for example, how to produce such a new compound and its technical effects might need to be disclosed for a person skilled in the art to make and use the invention.

Clarity requirement (or definiteness requirement)

Unless the claims are drafted clearly and distinctly, third parties will have difficulty analyzing what is and is not covered by a patent. The *clarity requirement*, which is commonly known as the *definiteness requirement* in the United States, is therefore one of the fundamental requirements relating to the claims.

Many national/regional laws require claims to be clear and concise. The claims must distinctly define the subject matter of the invention, using neither vague nor indefinite terms.

In most jurisdictions, the words in each claim are given the meaning that they normally have in the relevant art and hence the terms of a claim should typically be clear for a person skilled in the art. In particular cases, a patent drafter may include explicit definition of a word in the description, thereby giving it a special meaning as used in the claim.

The description and drawings may also be taken into account when interpreting the claims.

Module VI, section 3, offers insight into the more practical aspects of drafting clear and concise claims.

Best mode requirement

In some countries, at least one mode (i.e., one example) of carrying out the claimed invention must be disclosed in the description. In others, including the United States, an applicant must disclose in the specification the "best" mode of carrying out the claimed invention as contemplated by the inventor at the filing (or priority) date. The *best mode requirement* has a basis in the principle of equity, which requires inventors to be fair and prevents inventors from disclosing only what they know to be the *second-best* way of carrying out the invention while reserving the best way exclusively for themselves.

In the United States, however, the failure to disclose the best mode is not one of the grounds for cancellation or invalidation of a patented claim, or otherwise holding it to be unenforceable.

Key words

- Novelty
- Anticipation
- Inventive step (nonobviousness)
- Industrial applicability (utility)
- Patentable subject matter (patent eligibility)
- Disclosure requirement
- Support requirement
- Enablement requirement
- Clarity requirement
- Best mode requirement

Self-Test

☐ What is novelty?

☐ What is prior art?

☐ If your invention is published in an academic journal before you file a patent application, your application will be rejected in many countries. True or false?

☐ What is inventive step (nonobviousness)?

☐ What is the difference between inventive step (nonobviousness) and novelty?

☐ In contrast to the novelty requirement, for the determination of lack of inventive step, prior art references may be combined to show that the claims of a pending application are obvious. True or false?

☐ What is industrial applicability (utility)? Why is it required for patentability?

☐ To comply with the industrial applicability/utility requirement, an invention must be superior to existing products or processes. True or false?

☐ Why is meeting the industrial applicability/utility requirement sometimes a problem in relation to chemical compounds and processes?

☐ What kinds of invention are *not* patent-eligible subject matter in your country?

☐ What is the support requirement?

☐ What is the enablement requirement?

☐ Why must the patent claims be drafted clearly?

☐ What is the best mode requirement? Do all countries have this requirement?

Module III
Patent application preparation

1.	**Preparing patent applications**	**28**
1.1	Obtaining invention disclosures from inventors	30
1.2	Identifying patentable inventions	31
1.3	Understanding the invention (core inventive concept)	32
1.4	Inventorship	32
2.	**Typical parts of the patent application**	**33**
2.1	Request	33
2.2	Description	33
2.3	Claims	33
2.4	Drawings	34
2.5	Abstract	34
2.6	Application format	34

Preparing a patent application is a first step toward obtaining a patent that sets out clearly the scope of the legal protection granted to the patent owner. In this sense, drafting a patent application is different from writing a scientific or technical paper. Because the patent application contains technical subject matter, it will bear some similarities to such a paper. In general, however, scientific papers may pay greater attention to the theory underpinning the subject matter, while a patent application may focus on the structural details of the invention and the process for making and using it – even though it does not usually need to be a blueprint as such. The issued patent will be reviewed over years to come by public officials such as patent examiners, appeal board members and judges, as well as by business partners and competitors. The patent application should therefore be drafted with these audiences in mind.

A patent application typically includes a *request* (called an *application form* in some countries), a *description*, one or more *claims*, one or more *drawings* (where they are necessary to understanding the invention) and an *abstract*. The patent drafter is unlikely to prepare the patent application in this order and ordinarily prepares the claims first. This is because the claims are the heart of a patent and the content of the description will be dictated, in part, by the content of the claims.

In this module, we will explain each of these parts. We will discuss in detail how to draft claims in Modules IV–VI and the other parts of a patent application in Module VII.

Professional tip

Always ask the client and the inventor when the patent application needs to be filed – but do *not* rely on the client's or the inventor's interpretation of the law: check the facts yourself.

1. Preparing patent applications

The first question a patent drafter needs to ask upon receiving instruction to prepare a patent application is: *How soon does this application need to be filed?*

Each country's patent laws impose strict rules on when an application must be filed in relation to certain events. These events are as various as, for example, the first date of attempted commercial exploitation, the first date of export and the first date of public disclosure. The patent drafter therefore needs to gather the following facts.

(i)   In what territory/ies does the client want to protect their invention?
(ii) Has something already happened that might impair the client's ability to protect their invention in those specific territory/ies?
(iii) How soon does the client intend to do something that might jeopardize their ability to protect the invention in the territory/ies?

Even if there are no such time bars, the patent drafter – like any professional – should endeavor to complete and file the patent application as quickly as possible. There is always a risk that a third party might file an application for an invention similar to or the same as that created by the client, in which case any delay attributable to the patent drafter would be the primary reason for the client's application being denied. Likewise, if prior art might become available (e.g., an article is published), that could not have been used against the client's application, had it been filed earlier. Any professional patent drafter should recognize that their workload is largely driven by dates that are beyond their own control and they may frequently need to rearrange their work schedule to accommodate unexpected time-critical discoveries.

In principle, patent drafting is an iterative intellectual task shared between a patent drafter and the inventor. When there are several inventors, it is generally effective to position only one "contact inventor" as interlocutor – that is, as someone who knows most of the details of the invention, who can deal with and collect information from the rest of the inventors, and who has enough time to cooperate effectively with the drafter.

When drafting a patent application, the key question that the patent drafter has to answer is: *Am I able to draft claims that are worth being patented based on the inventor's knowledge and my own skills?*

Example

Engineer X calls to ask you about obtaining a patent on their invention in the United States. You ask them some preliminary questions, but they do not have time to speak in detail, so you agree to meet in two days. At the meeting, X hands you a large document describing the invention in great detail. You attempt to gather information about possible obstacles to patenting, so you ask the following questions.

(i)   Has this invention been shown to anyone in the absence of a nondisclosure agreement (NDA)? (An NDA is a confidentiality agreement under which the parties agree not to use or to disclose to others the subject of their communication.)
(ii) Has the company sold or attempted to sell this invention? (This is a time-barring event in some countries, such as the United States.)
(iii) Have you or your company published anything about this invention?
(iv) Have you told anyone outside your company or institution about this invention?
(v)   Have you demonstrated the invention in any public forum such as a trade show or conference, or on your website, social media, etc.?

Engineer X initially answers "no" to all these questions. They are not sure when their company plans to begin selling the invention. Believing that there is no pending bar date that would prohibit patenting, you continue to question X about the invention.

Toward the end of the interview, they remember that a co-worker displayed the invention at a scientific meeting "a couple of months or so ago." When you press Engineer X for the precise date, they leaf through their calendar and eventually exclaim: 'Wow, that was last October – so a year ago already!"

You know that, to enjoy the grace period in the United States, a patent application must be filed no later than one year from its first public disclosure by the applicant. So you ask X to confirm the exact date. Having called a colleague to be certain, they finally answer that today is in fact the first anniversary of the invention's public disclosure.

It is 15:00.

You know that this public disclosure at the scientific meeting may not serve as a bar to patentability if a patent application can be filed before midnight. But you cannot possibly prepare a full and complete patent application on the invention before midnight.

Fortunately, U.S. law provides for provisional patent applications. A provisional patent application must disclose the invention, but it does not need to include

Professional tip

When filing an application with the patent office in hard copy via mail or another mode of physical delivery rather than electronically, create a folder that contains a copy of everything sent, including all completed forms and evidence of any payments made. Include the original mail deposit receipt from the post office as evidence of the date of deposit.

When filing electronically, take care to save – and perhaps print – the electronic confirmation generated by the patent office after completion. In this way, if the patent office does not attribute the proper date of receipt to the patent application, you will have everything you need to prove the proper filing date – a date that is crucial in preserving your client's rights to obtain patent protection. *One day late is too late.*

patent claims. A provisional patent application will expire one year after its filing date and effectively serves as a placeholder if a regular utility patent application is filed within one year.

You know that you should not incur legal expenses without prior approval. So you call the president of the company (your contact person for patent work) to explain the situation. She authorizes you on the phone to proceed. As a precaution measure, you take care to follow up by writing an email to the company in which you summarize the agreement made via a phone call, so that you each have an additional written document confirming the authorization.

Luckily, Engineer X gave you a good invention disclosure and a technical document explaining the invention, and during your interview with them, you got a good understanding of the invention. You ask X for an electronic copy of the document. You inform your co-workers that you need to push all other work for the rest of the day to accommodate this rush provisional application.

You spend the rest of the day creating the best provisional application possible in the short time available.

After filing the application,[11] you create a folder for the provisional patent application.

Patent drafters must strive to protect their client's patent rights. Sometimes protecting the applicant's rights involves simply making sure that critical dates are observed. If the patent drafter in our example had forgotten to ask about possible bar dates or had not pressed the engineer for precise information, they might have returned to the office and spent the next two weeks drafting a beautiful legal document for an invention that could no longer be patented.

At the same time, the patent drafter must also check at an early stage whether the applicant wants to file in countries other than that in which they and the drafter are situated. Applicants from Paris Convention member states and from members of the World Trade Organization (WTO) can claim priority under the Paris Convention if they file their subsequent patent applications in those territories within 12 months of the filing date of the first application for the same invention (known as the *priority date*). Such priority based on the first application can also be claimed under the Patent Cooperation Treaty (PCT) when an international patent application is subsequently filed. The effect of validly claimed priority is that the subsequent application will not be invalidated by any actions that occurred between the priority date and the filing date of the subsequent application. For example, if someone files another application containing the same invention or discloses the same invention to the public between these two dates,

those actions will not affect the patentability of the subsequent application claiming the priority of the first application.

Module VIII, section 2, provides more information on foreign filing processes.

The patent drafter should docket the filing date of the first application and check in with the applicant well ahead of its first anniversary. Even when an applicant initially indicated no interest in foreign filing, they may have changed their mind a year later. Remember too that it is not necessary to wait a full year before filing abroad. While almost 180 countries are parties to the Paris Convention, the patent drafter should also determine – preferably before filing the priority application – whether the applicant is interested in obtaining protection in a country that is not a signatory to the Paris Convention. If so, the patent drafter will need to research that country's specific priority rules – although a patent drafter will likely not be allowed to directly represent their client before a foreign patent office.

1.1 Obtaining invention disclosures from inventors

Different clients may have different levels of capability when it comes to handling patent documents. Some clients may have fairly sophisticated administrative units that can provide completed invention disclosure packages to patent drafters, who are then able to conduct a follow-up review as necessary. At the opposite extreme are clients who have no intellectual property (IP) infrastructure and who require considerable guidance and assistance from the patent drafter.

The patent drafter will need to gather technical information and ideas about the invention from its inventors, as well as insight into business considerations that may come from other sources, such as the applicant's managers or marketing executives. The technical information will mainly be provided in writing – that is, as invention disclosures, sketches, technical drawings, laboratory reports, manuscripts of (unpublished) papers, prototypes, etc.

The patent drafter will learn over time which approach offers the best results for different types of client. For some clients, the patent drafter may want to provide a blank invention disclosure form and allow the inventor(s) to complete it on their own. For other clients, the patent drafter may want – or need – to obtain information about the invention by interviewing the inventor(s). In any event, the patent drafter should always attempt to have at least one meeting with the inventors in person, by telephone or through video conferencing. It is highly unlikely that an inventor will otherwise be able to supply a patent drafter with enough material to fuel an unambiguous understanding of the invention. Similarly, it is unlikely that the inventor will otherwise come to understand the legal context and reasons for the background information being sought about their invention.

In an ideal situation, the inventor will provide the patent drafter with an invention disclosure form and supporting documents well before their meeting. The patent drafter will review the disclosure materials as soon as possible thereafter and note any questions they may have – both technical (e.g., "How does A function with B"?) and legal (e.g., "Who else could be an inventor?") – or areas in which they believe additional disclosure would be helpful.

During the meeting, the patent drafter will check that they fully understand the invention, establish that there is no additional disclosure information that they should also receive, determine the most commercially significant aspects of the invention and confirm that there are either no pending bar dates (or verify any such dates).

1.2 Identifying patentable inventions

In reviewing an invention disclosure and/or in speaking with an inventor, the patent drafter must direct their focus to the patentable inventions described. It is likely that the disclosure text and the discussion will include not only detail of patentable novelty but also nonpatentable technical detail. It is commonplace for inventors to understand what they allegedly invented were only "discoveries" and not inventions in "patentability" terms. They may think that their prototype or the embodiment of the invention is the invention to be claimed, and will need assistance to explore the novel and inventive concept underpinning it. It is consequently often the patent drafter who articulates what constitutes the patentable invention – the concept. The patent drafter must remember that whether an invention is patentable or not cannot be determined without an understanding of the prior art. Exploring with the inventor the problem they think they have solved in light of the prior art will help the drafter to craft the essential elements of the patent claims.

Example

An inventor says they have taken well-known Widget A and combined it with Widget B, then burned the rim of their common edge for 5–10 minutes, before using epoxy to attach Widget C to the burnished common edges of Widget A and Widget B.

The patent drafter eventually realizes that they have never heard of a Widget A and Widget B attached to Widget C. Suspecting that this combination may be inventive – novel and nonobvious – the patent drafter asks the inventor if they have ever heard of anyone producing this combination of elements.

The inventor says that others have tried for years to combine these widgets and that there has been some success but that Widget C had always separated from Widgets A and B after a short time.

The patent drafter asks if the solution lies in burning the combined edge and the inventor affirms that this is correct.

Thus the patent drafter recognizes that one invention (for which they should draft claims) is Widget A coupled to Widget B and subjected to heat before application of Widget C.

Professional tip

You must *always* negotiate and discuss fees with your clients *before* incurring charges, especially when the client is an individual.

Professional tip

A sample invention disclosure form is provided as Annex B at the end of this manual. You should adapt a version of this form for your own use and ensure that it conforms to the legal requirements of your own jurisdiction. The sample invention disclosure form may be also modified to facilitate a full and complete disclosure in any other jurisdiction(s) of interest to your clients.

Professional tip

Never assume that an inventor actually knows what constitutes their invention. Inventors typically think in terms of products, discoveries or research results and not in terms of inventions or patent claims. You will have to ask questions to understand the invention – but do *not* be an arrogant patent drafter. You are not the inventor; your role is to support the client by describing the invention effectively and then protecting it.

1.3 Understanding the invention (core inventive concept)

The patent drafter should ordinarily not try to *become* the inventor but instead strive toward the clearest grasp of the invention that will allow them to draft a patent application with the broadest claims allowed by law. This means understanding the invention well enough to define the invention by means of the fewest possible elements – that is, understanding the invention well enough to know what elements are essential and what need not be recited.

Understanding the invention also means that the patent drafter is able to prepare an application that discloses all possibly patentable aspects of the invention and enough additional information so that a person skilled in the pertinent technical field can understand the invention and apply it. Understanding the invention also means that, on receipt of a prior art description, the patent drafter will be able to explain the differences between the invention and that prior art and/or the pending claims so as to minimize any risk of inadvertent reduction in claim coverage.

Example

The patent drafter understands that the invention involves Widgets A, B and C. The inventor disclosed that the common edge formed by the combination of Widgets A and B was burned before Widget C was attached. The patent drafter may want to ask the inventor whether the surface could be prepared in any way other than burning. If so, then the invention may be broader than only burning the surface material. The patent drafter may, for example, want to ask whether the surfaces can be burned *before* attaching Widget A to Widget B or whether they *must* be combined first.

There are many questions that the patent drafter in our example may ask the inventor. The answers to such questions help the patent drafter to understand the invention and draft the best possible claims and supporting description.

Of course, the patent drafter may discover that the inventor does not know all of the answers. In this instance, the inventor may be able to speculate about alternatives and, in some instances, may even have the time to conduct some additional research. The patent drafter must make sure, however, that the description discloses a working embodiment of the invention; hence if the inventor is uncertain about an answer, the patent drafter must use their best professional judgement to resolve the uncertainty. This may include, for example, directing the inventor to a design engineer for advice. And while there may be gaps in the technical disclosure that the patent drafter can fill, they should always confirm with the inventor that any material they have added is correct and within the spirit of the invention.

Sometimes, the patent drafter may even assist the inventor in considering possible alternative embodiments for the invention. Inventors often work to solve a very specific problem and have not really considered whether their invention could have applications in other areas.

1.4 Inventorship

A patent application as filed is required to include the name(s) of the inventor(s). Before filing the patent application, the patent drafter should ask their client who is/are the inventor(s) and then confirm whether the inventor(s) indicated by the client qualify for *inventorship* or not. The patent drafter should keep in mind that the would-be inventor(s) indicated by the client may not always be entitled as true inventor(s).

In some countries, for example, it may be a customary practice to list all members of a research team as joint inventors regardless of the degree of individual contribution to the invention. It may be culturally commonplace to list, as a mark of respect, a research and development manager or a lead professor who has made no substantial contribution to the invention. Incorrectly identifying the inventor(s) may cause problems after filing, for example giving rise to a challenge as fraud or misappropriation that may render the granted patent invalid or even unenforceable. It may also complicate the establishment of a priority claim. Since only some jurisdictions and not others will allow amendment of an incorrect indication of the inventorship after the patent application has been filed, it is essential to check it thoroughly at this stage.

Although the definition of inventorship differs across jurisdictions, the general test in the context of the patent system is that the person must have made a creative contribution to the inventive concept of the claimed invention. In other words, that person's creativity should have led in some way to the features of the claimed invention that distinguish it from the prior art. For example, in the United States, a person who contributed to the conception of the invention is entitled to be an inventor, while someone else who merely acted under the direction of that person is not. Similarly, in Japan, only a person who has substantially engaged in the creative process of the claimed invention is entitled to be an inventor. In contrast, a supervisor who simply manages inventors, a person who simply follows instructions from a researcher to collect data or conduct experiments, or a person who merely provided funds and facilities to the inventor may not be so entitled.

2. Typical parts of the patent application

Once a patent drafter understands the invention, they can begin to prepare the patent application, which will typically include:

– a request;
– a description;[12]
– claims;
– drawings; and
– an abstract.

Where an invention relates to nucleotide and/or amino acid sequences, a sequence listing, typically in electronic form, may also be required.

In addition, national/regional patent laws may demand various other documents and statements to be submitted to the respective patent office. These include a power of attorney, a document relating to the identity of the inventor, a document relating to the applicant's entitlement to apply for or be granted a patent and an oath or declaration of inventorship. Since these requirements vary from one country to another, a patent drafter should check the rules of the territory/ies in which patent protection is sought.

We will now describe each of these main parts of the application in brief. Modules IV–VI will look in more detail at how to draft claims, while Module VII will explore drafting of the description, drawings and an abstract.

2.1 Request

The *request* explicitly states that an applicant seeks patent protection and is signed by the applicant or its representative. Usually, each patent office provides a specific request form (known in some countries as a patent application form) for completion. While each request form is different, reflecting the specifics of national/regional law, the request form will generally contain:

– the title of the invention;
– the name and address of the applicant and their representative (e.g., a patent attorney);
– an indication of the inventor; and
– information relating to the priority claim, such as the application number and filing date of the earlier application on which the priority is based.

In general, all priority information, such as the information about the earlier application on which the priority is claimed or the information about the parent application in case of a divisional application, should be included in the patent application, whether on the request form or in an application data sheet.

In the United States, such indication of related applications can be described under the heading "CROSS-REFERENCE TO RELATED APPLICATION" in an earlier part of the form, following the title of the invention.

2.2 Description

The *description* discloses the invention sufficiently clearly and completely to the extent that a person skilled in the art will be able to carry out the claimed invention. To improve the readability of the description, it usually contains several sections.

While the format of the description is not the same across jurisdictions, in general, the follow elements appear on the description.

(i) The *title of the invention*, as appearing in the request, concisely identifies and broadly describes the invention for which patent protection is sought.
(ii) The *technical field* to which the invention relates may then be specified.
(iii) The *background art* in the field of the invention will be set out next, which can be useful for the understanding of the invention.
(iv) This is followed by a *summary of the invention*, which outlines its full scope and how it has solved the problem of the background art.
(v) The description then briefly explains *the drawings*.
(vi) Finally, the description discloses greater detail of the claimed invention by way of *examples (embodiments)*, making reference to the drawings. These examples often play an important role in meeting the support requirement and the enablement requirement (see Module II, section 2.5).

2.3 Claims

The *claims* define the scope of exclusive patent protection in terms of the technical features of the invention. The claims are the legally operative part of a patent application and whether or not an invention meets the patentability requirements is determined on the basis of the claims.

Claims must be clear and concise, as well as fully supported by the description. Claims are written in a peculiar format – for example:

1. An apparatus, comprising:
   – a pencil having an elongated structure including two ends and a center between the ends;
   – an eraser attached to one end of the pencil; and
   – a light attached to the center of the pencil.

2.4 Drawings

The *drawings* provide visual support in describing the invention and often facilitate better understanding of the claimed invention. They may include figures, tables, flow charts and diagrams. A representative drawing is usually positioned on the front page of a published patent document.

2.5 Abstract

The *abstract* is a summary (a digest) of the invention limited to a certain number of words. It typically includes key features recited in the claims and is primarily an aid for those conducting patent searches and readers of patent documents, delivering an overview of the invention.

2.6 Application format

Although these five parts are found commonly in the filing requirements of various countries and for international patent applications under the PCT, their detailed format is rarely the same. For example, while the description may be divided into several sections, the section headings may differ from one jurisdiction to the next. Some patent offices supply a sample application form to ensure that submissions conform to their requirements.

Key words

- Application (request)
- Description
- Drawings
- Claims
- Abstract
- Time-barring events
- Nondisclosure agreement
- Provisional application
- Invention Disclosure Form
- Embodiment
- Core inventive concept
- Priority claim under the Paris Convention
- Inventorship
- Common Application Format (CAF)

It is worth noting that a common application format (CAF)[13], establishing common headings and standardizing the order of sections in a patent application, is accepted by the European Patent Office (EPO), the Japan Patent Office (JPO), the Korean Intellectual Property Office (KIPO), the National Intellectual Property Administration of the People's Republic of China (CNIPA) and the United States Patent and Trademark Office (USPTO). The CAF is intended to reduce the burden on applicants when applying across multiple territories, allowing them to meet multiple specification requirements in the above jurisdictions.

Self-Test

- [ ] List the parts of a patent application.

- [ ] Give some examples of questions a patent drafter might ask an inventor when they meet for the first time.

- [ ] An inventor needs to disclose their invention to a potential investor before filing a patent application. What might you suggest the inventor does to maintain the possibility of obtaining patent protection in the future?

- [ ] To enjoy the right of priority under the Paris Convention, how much time does an applicant have in which to file a subsequent application in another Paris Convention country? Is there any special consideration to be made for subsequent filing in a country that is not a signatory to the Convention?

- [ ] What is an invention disclosure form and when should an inventor use it?

- [ ] The inventor will always know what their invention is. True or false?

- [ ] If the patent drafter helps to identify the invention or makes suggestions to the inventor, does this make the patent drafter one of the inventors?

- [ ] Why is it important for the patent drafter to understand the invention before drafting the patent?

- [ ] The description must disclose a working embodiment of the invention. True or false?

- [ ] Which part of the patent application should the patent drafter prepare first?

Module IV
Fundamentals of claim drafting

1.	**Theory of the patent claim**	**36**
1.1	Overview: inventions, embodiments and claims	36
1.2	Broad and narrow claims	37
1.3	Patent protection and infringement: all-elements rule	37
2.	**Patent claim format**	**38**
2.1	Parts of a claim	38
2.2	Grammar of a claim and other detail	41
2.3	Two-part claims or improvement claims	44
2.4	Alternative elements and Markush claims	45
2.5	Functional elements and means-plus-function claims	47
3.	**Claim sets**	**48**
3.1	Independent claims	48
3.2	Dependent claims	50
3.3	Multiple dependent claims	53
3.4	Claims referring to features of another claim	56
3.5	Claim sets based on set theory	57
3.6	Schematic example of drafting a set of claims	60

When an inventor tells a patent drafter that they want to file a patent application, the first set of questions that a patent drafter must ask themselves is:

– What has been invented?
– What is the essential inventive concept of this invention?
– Does the inventor know what they want to protect?
– How should we claim the invention?

1. Theory of the patent claim

1.1 Overview: inventions, embodiments and claims

The claims mark (define) the boundaries (the scope) of the protection provided by a patent, just as a physical boundary such as a fence marks the limits of a parcel of real property. The claims are thus a written approximation of the abstract concept created by the inventor. While courts in jurisdictions around the world may apply differing legal doctrines when interpreting claims, in the most prevalent theory, the claims establish the outer limits of patent protection (known as *peripheral claiming*). The claims clearly and concisely tell the world what the applicant claims as their invention. As a member of the Court of Appeals for the Federal Circuit (and its predecessor, the Court of Customs and Patent Appeals) of the United States said in 1990, "The name of the game is the claim."[14]

The patent drafter needs to understand the differences between three legal constructs related to patents: inventions, embodiments and claims.

– An *invention* is a construct inside the mind of the inventor and has no physical substance.
– An *embodiment* of an invention is a physical form of the invention in the real world.
– The *claims* must protect *at least* an "embodiment" of the invention – *but* the best patent claims will protect the "invention" itself, so that no physical embodiments of the invention can be made, used or sold by anyone without infringing the claims.

The logical conclusion of these differences between the invention, embodiment(s) and claims is that the claims do not define the invention. Nevertheless, patent practitioners commonly use the expression *claimed invention* to mean the subject matter defined by claims in a patent application or in a granted patent.

Example

An inventor conceives of the first cup to have a handle. They make a physical embodiment of their invention in the form of a red clay cup with a handle. Their patent drafter could claim only the physical embodiment of the red clay cup with a handle, but this would allow others to make noninfringing cups, such as plastic cups with handles.

If the patent drafter understands the invention, they will position the *invention* of the cup with a handle as their broadest claim and the *embodiment* (the red clay cup) in a subsequent narrower claim (see section 1.2 of this module regarding the concept of broader and narrower claims).

Early patents did not include claims and the scope of the patented invention was determined in court proceedings during patent infringement litigation by reviewing the description of the invention filed by the inventor. Unsurprisingly, this process eventually became unworkable and the process of patent claiming was born to give notice of the boundaries of the patent. Thus claims were originally intended to serve as a guideline, explaining what the inventor perceived as their invention at the time they filed their patent application. Today, claims define the protection given by a patent and lie at the heart of any invention. The claims are typically the first portion of the patent examined and scrutinized by anyone interested in the patent, including the courts. Additionally, in a substantive examination patent system (see Module II, section 1.1), a patent examiner will review the claims before granting a patent, which typically provides the courts and the public with some assurance that the patent does not exceed the maximum scope of protection the inventor should receive.

As noted throughout this manual, the description set out in the patent application must support the patent claims. Consequently, after drafting the claims and writing the description, the patent drafter must revisit both to ensure that every single claim is adequately supported in the description. The choice of terminology – the words and phrases – used in claims should track through the description consistently; a claim that is not supported by the description can easily be thrown out for lack of support. If a patent drafter claims a glass table with four legs, they must ensure that there is support for a glass table with four legs in the description and not only, for example, a description of wooden tables or of tables with three legs. In the jurisdictions in which the support requirement is evaluated strictly, such as at the European Patent Office (EPO), the description must also specifically include at least one embodiment that explicitly demonstrates the combination of glass and four legs.

While jurisdictions may differ in terms of format and interpretation, the theory of what constitutes a good patent claim is essentially the same worldwide. The EPO summarizes this as follows:

The application must contain "one or more claims." These must:

(i) "define the matter for which protection is sought";
(ii) "be clear and concise"; and
(iii) "be supported by the description."

Since the extent of the protection conferred by a […] patent or application is determined by the claims (interpreted with the help of the description and the drawings), clarity of the claims is of the utmost importance.[15] In general, the concept of invention is associated with the concept of *technology*, the latter being generally defined as the use of scientific knowledge to solve practical problems. The EPO recommends that claims be drafted in terms of the "technical features of the invention" – that is, that claims should not contain statements relating, for example, to commercial advantages or other nontechnical matters, although "statements of purpose are allowed if they assist in defining the invention."[16]

This is sound advice for patent drafters in any jurisdiction.

1.2 Broad and narrow claims

If it is the patent examiner's role to prevent a typical patent claim from *exceeding* the scope of its invention (i.e., the claim's theoretical maximum), whose role is it to make sure that the claims *approach* their theoretical maximum?

The quick answer is that it is the patent drafter's responsibility to aim at a broad set of claims that covers various aspects of the invention at various levels of detail. The patent drafter may not want the claims to reach only to their theoretical maximum, since subsequent litigation will likely raise invalidity arguments not contemplated by either the applicant or patent examiner; hence some narrower claims will be useful in the event that the broadest claims are invalidated. A narrower set of claims may be upheld during litigation and may still be "broad enough" to prove protection against the patent infringer.

This is, to some extent, easier said than done. At the time of drafting a patent application, it is difficult to predict the legitimate scope of the protection for an invention, since this scope will be revealed only in light of all relevant prior art. A search of the prior art will never be exhaustive and an applicant may find out only after filing that part of their initially claimed subject matter was not novel. To complicate matters further, patent applications already filed but not yet published at our own filing date may subsequently emerge as novelty-destroying prior art in many jurisdictions. As a general

rule, the description of a patent application should therefore disclose the claimed subject matter in the form of embodiments making use of the inventive concept of an invention and, in the claims, define the subject matter for which protection is sought.

While some jurisdictions place limits on the degree to which an applicant may amend claims or cancel and replace them with new claims on their own initiative, amendment may occur during patent prosecution or during examination should the patent examiner raise an objection. The patent drafter may have some flexibility to adjust pending claims to avoid reading on newly discovered prior art, to satisfy legal requirements that have not been met or to reflect changing interests in the scope of protection, etc. In some jurisdictions, there may also be scope to respond to hindsight when a client or the patent drafter realizes belatedly that the claims as filed might have been more broadly recited.

Unsurprisingly, claiming strategy is a complicated issue and we will address it in detail in Module VI.

1.3 Patent protection and infringement: all-elements rule

As explained in the earlier modules, a patent generally grants the patent owner the exclusive right, with certain exceptions, to control who makes, uses, sells, offers for sale and/or imports any product or process defined by the patent's claims. In other words, competitors need permission from the patentee to make, use, etc. the claimed invention. Without such permission, they infringe on the patent claims and hence infringe the patent. This means that, when drafting claims, patent drafters should always try to ensure that competitors, either actual or potential, cannot circumvent the claimed invention and freeride on the "ideas" or "inventive concepts."

Example

A patent claim reads:

1. A writing apparatus, comprising:
   – a pencil having an elongated structure including two ends and a center between the ends;
   – an eraser attached to one end of the pencil; and
   – a light attached to the center of the pencil.

According to the all-elements rule, a competitor infringes the claim if it produces a writing device that has *all* of:

(i) a pencil with an elongated structure, including two ends and a center between the ends;
(ii) an eraser attached to one end of the pencil; and
(iii) a light attached to the center of the pencil.

A competitor produces a writing device that has the elements of a pencil and an eraser attached to one end of the pencil, but no light attached on the pencil. Another competitor produces a pencil with an eraser attached to one end and a light *also attached to one end* of the pencil (i.e., not to the *center* of the pencil).

In these cases, there is no patent infringement.

But what exactly is meant by *infringing* a patent claim?

Every act of infringement allegedly done by a third party is associated with what is called an *accused embodiment* that is either an object (e.g., an apparatus that a third party has manufactured, a chemical compound that a third party has sold, etc.) or an activity (e.g., a manufacturing process that a third party has used). In some cases, a third party might have another patent relating to the accused embodiment.

To determine whether the accused embodiment infringes patent claims, it will be directly compared with the subject matter defined by the claims.

The basic rule of patent claim infringement is sometimes referred to as the *all-elements rule*. In essence, it means that, to assert patent infringement, all of the elements of a claim must be reproduced in the third party's accused embodiment.

As this example illustrates, the comparison between the accused embodiment and the allegedly infringed claim should be conducted element by element – a principle widely adopted in many jurisdictions. The term *element* is commonly used across jurisdictions, and it is used synonymously with the term *technical feature* that appears in the European Patent Convention (EPC) and *limitation*, which appears in U.S. patent law and practice.

Depending on the subject matter claimed, various kinds of element may appear, including the following.

– *Structural elements* are defined by what they are, for example "a screw," "a DVD," "hydrogen peroxide," "talc," etc.
– *Functional elements* are defined by the functions they perform, for example "a fastening means," "a computer-readable storage medium," "an oxidizing agent," "a pharmaceutically acceptable excipient," etc.
– *Relational elements* subsume the relationships between other elements, for example "attached," "electrically connected," "dissolved in the same solution," etc.
– *Intentional elements* define an intention or purpose and are typically introduced with the preposition *for*, for example "for coagulation," "for treating cancer," etc.
– *Parametric elements* are parameters (i.e., values of directly measurable properties), for example the flexural strength of a metal, the resistance of an electric conductor, the melting point of a substance, etc.
– *Activity elements* subsume the *steps* used when defining the subject matter of process or activity claims, and are typically introduced with verbs in gerund form, for example "fixing" together, "reading" information from, "reacting" with, etc.

2. Patent claim format

There is no universal format for a patent claim and different drafting styles are found in different jurisdictions. Nevertheless, there are generally accepted formats and styles, as you will see in this section.

In this manual, unless specified, the rules explained are those under the Patent Cooperation Treaty (PCT).

A patent claim is traditionally written as a single sentence and in the present tense. Each claim begins with a capital letter and ends with a period. Periods may not be used elsewhere in the claims, other than in abbreviations. Usually, semicolons are used to separate clauses and phrases. Although a patent claim is a single sentence, it is consequently usually a heavily punctuated single sentence.

Claims are numbered consecutively and that number becomes the claim's identifier (e.g., "Claim 1").

All of the claims, appropriately grouped and numbered, appear in a separate section headed "Claims," which must be clearly separated (by page breaks) from the other parts of the application. The patent claims typically appear toward the end of the application and an issued patent. In the printed documents of some patent offices, such as the China National Intellectual Property Administration (CNIPA), the Japan Patent Office (JPO) and the Korean Intellectual Property Office (KIPO), the claims section is placed before the description section. In the United States, the claims section and the description section are distinguished only with expressions of the type "I/we claim" or "What is claimed is."

2.1 Parts of a claim

A patent claim is generally in three parts – the preamble, the transitional phrase and the body – although different styles of claim may be permitted in various jurisdictions.

Preamble
The *preamble* is an introductory phrase that identifies the category of the invention protected by that claim. For example,

the invention may be an apparatus, article, composition, compound, device, system, method or process.

The preamble is typically written in the form of a singular noun phrase. The noun phrase may be accompanied by premodifiers, such as adjectives, for example "a chemical composition." It may be also accompanied by postmodifiers, such as complements typically introduced with a preposition, for example "a chemical composition *for* moisturizing." The more adjectives or complements are added, the narrower the scope of the preamble becomes.

It is important that the preamble is chosen carefully and is at the right level of breadth. Sometimes, it is a good idea to keep the preamble consistent with the title of the invention. The claim can also recite an object of the invention in the preamble, but – for the same reasons noted elsewhere in relation to drafting the description (see Module VII) – the patent drafter must be cautious of accidentally limiting the scope of the invention.

Let us take a look at some examples.

Example 1

A patent applicant has invented a rice cooker. Since an object of this invention is to cook rice, the preamble and title might read:

"An apparatus for cooking rice,"

Suppose that the patent applicant knows their invention could be used for cooking all kinds of grains. In this case, a broader preamble might read:

"An apparatus for cooking grains,"

Suppose further that the patent applicant knows their invention could be used for cooking vegetables – or even melting cheese for fondue. An even broader preamble might simply read:

"An apparatus for cooking,"

Example 2

A patent applicant wants to claim a unique method of making tea. Here, the preamble might read:

"A method for making tea,"

If the inventor believes their method would be applicable to making any beverage arising from a plant substance, a broader preamble might read:

"A method for making a plant-based beverage,"

If the inventor instead believes their method would be applicable to making any warm beverage, the preamble might read:

"A method for making a warm beverage,"

The second and third preambles are broader, in some ways, than the first: the second preamble applies to any plant-based beverage, whether warm or not; and the third preamble applies to any hot beverage, whether plant-based or not. The patent drafter can add claims to a patent application based on any or all of these preambles – assuming that they accurately reflect the invention.

One potential disadvantage of using these preambles is, however, that the patent office might find multiple inventions in the one application and require certain claims be moved to a divisional application, which would increase the fees payable (see Module VI, section 11, for more on unity of invention).

The patent drafter must ensure that the preamble relates accurately to the invention. This means that if an invention were supposed to cover "bicycles" and the inventor to believe their invention adaptable to all kinds of nonmotorized vehicles, it would be a good idea to keep the preamble broad enough to cover all forms of nonmotorized land vehicle but perhaps not *motorized flying* vehicles.

The preamble may not necessarily be accorded the same weight during patent litigation as the body of the claim and the weight given to preambles can vary from jurisdiction to jurisdiction. In some jurisdictions, the courts will look at whether the preamble "breathes life" into the claim as a whole and, if so, the preamble will be accorded patentable weight.

Example

An invention comprises a mounting for attaching a telephone to a wall. The patent drafter will be unlikely to claim a telephone as part of this invention, because this could narrow the range of potential infringers to persons who sell telephones *and* their mountings, rather than anyone who sells only mountings.

Consequently, the preamble for the mounting could read:

"A device for mounting a telephone,"

In this way, both making, using or selling a mounting device alone *and* making, etc. a mounting device together with a telephone will most likely infringe the claim.

Transitional phrases

There are two types of *transitional phrase*: open-ended and closed.

Open-ended phrases do not exclude any additional elements or method steps that are not recited in the claim. In other words, open-ended phrases are inclusive, not exclusive. In the United States, for example, open-ended phrases include words such as "comprising," "including," "containing" and "characterized by." These terms have been construed or interpreted to mean "including the following elements but not excluding others." The words "comprising" and "including" are the most commonly used transitional phrases in the United States.

Let us take a look at a sample claim using the phrase "comprising."

Example

The invention relates to a pencil with an eraser and a light attached to it. A claim may read:

1. An apparatus, *comprising*:
   – a pencil having an elongated structure including two ends and a center between the ends;
   – an eraser attached to one end of the pencil; and
   – a light attached to the center of the pencil.

In this claim, by using the open-ended phrase "comprising," we have expanded its scope to allow for other elements or limitations. For example, this claim leaves open the possibility of including a cap for the pencil. In other words, an accused infringer could not successfully argue that their product does not infringe because it has a pencil cap.

To reiterate, while in everyday language the word "comprise" may be interchangeable with the words "include," "contain," "comprehend" or "consist of," in drafting patent claims, legal certainty normally requires it to be interpreted as more broadly meaning "include," "contain" or "comprehend."

Closed phrases are the opposite of open-ended phrases. Closed phrases such as "consisting of" limit the claim to nothing more than the specifically recited elements: the claim covers *only* the elements named and nothing more.

Example

We might rewrite the previous open-ended example in closed form as:

1. An apparatus, *consisting of*:
   – a pencil having an elongated structure including two ends and a center between the ends;
   – an eraser attached to the pencil; and
   – a light attached to the pencil.

By using the phrase "consisting of," this claim has become a closed claim that includes only the three recited elements of pencil, an eraser and a light – and nothing more.

The patent drafter may sometimes draft a claim for a chemical compound that refers to it as "consisting of components A, B and C," each of which will include proportions expressed in percentages. Such claims are acceptable in most jurisdictions. However, the presence of any additional component will be excluded and therefore the percentages should add up to 100 percent. In drafting such a claim, the patent drafter must know for certain that third parties may avoid patent infringement by including another chemical compound – however small its percentage might be. Alternatively, the patent drafter could make sure that one of the terms included in the percentage is so broad (for example, "metal") that it could refer to many things.

A patent drafter will rarely write – and must think twice before filing – a closed claim, because infringers can easily avoid infringement by simply adding another element. In some jurisdictions, a patent drafter might use a closed transitional phrase when an invention is a simplification of an apparatus that is already in use. Since the simplification has fewer elements than the original, some jurisdictions might consider that a closed phrase overcomes the prior art of the original for anticipation (i.e., novelty) purposes. However, the patent office might still consider the original reference to be relevant prior art for obviousness (e.g., inventive step) purposes. There may also be particular instances in which, for a specific technological invention type such as biotechnology, closed phrases may be slightly more likely to arise.

When drafting claims, the patent drafter will therefore need to check carefully not only which transitional phrases are considered open-ended or closed in the jurisdiction(s) of interest but also whether the subject matter and the laws of the jurisdiction(s) of interest support an interpretation of closed transitional phrases that will help the client to achieve their goals. Using the wrong phrase could significantly limit the scope of protection provided by the patent. In Australia, for example, the term "comprising" has sometimes been interpreted as a narrow, closed transitional phrase – precisely the opposite of its interpretation in many countries. Thus an open-ended claim in the United Kingdom might use the transition "comprising," while a claim of precisely the same scope in Australia might use "including" as its transitional phrase.[17]

Body of the claim

The *body of the claim* is the portion that follows the transitional phrase. The body of the claim recites the elements and limitations of the claim. The body also explains how the different elements exist in relationship to one another. Basically, the body of the claim recites and interrelates all of the elements of the claim; hence the body of the claim may include any of a variety of structural, functional, relational or parametric elements or active steps.

Example

The body of an apparatus claim covering a table might read:

1. An apparatus for holding items, comprising:
   – at least one leg; and
   – a top configured to be supported by at least one leg.

In this claim, the body recites the two elements, "at least one leg" and "a top" that is supported by the one leg. The body of the claim also connects the leg to the top.

A patent claim cannot be merely a list of parts; they must be connected in some manner. Most patent offices will not knowingly allow patent claims that merely list parts and hence the claim in our example would likely be *rejected* if it were to be written:

1. An apparatus for holding items, comprising:

   – four legs;
   – 16 screws; and
   – a top.

The number and types of element included in a claim very much depends on the technical field and on the particular invention. In the field of chemistry, for instance, such elements may be isolated chemical entities, defined as alternatives and represented by either specific formulae or names or by general formula with variables.

We have discussed the open-ended phrase "comprising" and the closed phrase "consisting" in relation to the transition phrase. These phrases can equally be used in the body of the claim to define the elements in either open-ended or closed ways.

2.2 Grammar of a claim and other detail

Punctuation

While many topics related to patent claims may be more exciting than their punctuation, nearly every patent office stipulates requirements in this regard. If the patent drafter focuses solely on attuning their patent claims to the client's business needs and does not pay attention to the minute detail of full stops and semi-colons, they may find that their otherwise well-crafted patent claims are rejected by patent offices the world over.

Professional tip

You will almost always better serve your client's interests by amending claims to avoid the prior art but in a manner that still makes it difficult for a competitor to avoid the claim easily – and the best way of doing this is usually to add clarifying amendments to the claims rather than to use a closed transitional phrase.

Professional tip

Most countries follow a "peripheral claiming" doctrine in which the claims establish the outer limits of patent protection. Unless you happen to file the claims in a now-rare jurisdiction that allows claims that follow a "central claiming" doctrine (i.e., the claims identify the "center" of the patented invention), it is critical that you draft the claims to set the limits of the scope of the protection sought.

For the sake of clarity, claims are frequently more extensively punctuated than grammatically required. A comma typically separates the preamble from the transitional phrase and a colon typically separates the transition from the body. The body itself is typically broken into small paragraphs that define the logical elements of the claim. Many jurisdictions do not have specific laws requiring such punctuation, but the patent drafter should strive to make sure that the claim will be interpreted as they intend. The patent drafter must write with the patent examiner – and, later, the courts and potential licensees – in mind. Thus the "elements" of a claim are typically separated by semi-colons and the penultimate element is followed "; and," before the last ends with a full stop.

The model is this:

Preamble, transitional phrase:

– Element (#1);
– Element (#2); and
– Element (#3).

In practice, it might look like this:

An apparatus, comprising:

– a plurality of printed pages;
– a binding configured to hold the printed pages together; and
– a cover attached to the binding.

In some countries, such as the United States, each element or combination of elements of the claim should be separated by a line indentation, as demonstrated here. In some other countries, the line indentation is accepted but not required.

Proper antecedent basis
The elements in a patent claim must demonstrate the correct antecedent basis. This means that an element is introduced with the indefinite article "a" or "an" on its first use. When referring back to that element, the definite article "the" will appear. Not only is this grammatically appropriate but also proper antecedent basis is a matter of law.

The following set of claims will help to explain:

1. *A* device, comprising:
   – *a* pencil; and
   – *a* light attached to *the* pencil.

2. *The* device recited in claim 1 wherein *the* light is detachably attached to *the* pencil.
3. *The* device recited in claim 2 wherein *the* pencil is red in color.

In Claim 1, we introduce the "pencil" for the first time by referring to it as "*a* pencil." In the same claim, we also introduce the light for the first time as "*a* light." However, when we go on to specify that the light is attached to the pencil, we refer to the pencil as "*the* pencil." The use of the word "the" signals that the pencil is the same one we previously defined in the claim; otherwise, there may be ambiguity – *is it the same pencil or another pencil?*

Professional tip

While the words "the" and "said" are interchangeable in claims drafting (e.g., "the pencil" or "said pencil"), the latter is increasingly old-fashioned and the trend in many jurisdictions is toward plain language even in law. If your patent is litigated in court in the United States, a nonlawyer jury may read the claims and you will not endear yourself to them if you lean on "legalese."

If we want to draft another claim that refers to another pencil, then we will need to distinguish the first pencil from the second. One way to do this is by reciting a "first" element and then reciting a "second" element – and so on. An alternative where there will be only a small number of elements is to refer to the first as "an" element and the second as "another" element, for example:

– A first widget, connected to a second widget, wherein the first widget…
– A foomerantz, coupled to another foomerantz, wherein another foomerantz has a higher capacitance than the foomerantz…

In each new claim *set*,[18] the antecedent basis must be re-established. Thus, in another claim set, the patent drafter will provide a proper antecedent basis for the element "pencil" all over again. In other words, each new claim needs to be drafted independently of the others.

If we draft a new claim (Claim 4) for our pencil invention, it might read:

4. *A* device, comprising:
   – *a* pencil; and
   – *a* light attached to *the* pencil, wherein *the* light is detachably attached to *the* pencil.

Reference numerals and expressions in parenthesis

In some jurisdictions, claims are encouraged and/or required to recite reference numerals with which particular elements in the patent application's drawings are labeled. For PCT international applications, such reference numerals shall preferably appear in parentheses after each of the corresponding elements in the claims. Thus if figure 1 of a patent application shows a computer memory and this computer memory is labeled "123," for example, any reference to this particular computer memory element in the claims will be followed by the reference numeral "(123)."

In those jurisdictions in which the use of reference numerals is encouraged, this practice can support comprehension of the claims by establishing clear connection between the claims and the drawings. If, however, there are a large number of different embodiments, only the most important embodiments typically need to be incorporated in the claim(s) and indicated in this way.

In many countries, the patent laws explicitly state that reference numerals shall *not* be interpreted as limiting the extent of the matter protected by the claims. Their sole function is to make claims easier to understand. The patent drafter may even want to make a comment themselves to that effect in the description.

In some countries, however, and particularly in the United States, patent drafters either avoid or are prohibited from including any such reference numerals, likely because of the risk that infringers and the courts may indeed interpret them as limiting the claims. If text is added to reference numerals within the parentheses, lack of clarity can arise. Expressions such as "securing means (screw 13, nail 14)" or "valve assembly (valve seat 23, valve element 27 & valve seat 28)" may not be considered to be mere reference signs but "special features."[19] Consequently, it may be unclear whether the features added to the reference signs are limiting or not.

In some jurisdictions, a lack of clarity can also arise with expressions in parenthesis that do not include reference numerals, such as "(concrete) molded brick," and hence these may be rejected. In contrast, expressions with a generally accepted meaning are allowable, such as "(meth)acrylate," which is known as an abbreviation for "acrylate and methacrylate." The use of parentheses in chemical or mathematical formulae is, of course, also typically unobjectionable.

It is important to remember that the inclusion of reference numerals in the claim does not mean that the respective drawings are incorporated in the claims – a practice that is impermissible in most countries.[20] Claims should therefore be drafted as clearly as if there were no drawings.

Example

A claim with reference numerals may read:

1. An apparatus, comprising:
   – a plurality of printed pages (11);
   – a binding (14) configured to hold the printed pages (11) together; and
   – a cover (21) attached to the binding (14).

The numbers in parentheses are the reference numerals that appear as labels in the drawings attached to the patent application.

Claim phrases

We have already seen that words such as "comprising" have a special meaning when applied to claims. Similarly, other words can have special meanings when applied to patent claims. Some words are used to further define a structure or provide a function associated with a given structure. Such words include "wherein," "whereby" and "such that," and "so as to." The patent drafter must know how the courts in the jurisdictions of interest have opted to interpret these words and then use them in a manner appropriate to the protection sought.

For example, a "wherein clause" is generally used to describe a function, operation or result that flows from the previously recited structure or function of the claim; hence "wherein clauses" should be used where the result necessarily follows the recited structure or function.

Example

We want to claim a folder for storing files. Using "wherein," the claim might read:

1. A folder for keeping files, wherein the folder is configured to receive the files…

In claim drafting, the word "wherein" is also used to add a selection of elements in a dependent claim, as we will explain later in section 3.5 on claim dependency.

Multiple elements

Many patent offices require claims to recite at least two elements. A patent claim without many limitations can be impossibly broad.

The necessity for this rule is readily evidenced by a comparison of two claims.

Example

Compare:

A computer, comprising:

– a processor.

with:

A computer, comprising:

– a processor;
– a memory; and
– a bus configured to transmit data between the memory and the processor.

The first claim tells us little about a computer other than that it is something containing a processor. The specification will, of course, define a processor for us and we can also assume that processors exist in the prior art, but the applicant appears to be claiming anything that contains a processor – especially if the preamble is not considered to be limiting.

Such a claim is impossibly broad: it reads on (see Module II, section 1.2) a box in which a processor is shipped, since we do not know anything more about computers other than that they are structures that contain processors.

The second claim provides a lot more structure and definition for computers. It is therefore narrower in scope than the first.

2.3 Two-part claims or improvement claims

Most of the explanation in the previous sections about the parts and other detail of a claim also applies to a claim written in the two-part format, which is also known as an *improvement claim* or (in the United States) a *Jepson claim*.[21] In a two-part claim, the preamble of the claim sets out the most relevant known prior art and the body characterizes the improvement of the invention. The preamble and body are connected by a specific transitional phrase that signals that the claim is in two parts. Thus two-part claims still have a preamble, a transitional phrase and a body, but the preamble is the statement (an implied admission) of the *single* most relevant prior art, the transition is a phrase such as "characterized by" or "characterized in that" in Europe, or "wherein the improvement comprises" in the United States, and the body provides the element(s) that the applicant considers novel (not found in the closest prior art).

Example 1

1. A pencil having an eraser attached to one end of the pencil, wherein the improvement comprises a light attached to the pencil.

In this claim, "a pencil having an eraser" is the relevant known prior art and the claimed improvement is the attached light.

Using the standard claim format, we might rewrite the claim, without altering its scope, as:

1. A writing device, comprising:
   – a pencil having an elongated structure including two ends;
   – an eraser attached to one end of the pencil; and
   – a light attached to the pencil.

Example 2

1. A writing device, comprising: a pencil having an elongated structure including two ends and a center between the ends; an eraser attached to one end of the pencil; and a light attached to the pencil, characterized in that the light is attached to the center of the pencil.

In this claim, the applicant admits that a writing device comprising a pencil with an eraser on one end and a light is the known prior art and states that the claimed *improvement is the position of the light, which is at the center of the pencil.*

As Example 2 demonstrates, the two-part format clearly highlights the element of the claimed invention that the applicant considers inventive over the prior art. However, patent drafters should be mindful that, where the two-part claim format is used, the applicant explicitly admits that the subject covered by the first part of the claim was not novel on the filing (or priority) date of the patent application.

Some jurisdictions, such as the EPO, prefer the two-part format, wherever appropriate. The EPO advises that applicants should follow the two-part formulation in claims where, for example, it is clear that the invention resides in a distinct improvement on an old combination of parts or steps. As with many rules created for administrative efficiency, this "preference" is somewhat flexible in actual practice (a cursory review of EPO-issued patents will reveal many claims not in a two-part format). Thus patent drafters need to consider whether a two-part claim is in their client's best interest given that it requires an explicit admission that the first part is definitely in the prior art. Some patent drafters may wish to recite their claims initially in the standard format, then see whether the examiner enforces the preference and requires instead the two-part form. On other occasions, if the client is filing before the EPO only, they may be best served by claims drafted in the two-part format from the outset, given the nature of the invention and the prior art.

The EPO recommends that the first part of such claims contain a *statement* indicating "the designation of the subject matter of the invention" – that is, the general technical class of apparatus, process, etc. to which the invention relates – followed by a statement of "those technical features which are necessary for the definition of the claimed subject matter but which, in combination, are part of the prior art."[22] This statement of prior art features applies only to independent claims and not to dependent claims. Thus such statements are necessary only when prior art features are relevant to the invention. For example, if the invention relates to a photographic camera but the inventive step relates entirely to improvement of the shutter, it would generally be sufficient for the first part of the claim to read: "A photographic camera including a focal plane shutter…" There is no need to refer to other known features of a camera, such as the lens and view-finder, unless recitations of other components are required as representing essential elements of a camera.

The second part, or *characterizing portion*, should summarize the features that the invention adds to the prior art – that is, the technical features for which, in combination with the features stated in the first part, protection is sought.

While expressing a preference for two-part claims, the EPO concedes that such claims are inappropriate in some circumstances. The nature of an invention may be such that this form of claim is unsuitable, for example because it would give a distorted or misleading picture of the invention or the prior art. Examples of the kind of invention that may require a different presentation are:

- the combination of known integers of equal status, the inventive step lying solely in the combination;
- the modification of, as distinct from addition to, a known chemical process, for example by omitting one substance or substituting one substance for another; or
- a complex system of functionally interrelated parts, the inventive step concerning changes in several of these or in their interrelationships.

In the first two of these examples, the two-part form of claim may be artificial and inappropriate, while in the third it might lead to an inordinately lengthy and convoluted claim.

Another example of an instance in which the two-part form of claim may be inappropriate is where the invention is a new chemical compound or group of compounds.

The EPO further advises that other cases will arise in which the applicant is able to provide convincing reasons for structuring the claim other than in the two-part form.

2.4 Alternative elements and Markush claims

Many jurisdictions allow a single patent claim to contain alternative elements. In everyday language, the word "or" is used to express more than one alternative. However, in patent language, especially in claims, expressions such as "metal or plastic" are generally regarded as lacking clarity. If accepted practice in the respective country, the phrase "metal and/or plastic" or "at least one composition selected from metal and plastic" may be used when an inclusive "or" is meant, and "either metal or plastic" may be used when an exclusive "or" is meant.

To claim multiple exclusive alternative elements in a single claim, a special claim format, often referred to as a *Markush claim* after the inventor whose case gave rise to this format, is acceptable in many countries. Such claims can simplify the patent drafter's task in preparing a full claim set (see section 3 on claim sets and dependent claims). A claim, whether independent or dependent, may refer to alternatives, provided that the number and presentation of alternatives in a single claim does not make the claim obscure or difficult to construe.

The typical drafting style of Markush claims is "wherein element A is selected from the group consisting of X, Y and Z."

Example

A chemical process can be performed with either "copper," "lead" or "gold." The patent drafter might think of a more abstract term that unites the three choices, such as "metal," but neither the patent drafter nor the inventor might be certain that the process would work with *any* metal. In fact, the inventor may know for certain that the process would not work with mercury. The patent drafter therefore cannot use the more abstract term "metal" without further qualification.

The patent drafter and the inventor may not know a better abstract term for only the three metals that work with the invention. The patent drafter could write three independent claims – one directed toward "copper," one directed toward "lead" and one directed toward "gold" – but, thanks to Markush, the patent drafter can simply draft one independent claim that reads "a metal selected from the group consisting of copper, lead and gold."

The use of Markush groups is not limited to chemical inventions; they can be used in other technical fields, for example "a fastener selected from the group consisting of a nail, a screw and a rivet." In practice, however, Markush groups are often neither desirable nor necessary in these other fields, since generic words that describe the alternative elements (e.g., "a fastener") or functional elements (e.g., "a fastening means") will provide a broader definition of alternatives.

In contrast, Markush groups are commonly employed in chemical claims to define, for example, alternative chemical ingredients that can be used in a composition, alternative steps in a chemical process or alternative values for radicals in a formula. In product claims that structurally define a group of chemical products using a general formula, it is very common to use a Markush formula.

Example[23]

Claim 1. A compound of the formula:

wherein

- R1 is selected from the group consisting of H, C1-C3 alkyl, C3-C5 cycloalkyl and C1-C3 perfluoroalkyl;
- R2 is … ; R4 is … ; R5 is … ; R6 is … ; and
- R7 and R8 are each independently H, C1-C4 alkyl, (C1-C3 alkoxy)C2-C4 alkyl or hydroxy C2-C4 alkyl;
- and pharmaceutically acceptable salts thereof.

This claims that the structurally defined compounds resulted from all combinations of radicals R1–R8 (defined by the corresponding eight Markush subgroups), as well as the salts of these compounds, with all the acids that are not toxic to animals or humans (defined by the functional element "pharmaceutically acceptable salts thereof").

Like any other claims, a Markush claim must meet the requirements for unity of invention. We will explain the application of unity of invention to Markush claims in Module VI, section 11.

If a patent drafter intends to provide for selection of more than one member of the Markush group at the same time (in addition to the selection of only one), the claim must explicitly say that; otherwise, the claim will be interpreted as allowing only one member to be selected at a time. For example, the phrase "wherein the solvent is selected from the group consisting of A, B and C" is interpreted as allowing *only one* of A, B and C to be used as the solvent and not two of them. Thus, if it is possible to use various combinations of the members, the expression "wherein the solvent is selected from the group consisting of A, B, C and combinations thereof" (or an equivalent) should be used.

A Markush group must not be ambiguous. Additionally, the patent drafter must be certain that a Markush group is the most appropriate method of claiming the invention before they employ it. In the example above, if iron would also work with the invention, the proposed Markush group would not directly protect embodiments of the invention that used iron. The patent drafter must remember always to strive to draft claims that cover all patentable embodiments of the invention.

Markush groups should be used with extreme caution, since if one of the alternatives covered by the Markush claim is found in the prior art, the whole claim will lack novelty. Although a Markush claim is very useful for drafting an independent claim that meets unity of invention, an applicant may prefer to claim members of the group in a set of separate, dependent claims (see section 3 of this module).

2.5 Functional elements and means-plus-function claims

As some examples have illustrated, functional language can be used to define a claim element in terms of what it accomplishes (i.e., the function it performs) rather than in terms of what it is. In general, a functional element may be included in a claim, provided that a person skilled in the art would have no difficulty in performing the function without exercising inventive skill.

Functional language can be achieved in several ways.

- The element can be defined by using a phrase defining its function, such as "a computer-readable storage medium," "an oxidizing agent" or "a pharmaceutically acceptable excipient."
- The element can be defined by a generic structural word that intrinsically implies a function, such as "a heater," "a fastener" or "a solvent."
- Functional language can also be introduced by a phrase that appears immediately after the relevant element, such as:
  - "providing [some operation]";
  - "creating [some physical or chemical property]";
  - "such that [something is achieved]";
  - "whereby [some effect happens]";
  - "so that [some end is achieved]"; or
  - "configured to [achieve some result]."

Among the various possibilities, means-plus-function claims recite elements that do not have specifically defined structures but instead are means of performing functions disclosed in the specification. The interpretation of means-plus-function claims varies from jurisdiction to jurisdiction and even within jurisdictions over time. For example, a given jurisdiction may interpret a means-plus-function claim as the means disclosed in the patent's specification for performing the recited function, as well as the reasonable equivalents of those means.

In other words, a means-plus-function claim may not encompass any or all elements for performing the recited function. Means-plus-function claims can be interpreted both broadly and narrowly, since the claims do not specifically define the structure. Indeed, litigants in patent infringement cases sometimes expend considerable energy arguing over whether or not an asserted claim even *is* a means-plus-function claim.

The format of a classic means-plus-function claim is the word "means" followed by a function. For instance, if the invention is a rice cooker, a claim in the means-plus-function format might read:

1. An apparatus for cooking rice, comprising:
   - a *means* for holding rice; and
   - a heater configured to heat the rice-holding means.

In this example, instead of reciting a rice-holding structure by name (e.g., a bowl), we have referenced a device that performs the function of holding rice. By doing so, we have avoided using a specific name and have instead recited the function that it performs; hence we avoid a competitor simply using something other than a bowl to hold the rice.

Not all of the elements in a means-plus-function claim need to be means elements. In fact, each element may be treated differently. If a claim recites three elements, two in means-plus-function format and one that recites a structural element (such as the "heater" above), the structural element will typically be construed according to its ordinary meaning in the art, while each of the two means-plus-function elements will be construed by first determining the recited function and then respectively determining the structure disclosed in the specification for performing that function.

Means-plus-function claims are helpful in jurisdictions where such claims are interpreted more broadly than claims that specifically recite a structural element. Means-plus-function claims are even helpful in jurisdictions that do not necessarily afford a broad interpretation to means-plus-function claims but nevertheless interpret such claims differently from claims in which the structural limitations are affirmatively recited. The "difference," whatever it might be, allows for a more complete range of claim coverage – assuming that the patentee includes both types of claim in their application. Remember too that the way in which the courts interpret claims tends to change over time: in the 20-year lifetime of a patent, a court that narrowly interpreted the means-plus-function claims in its first year might have adopted a relatively broad interpretation by the time it is first litigated, in the patent's 11th year in force.

Either way, the patent drafter must keep in mind that means-plus-function clauses must typically be accompanied by adequate description in the specification that clearly defines a structure for performing the recited function. Sufficient

WIPO Patent Drafting Manual

structures must always be defined in the description of the patent application regardless of the claim type being used.

A more special concern for the patent drafter when using means-plus-function claims is to avoid reciting unnecessary structures and/or failing to make it clear in the specification precisely which set of structures perform the function, thus inadvertently allowing a defendant in patent infringement litigation to argue for narrow interpretation. For example, if the claim uses the phrase "means for fastening," then the specification should clearly define what those fastening means are, for example "tapes, adhesives, rivets and/or any one of these fasteners." Otherwise, the patent holder will risk the courts upholding a much narrower interpretation of "means for fastening" than that which the inventor actually had in mind.

In the event that all of the elements of a claim are defined functionally, either with means-plus-function expressions or otherwise, there will also be a high risk that the application may be rejected as claiming a mere desideratum (i.e., a desired result without saying how it is achieved). The area defined by the claims must be as precise as the invention allows.

It is possible to mix, in one patent, means-plus-function claims and claims that are not reliant on such language.

3. Claim sets

A patent specification typically contains more than one claim. We have seen the following example already:

1. *A* device, comprising:
   – a pencil; and
   – a light attached to *the* pencil.

2. *The* device recited in claim 1 wherein *the* light is detachably attached to *the* pencil.
3. *The* device recited in claim 2 wherein *the* pencil is red in color.

A set of claims in a patent specification will normally include one or more independent (or main) claims and a number of dependent or subsidiary claims (or subclaims), which depend from one or more preceding independent and/or dependent claim(s). In the above example, Claim 1 is an independent claim; Claims 2 and 3 are dependent claims.

All patent applications must contain at least one *independent claim* directed to the essential features of the invention – that is, those features necessary to satisfy the legal patentability requirements such as novelty and inventive step.

Each independent claim may be followed by one or more *dependent claims* that relate to more specific embodiments

of the invention recited in the independent claim. *Dependent claims contain references to other claims.* A dependent claim that refers to another claim will include all features of the other claim even if they are not explicitly recited. Also, in some cases, a dependent claim may define a particular feature (or features) that may appropriately be added to more than one previous claim (independent or dependent). It follows that there are several possibilities: a dependent claim may refer back to one or more independent claims, to one or more dependent claims, or to both independent and dependent claims.

Patent applications with only one claim are relatively rare. This is because, in general, patent drafters aim to deliver a broad set of claims that protect various aspects of the invention at various levels of detail – that is, a number of claims, each of which has a different scope. Nonetheless, while patent laws rarely set an upper limit to the number of claims, drafting as many as possible is not the best practice – not least because of the cost to the client.

Patent drafters should take costs and other factors into account when preparing a set of claims. First, many patent offices require additional filing fees for claim sets in excess of a particular number of claims, and claim fees may not be refunded if the number of claims is later reduced by an amendment. Other fees, such as examination fees and grant fees, may also depend on the number of claims. When counting the claims, some offices count the numbered claims only (e.g., Claim 1, Claim 2, etc.) for the purpose of calculating fees; other offices, for example the United States Patent and Trademark Office (USPTO), charge an additional fee for each claim written in the multiple dependent form (see section 3.3) whether numbered or not.

Second, drafting claims that are obviously too broad or too narrow does not help applicants to seek meaningful patent protection for their inventions. Claims that are too broad are likely to be rejected for failing to meet the novelty or inventive step requirement. Conversely, claims that are too narrow may, even if granted, have limited utility for a patentee given that competitors can easily avoid infringement of the patent by designing around the scope of the claims.

Third, patent laws generally require claims to be clear and concise; hence a proliferation of dependent claims may unreasonably complicate matters, and the number of claims should be reasonable in relation to the nature and complexity of the claimed invention.

3.1 Independent claims

The independent claims in a patent represent the broadest claims. Some independent claims are broader than other independent claims, but a given independent claim is always broader than any claim that depends on it. An independent claim is a claim that stands alone and does not need a limitation from another claim to be complete. Each claim set begins with an independent claim.

A patent application may have more than one independent claim. For instance, a single invention may encompass several different aspects of the invention, in which case it may not be possible to have one broad claim that covers all the different aspects. In general, it will be wise to prepare several independent claims, each of which separately covers a different aspect.

The various types of claim, which we discuss below, are a different issue from the breadth of the claim. A patent drafter may want to prepare several independent apparatus claims, each covering a different aspect of the apparatus. Even when they cover to the same aspect, the patent drafter may want to draft several claims of differing scope or breadth. This may be an important consideration in attempting to capture different kinds of activity by potential infringers. A patent drafter will certainly want the claim to prevent competitors from manufacturing products embodying the inventive concept; at the same time, a claim that can be infringed only by end-users of a product (that means, customers) is unlikely to be so useful.

The legal requirement called *unity of invention* typically requires that multiple independent claims contained in one patent must relate to one invention only, or to a group of inventions so linked as to form a single general inventive concept (see Module VI, section 11, for more on unity of invention). This does not mean that multiple inventions cannot be claimed in one patent application, but that the patent office will not grant a patent unless they all relate to only one invention at their core.

In the USPTO, there is a fee payable for each additional independent claim beyond an initial three. Some jurisdictions, such as the EPO, may require that the number of independent claims be limited to one in each category (e.g., one independent product claim and one independent process claim within one application), thus discouraging applicants from filing applications making swathes of independent claims in a rule that supports administrative efficiency. The EPO does offer exceptions to this rule, however:

(i) Examples of a plurality of interrelated products …
plug and socket
transmitter – receiver
intermediate(s) and final chemical product
gene – gene construct – host – protein – medicament
[…]

(ii) Examples of a plurality of different inventive uses of a product or apparatus …
claims directed to further medical uses when a first medical use is known …
[…]

(iii) Examples of alternative solutions to a particular problem …
a group of chemical compounds
two or more processes for the manufacture of such compounds[24]

Varying the breadth of claims can offer insurance against arguments that a patent is invalid based on the prior art – sometimes in cases brought long after a patent examiner has approved an application and the patent has been granted. It is not uncommon for the best prior art to be found by an alleged infringer only during

Professional tip

When drafting a set of claims, you must carefully consider and strike a balance between the scope of protection sought, the likely cost of that protection and the need to meet requirements under the applicable law.

Professional tip

You should strive to ensure that your client has been accorded the appropriate number of claims for their invention. With experience, you will start to recognize the point at which the costs of making such claims (in terms of excess claim fees, annuity fees, etc.) tips toward diminishing returns.

WIPO Patent Drafting Manual

patent infringement litigation and claims of varying scope help to defend the inventor against instances of prior art not known to them, the patent drafter or even the patent examiner.

An independent claim should typically specify the essential features needed to define the invention. Although the standard varies among different patent offices, typically these features may not be required if they are implied by the generic terms used (e.g., a claim to a bicycle does not typically need to mention the presence of wheels). Where patentability depends on a technical effect, the claims should typically be drafted so as to include all of the technical features of the invention that are essential for the technical effect. In other words, *claims must be clear and be directed to the heart of the invention.*

If a claim is directed to a process for producing a product X, the process claimed should be such that, when carried out in a manner reasonable to a person skilled in the art, it necessarily leads to product X as its end result; otherwise, there is an internal inconsistency and therefore a lack of clarity in the claim. In the case of a product claim, if the product is of a well-known kind and the invention lies in modifying it in certain respects, it is typically sufficient that the claim clearly identifies the well-known product and specifies what is modified and in what way. Similar considerations apply to claims for an apparatus.

3.2 Dependent claims

Patent drafters commonly prepare a combination of broad and narrow claims that effectively capture the complete scope of an invention. As a practical matter, they approach this by first drafting the broadest independent claim and then drafting a number of dependent claims covering various ranges of the scopes narrower than that of the independent claim.

Dependent claims also reflect the "fallback" position of the patent drafter. Even if they conduct a prior art search, they cannot be certain of finding all of the relevant prior art published all over the world; there is always a risk that a patent examiner will find relevant prior art that denies the novelty or inventive step of the claimed invention. But if a patent examiner finds a piece of prior art that denies patentability to the broad independent claim and not the narrower dependent claims, a patent may still be granted with that narrower scope of protection. The narrower dependent claims are not as "strong" as the independent claim, but they may suffice for the applicant's purposes – that is, allowing them to obtain competitive advantage in the marketplace.

Format and structure of dependent claims
A dependent claim is one that "depends from" (not, in patent language, "depends on") another claim – either from

an independent claim or from another dependent claim. Dependencies to another claim are signaled by the identification of a parent claim from which it depends. For example "2. The apparatus of Claim 1, further comprising…" indicates that Claim 2 is dependent from Claim 1.

The format of a dependent claim makes the claim more concise, avoiding repetition of the whole text of the claim to which it refers. By referring to another claim, the dependent claim includes *everything* from the parent claim *plus* whatever is newly recited in the dependent claim itself. Dependent claims tend to be considerably shorter than independent claims and patent novices sometimes mistakenly believe that dependent claims are broader than independent claims when the opposite is in fact true.

Example

An independent claim (Claim 1) reads:

1. An apparatus, comprising:
   – a pencil; and
   – an eraser attached to the pencil.

A dependent Claim 2 reads:

2. The apparatus of Claim 1, further comprising:
   – a light attached to the pencil.

A dependent Claim 3 reads:

3. The apparatus of Claim 2, further comprising:
   – a pencil lead release button attached to the pencil.

A further dependent Claim 4 reads:

4. The apparatus of Claim 2,
   – wherein the light is an LED light.

The entirety of the dependent Claim 2 includes all the text affirmatively recited in Claim 2 *plus* all the text of Claim 1. Thus Claim 2 *actually* reads:

2. An apparatus, comprising:
   – a pencil;
   – an eraser attached to the pencil; and
   – a light attached to the pencil.

Similarly, Claim 3, which depends from Claim 2, which itself refers to Claim 1, actually has the same scope as would the following independent claim:

3. An apparatus, comprising:
   – a pencil;
   – an eraser attached to the pencil;

- a light attached to the pencil; and
- a pencil lead release button attached to the pencil.

As illustrated, all dependent claims that relate to an independent claim share the same preamble. Although it is not a universal practice, an independent claim typically begins with the indefinite article "A" or "An," while a dependent claim starts with the definite article "The."

Dependent claims are always narrower than the claim from which they depend. For example, a competitor's pencils that do not include any sort of a light will not infringe Claim 2, even though they may infringe Claim 1, which is the broader claim.

A word or a phrase that indicates dependency from another claim typically follows the preamble. Such a word or a phrase is interpreted as including everything recited in the parent claim. Our example uses the wording "The apparatus of Claim 1… ." Other typical phrases are "The apparatus according to Claim 1" and "The apparatus as in Claim 1." Equally, the words "as claimed in," "as per," "as set forth in" and "as recited in" may be used to signal the dependency from another claim.

Immediately after the reference to another claim, a dependent claim states at least one additional feature that is not present in that other claim. It does so in one of three ways:

(i) by adding at least one new element, E, which is typically written as "further comprising E" (e.g., in our dependent Claim 2, a light attached to the pencil is a new element not found in Claim 1);
(ii) by selecting at least one element, E1, from a broader element E, mentioned in the parent claim, which is typically written as "wherein E is E1" or "in which E is E1" (e.g., in our dependent Claim 4, the broader concept of the light is narrowed down to an LED light), or by further characterizing at least one element in the dependent claim (e.g., "wherein the light is detachable"); or
(iii) as a combination of (i) and (ii).

Dependent claims should be grouped together in the most appropriate way possible. The arrangement must therefore enable a ready reckoning and construction of the association of related claims and their meaning. All dependent claims must refer back to at least one previous claim and they cannot refer forward to a subsequent claim. In no way can a dependent claim extend the scope of protection of the invention defined in the corresponding independent claim.

The relationships of the independent and dependent claims can be usefully imagined as a claim tree, in which each claim is represented by its respective claim number, which is linked with an arrow or a line. A claim tree for our example can be drawn as:

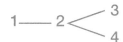

Sometimes, a patent examiner finds prior art references that deny patentability to an independent claim but not that of a dependent claim. Although a patent drafter and their client may decide to fight for the patentability of the parent claim, they may instead choose to pursue a patent simply by cancelling the rejected independent claim (and any other intervening dependent claims) and drafting a new independent claim by combining the limitations in the now-cancelled independent claim with the limitations in the allowable dependent claim. The patent drafter can also then amend the other claims in the application to depend from the now newly independent (formerly dependent) claim.

Example

An application contains one independent claim (Claim 1) and 10 other claims that depend, ultimately, from Claim 1.[25]

The first three claims read:

1. An apparatus, comprising:
   - a pencil; and
   - an eraser attached to the pencil.

2. The apparatus of Claim 1, further comprising:
   - a light attached to the pencil.

3. The apparatus of Claim 2, further comprising:
   - a pencil lead release button attached to the pencil.

The patent examiner has rejected Claim 1 but has found Claim 2 allowable and objected to Claim 2 only because it depends from rejected Claim 1.

If the client approves the plan of action, the patent drafter could rewrite Claim 2 to become a new independent Claim 1 by specifically reciting all the limitations of Claim 1 (as we did earlier). Old Claim 2 will now be renumbered Claim 1:

1. An apparatus, comprising:
   - a pencil;
   - an eraser attached to the pencil; and
   - a light attached to the pencil.

Claim 3 already depends from former Claim 2, which is now Claim 1. So Claim 3 does not need substantive amendment but only amendment such that it now refers back to "Claim 1" and is renumbered Claim 2:

2. The apparatus of Claim 1, further comprising:
   - a pencil lead release button attached to the pencil.

WIPO Patent Drafting Manual

Once the patent drafter files their amendment, the patent examiner will likely allow the patent application and the client will eventually obtain a patent with a total of 10 claims rather than 11.

While formats vary from jurisdiction to jurisdiction, the request to amend Claim 2 to render it independent might look like this:

12. An apparatus, comprising:
 – a pencil;
 – an eraser attached to the pencil; and
 – a light attached to the pencil.

The strikethrough shows deleted words and the underlining shows newly added words.

Alternatively, the amendment might be to the original Claim 1 by adding the limitations that were found in the original Claim 2:

1. An apparatus, comprising:
 – a pencil;
 – an eraser attached to the pencil; and
 – a light attached to the pencil.

We will explain more on amendments in Module IX, section 3.

A dependent claim can only add elements or limitations to the claim from which it depends; it cannot subtract any elements or limitations. In other words, a dependent claim may only narrow the scope of the claim to which it refers not broaden it. For example, dependent Claim 4 cannot read as follows:

4. The apparatus in Claim 2 wherein the light is *not* attached to the pencil.

This claim would be improper because it subtracts an element from the independent claim – namely, the light.

Dependent claims can be also used to support a broader interpretation of independent claims. For example, if Claim 1 recites "a box" and dependent Claim 2 recites "wherein the box is wooden," then clearly Claim 1, by implication, can be made of any material including and other than wood. Of course, one could always argue that the box in Claim 1 could be a nonwood material; it is also possible that an opponent might argue that the specification provided no support for a nonwooden box. The recital "wooden box" in Claim 2 makes it much clearer that Claim 1 refers to a box of any material. An opponent can still argue that there is no support in the specification for nonwooden boxes, but the patentee can now additionally argue that the patent examiner themselves must have considered the enablement requirement (see Module II, section 2.5) and concluded that both wooden and nonwooden boxes covered by Claim 1 are supported by the specification.

Dependent claims regarding two-part claims and Markush claims
In all of the examples of dependent claims described so far, the independent claim from which they depend is written in the standard format. Now, let us consider the cases in which a dependent claim depends on an independent claim written in the two-part format. In such cases, by definition, the dependent claim includes everything recited in the independent claim – that is, the two parts separated by the

Professional tip

Remember that if the independent claims are considered allowable over prior art by a patent examiner, then dependent claims will also be allowable. You will not need to make any amendments.

expression "characterized in that" or "characterized by." Those expressions are consequently unnecessary in the dependent claims (although they are permissible).

Example

Claim 1 is written in the two-part format as:

1. A writing device, comprising: a pencil with two ends and an eraser attached to the pencil; characterized in that the eraser is attached to one end of the pencil.

A dependent Claim 2 that recites a light attached to the pencil as an additional element to the writing device in Claim 1 can be drafted as:

2. The writing device of Claim 1, further comprising a light attached to the pencil.

Where an independent Claim 1 is a Markush claim, a typical dependent claim may define a narrower subset of the Markush group in Claim 1.

Example

Using the example in section 2.3 of this module, a set of claims could read as follows:

1. A compound of the formula:

wherein

– R1 is selected from the group consisting of H, C1-C3 alkyl, C3-C5 cycloalkyl and C1-C3 perfluoroalkyl;
– R2 is … ; R4 is … ; R5 is … ; R6 is … ; and
– R7 and R8 are each independently H, C1-C4 alkyl, (C1-C3 alkoxy)C2-C4 alkyl or hydroxy C2-C4 alkyl;
– and pharmaceutically acceptable salts thereof.

2. The compound as claimed in claim 1, wherein R1 is selected from the group consisting of H, methyl or ethyl; R2 is C1-C3 alkyl; … ; R7 is… .
3. The compound as claimed in claim 2, wherein R1 is methyl; R2 is n-propyl; …

Claim 2 defines a narrower scope than Claim 1 by narrowly defining a set of values for the radicals R1–R7. Claim 3 depends on Claim 2, further narrowing down the Markush group.

3.3 Multiple dependent claims

Format and structure of multiple dependent claims

Multiple dependent claims are subsets of dependent claims. The preamble of a multiple dependent claim will refer to more than one claim in the alternative, for example "the apparatus of Claim 1 *or* Claim 2" or "the apparatus of *one of* Claims 1 and 2." This means that the claim depends from either Claim 1 or Claim 2 but not both.

Like dependent claims, the body of a multiple dependent claim must narrow the claim from which it depends.

Example

Recall our pencil:

1. An apparatus, comprising: a pencil and a light attached to the pencil.
2. The apparatus of Claim 1, wherein the light is detachably attached to the pencil.

Here, another claim with a multiple dependent claim format may be recited as:

3. The apparatus as recited in Claims 1 *or* 2, further comprising an eraser.

This multiple dependent Claim 3 covers an apparatus comprising either:
– a light attached to the pencil and an eraser; or
– a light detachably attached to the pencil and an eraser.

Thus, to infringe this claim, an accused apparatus will have to contain either of these limitations.

This means that, in fact, a patent drafter can choose to write a set of claims by using only single dependent claims or by using multiple dependent claims.

The following two sets of claims are equivalent in terms of both claiming scope and protection.

Example

Alternative A, using a multiple dependent Claim 3:

1. An apparatus, comprising: a pencil and a light attached to the pencil.
2. The apparatus of Claim 1, wherein the light is detachably attached to the pencil.
3. The apparatus of Claims 1 or 2, further comprising an eraser.

Alternative B, using only single dependent Claims 2–4:

1. An apparatus, comprising: a pencil and a light attached to the pencil.
2. The apparatus of Claim 1, wherein the light is detachably attached to the pencil.
3. The apparatus of Claim 1, further comprising an eraser.
4. The apparatus of Claim 2, further comprising an eraser.

A claim tree (see section 3.2) can graphically depict the relationships of multiple dependent claims with an independent claim and single dependent claims.

Our example can be drawn as:

Here, "3/1" and "3/2" denote that Claim 3 is a multiple dependent claim that depends from Claim 1 or Claim 2; hence 3/1 hangs to Claim 1 and 3/2 hangs to Claim 2.

To refer to more than one claim in the alternative in a multiple dependent claim, many other expressions are generally accepted in many jurisdictions, such as:

– "A pencil according to Claim 1 or Claim 2, wherein…"
– "A pencil as in either Claim 1 or Claim 2, further comprising…"
– "A pencil as in any one of Claims 1, 3 or 9–13 inclusive, in which…"
– "A pencil as in any of Claims 1, 4, 5–7 in which…"
– "A pencil as in any of Claims 2 or 3, further comprising…"
– "A pencil as in any of the preceding claims in which…"

Wording that would cause the claims to become cumulative is *not* permitted, for example "according to Claims 1 and 2," "according to Claims 1–3," "as in Claims 1, 2 and/or 3," etc.

Pros and cons of multiple dependent claims

The multiple dependency format usually reduces the countable number of claims. This can inform a client's decision whether or not to use it because, on the one hand, it may be more convenient to group more than one dependent claim and, on the other hand, the claim fee structure of the respective patent office makes the claim fee prohibitive.

In the United States, multiple dependent claims trigger extra claim fees and they are consequently uncommon drafting practice. For the EPO, however, using multiple dependent claims may save fees because the EPO's claim fee structure is based on countable numbered claims (Claim 1, Claim 2, etc.). The number of equivalent single dependent claims would easily force up costs.

There are other considerations involved in using multiple dependent claims. In general, the disclosure in the patent application as filed cannot be substantively amended in a manner that the amendment introduces new matter. In some jurisdictions, such as the EPO, an applicant may be able to justify amendment with less difficulty in certain cases if they have used the multiple dependent claim format.

Let us look at an example.

Example

A claim set includes only single dependent claims:

Claim 1. A composition, comprising: an element A selected from the group consisting of A1 and A2; and an element B selected from the group consisting of B1, B2 and B3.
Claim 2. The composition according to Claim 1, wherein A is A1.
Claim 3. The composition according to Claim 1, wherein A is A2.
Claim 4. The composition according to Claim 1, wherein B is B1.
Claim 5. The composition according to Claim 1, wherein B is B2.
Claim 6. The composition according to Claim 1, wherein B is B3.

An examiner found prior art references for the various combination of elements A and B, except the combination of A1 and B3, and now the applicant wishes to amend the claim as:

[new] Claim 1. A composition, comprising: element A1; and element B3.

Unless there is a specific indication concerning this particular combination in the application as filed, in the

Module IV. Fundamentals of claim drafting

EPO such amendment would likely be subject to objection on the ground that the selection of the two characteristics is not clearly and unambiguously evident from the application as filed. However, according to EPO case law, such an objection would not be raised if there were a dependent claim specifically claiming a composition comprising elements A1 and B3.

Unfortunately, the above set of six claims do not recite this specific combination.

Had they used multiple dependent claims, however, the applicant could claim various combinations within the same number:

Claim 1. A composition, comprising: an element A selected from the group consisting of A1 and A2; and an element B selected from the group consisting of B1, B2 and B3.
Claim 2. The composition according to Claim 1, wherein A is A1.
Claim 3. The composition according to Claim 1, wherein A is A2.
Claim 4. The composition according to any one of Claims 1–3, wherein B is B1.
Claim 5. The composition according to any one of Claims 1–3, wherein B is B2.
Claim 6. The composition according to any one of Claims 1–3, wherein B is B3.
Claim 6, insofar as it refers back to Claim 2, covers the specific combination of elements A1 and B3.

Having many claims drafted in the multiple dependency format is also very convenient for a patent owner. They may be able to easily amend their claims where a third party challenges the validity of a granted patent or where they want to limit the scope of protection on their own initiative, for example to a very narrow (and very strong) claim that protects the only commercial product that is susceptible to imitation. However, in these cases, claim amendments will be allowable only if they do not extend the protection conferred by the granted patent.

This can be illustrated by looking at how our two groups of six claims without and with multiple dependencies might impact a nullity action.

Example

Let us imagine that the only embodiment of interest is "Preamble-P comprising A1 and B3" (e.g., the only active pharmaceutical ingredient authorized for sale, which is the only one that competitors want to exploit).

In a nullity action, a prior art document disclosing "Preamble-P comprising A2 and B3" would be novelty-destroying for Claim 1 and Claim 6 of the first set, invalidating the two granted claims that protect the embodiment of interest.

However, this prior art document would *not* be novelty-destroying for Claim 6 of the second set, dependent from Claim 2. That particular claim would read "Preamble-P comprising A1 and B3" and specifically protects the embodiment of interest.

Multiple-multiple dependent claims
So far, all examples of multiple dependent claims refer back to either an independent claim or a single dependent claim – but could a multiple dependent claim serve as a basis for *another* multiple dependent claim? In some jurisdictions, such as the EPO and Japan, it is permissible, while in other jurisdictions, such as the United States and the Republic of Korea, it is not.

Professional tip

Bear in mind that multiple-multiple dependent claims complicate the application. If you make excessive and unnecessary use of multiple-multiple dependent claims, you risk preparing claims that combine the features of so many referred claims that the claims become difficult to comprehend.

55

WIPO Patent Drafting Manual

Claim 4, below, is an example of such a multiple-multiple dependent claim:

Claim 1. An apparatus, comprising: a pencil and a light attached to the pencil.
Claim 2. The apparatus of Claim 1, wherein the light is detachably attached to the pencil.
Claim 3. The apparatus of Claims 1 or 2, further comprising an eraser.
Claim 4. The apparatus of any one of Claims 1–3, wherein the light is an LED light.

3.4 Claims referring to features of another claim

In some jurisdictions, such as the EPO, an independent claim may contain a reference to another claim, incorporating the defined features of the other claim, and yet not be a dependent claim. A claim referring to another claim of a different category (e.g., "Apparatus for carrying out the process of Claim 1 … ," or "Process for the manufacture of the product of Claim 1 …") is one example. Similarly, in a situation such as a plug and socket, a claim to the one part referring to the other cooperating part (e.g., "plug for cooperation with the socket of Claim 1 …") incorporates the features of another claim, but it is not a dependent claim. However, in some other jurisdictions, such as the United States, an independent claim cannot contain a reference to any other claim.

In any case, it is important to carefully review the features incorporated through such referencing and whether all such features are indeed essential to the claimed invention. The patent drafter must also verify that this approach is permissible in the jurisdiction(s) of interest to their client before employing it.

A definitional reference to another claim is one type of such reference frequently used in claims directed to computer-implemented inventions, where different types of claim (for a computer-implemented method, a data-processing apparatus, a computer program product, a computer-readable storage medium, etc.) are drafted to obtain comprehensive protection.

Example

A computer-implemented method Claim 1 recites the essential steps (i)–(x). A claim for a data-processing apparatus may read:

2. A data-processing apparatus comprising means for carrying out the method as defined in Claim 1.

Similarly, a computer program product claim may read:

3. A computer program product comprising instructions which, when the program is executed by a computer, cause the computer to carry out the method as defined in Claim 1.

This type of reference to another claim is also found in the pharmaceutical area, where a number of different types of claim are foreseen, such as claims on a new chemical compound, a pharmaceutical composition comprising that compound and a method of manufacturing the compound, etc.

Example[26]

Claim 1. A compound of the formula:

wherein

– R1 is selected from the group consisting of H, C1-C3 alkyl, C3-C5 cycloalkyl and C1-C3 perfluoroalkyl;
– R2 is … ; R3 is … ; R4 is … ; R5 is … ; R6 is … ; and
– R7 and R8 are each independently H, C1-C4 alkyl, (C1-C3 alkoxy)C2-C4 alkyl or hydroxy C2-C4 alkyl;
– and pharmaceutically acceptable salts thereof.

Claim 2. A compound as claimed in Claim 1, wherein R1 is selected from the group consisting of H, methyl and ethyl; R2 is C1 C3 alkyl; […].
Claim 3. A compound as claimed in Claim 2, wherein R1 is methyl; R2 is n-propyl; […].
Claim 4 A compound as claimed in Claim 3, wherein the compound is selected from [seven systematic chemical names]; and pharmaceutically acceptable salts thereof.
Claim 5. *A pharmaceutical composition* comprising a compound of the formula (I) or a pharmaceutically acceptable salt thereof, *as defined in any one of Claims 1–4*, together with a pharmaceutically acceptable diluent or carrier.
Claim 6. *A compound* of the formula (I) or a pharmaceutically acceptable salt thereof, *as defined in any one of Claims 1–4*, *for use* in medicine.
Claim 7. *A use* of a compound of the formula (I) or a pharmaceutically acceptable salt thereof, *as defined in any one of Claims 1–4*, for the manufacture of a medicament for the treatment of angina, hypertension and […].

Here, Claims 1–4 relate to compounds of certain formulae "and pharmaceutically acceptable salts thereof." Claim 5, which relates to a pharmaceutical composition, refers to the features of "any one of Claims 1–4." This means that a single Claim 5 incorporates the features of all of

Figure 3: Scopes of Claims 1, 2 and 3 and their embodiments

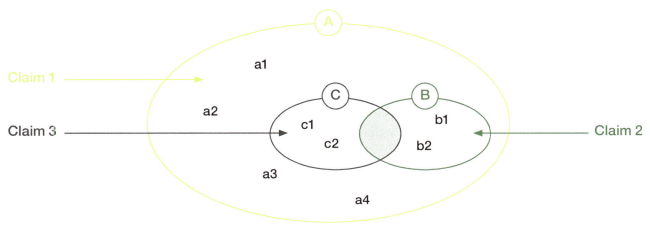

Claims 1–4 with a multiple reference. Similarly, using a multiple reference to Claims 1–4, Claim 6 covers first medical use of the compound and Claim 7 covers a second medical use of the compound.

With the use of reference to the features of multiple claims, the total number of claims is considerably reduced.

In some jurisdictions, such as the EPO, if a claimed process results in a product defined by a product claim and if the product claim is patentable, no separate examination for the novelty and nonobviousness of the process claim is necessary, provided that all features of the product as defined in the product claim inevitably result from the claimed process. This also applies in the case of a claim for the use of a product, when the product is patentable and is used with its features as claimed. In all other instances, the patentability of the claim referred to does not necessarily imply the patentability of the independent claim containing the reference. (See also Module VI, section 12, for more on the claim point of view.)

3.5 Claim sets based on set theory

As we saw in Module IV, section 1.1, just as a fence marks the limits of a parcel of land protected as real property, a patent claim marks the boundaries of an area of technical subject matter for which patent protection is claimed. Today, most patent offices follow a "peripheral claiming" doctrine whereby the claims establish the outer boundaries or limits of the scope of protected subject matter.

To illustrate, let us consider three claims with different scopes.

Example

Claim 1. A cup with a handle.
Claim 2. A cup with a handle, wherein the cup is made of clay.
Claim 3. A cup with a handle, further comprising a spoon detachably attached to the handle.

In Figure 3, the whole area surrounded by the red closed curve (set A) depicts the scope of Claim 1. Claim 1 coves *any* cup with a handle, regardless of its material, its shape or any other additional elements.

The area surrounded by the purple curve (set B) shows the scope of Claim 2. Since Claim 2 is a certain kind of the cup defined in Claim 1 (i.e., made of clay), set B is described within the area of set A.

Similarly, the scope of Claim 3 is shown by the area surrounded by the green curve (set C).

The area with the blue stripes, which is the overlapping area of sets A, B and C, depicts a cup that has all the elements (limitations) of Claims 1, 2 and 3. In the claim-style language, the blue-striped area can be expressed as:

Claim 4. A cup with a handle, wherein the cup is made of clay and the cup further comprising a spoon detachably attached to the handle.

Embodiments of each claim are shown as a1, a2, b1, c1, etc. For example, a1–a4 are shown within the area of set A, but outside sets B and C. This means that embodiments a1–a4 are cups with a handle, but they are *neither limited* to the cup made of clay *nor restricted to* the cup having a handle to which a spoon is detachably attached. For example, embodiment a1 may be a cup with a handle made of metal with an isolation layer on the inner surface of the cup (and no spoon attached on a handle). Or embodiment a2 may be a cup made of wood (and no spoon attached on a handle). Similarly, embodiment b1 may be any clay cup with a handle, but no spoon is attached on a handle (because embodiment b1 is outside the area of set C).

The Venn diagram (of which Figure 3 is an example) is used in set theory to illustrate all possible logical relationships between different sets. These relationships among claims, for example between an independent claim and a dependent claim, as well as relationships between a claim and its embodiments, can be explained with set theory.

Illustrating the relationships between an independent claim and dependent claims

According to set theory, a *set* is a single collection or aggregate of individual things – referred to as *members* – that belong to the set. A set is defined by a sentence such as, "The persons who are in this classroom." The set of *all* things under discussion in any context is called the *universal set* of this particular kind of things (all persons of the world, for example).

Note that a defining sentence is not a complete proposition or statement by which something (the predicate) is affirmed or denied of somebody or something (the subject), such as, "The persons who are in this classroom are interested in patent claim drafting." A statement is either true or false – but a *defining sentence* merely defines a set of members and it is neither true nor false in its own right.

Using set terminology, *a patent claim is a defining sentence of an area (scope) of technical subject matter* within a given technical universe. Technical subject matter can be very diverse in nature and breadth (electromechanical entities, chemical entities, biological matters, processes of obtaining products, industrial methods of doing something, etc.).

Figure 4: Scopes of independent Claim 1 and dependent Claims 2 and 3

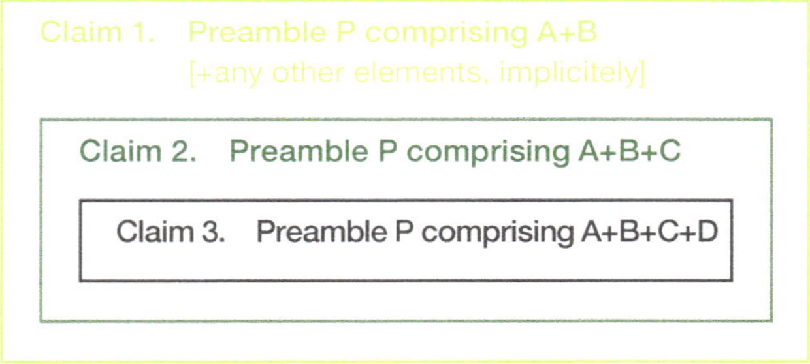

Claim 1.   Preamble P comprising A+B
[+any other elements, implicitely]

Claim 2.   Preamble P comprising A+B+C

Claim 3.   Preamble P comprising A+B+C+D

For teaching purposes, the scope of a set is usually represented by a closed surface – typically, a circle or ellipse (as in the Venn diagram). Analogously, the scope of a claim (i.e., an area covering the claimed subject matter) can be illustrated by a closed surface – although most commonly by a rectangle, as in Figure 4. In these schemes, the *universal* set will not be shown, but it will be determined by the wording of the *claim preamble*.

Set A2 is a *subset* of set A1 (that is, A1 includes A2) if every member of A2 is a member of A1. This is represented as "$A2 \subset A1$," in which the Greek letter epsilon $\subset$ denotes belonging. In particular, if A2 is completely contained in A1 and A2 cannot be the same scope as A1, A2 is a proper subset of A1, which is represented by $A2 \subset A1$. As will be explained later, when a patent claim A2 has a scope that is a subset of the scope of another claim A1, it is said that *claim A2 is dependent from claim A1*.

In set theory, if $A2 \subset A1$ and $A3 \subset A2$, then $A3 \subset A1$. Concerning patent claims, if Claim 2 is dependent from Claim 1 and Claim 3 is dependent from Claim 2, then Claim 3 is dependent from Claim 1 – a situation that is illustrated in Figure 4.

In the claim group represented in Figure 4, Claim 1 is the only *independent* claim, because it is the only claim that does not depend from any other previous claim. Claim 2 is dependent from Claim 1 and Claim 3 is dependent from Claim 2. Logically, Claim 3 is also dependent from Claim 1, because the scope of Claim 3 is also a subset of the scope of Claim 1.

Whether a claim is dependent from another claim or not depends on their respective claimed subject matters and on whether a reference is made from one claim to another. In the claim group represented by Figure 4, Claim 3 is *written in singular dependent form* with Claim 2 as its base claim; Claim 2 is written in singular dependent form with Claim 1 as its base claim; and Claim 1 is *written in independent form*. What is not illustrated in Figure 4 is the possibility that a dependent claim can be *written in multiple dependent form* with *several* base claims. In other words, the illustration in Figure 4 shows only the scope of subject matter covered by each claim but does not necessarily show the form of each claim in which it is written.

Based on a simple claim dependency relationship between three claims, as illustrated in Figure 4, let us consider a claim set that is more complex.

Figure 5 illustrates the same dependency *chain* as Figure 4 for Claims 1–3, supplemented with three additional dependent claims (Claims 4–6) whose scopes are not overlapping – that is, whose subject matters are mutually exclusive, a situation sometimes referred to as a *dependency pyramid*, in this case with its 'vertex' in Claim 3. In both Figures 4 and 5, Claim 1 is the only *independent* claim – that is, the only claim that is not dependent from any other.

In the particular example shown in Figure 5, the scopes of Claims 4–6 derive from three separated alternatives of an element D, defined in Claim 3 as a Markush group, for example with the expression "D is an element selected from the group consisting of D1, D2 and D3" or, more simply, with the expression "element D being D1, D2, or D3." When a specific element (e.g., D1) is a selection from a broader element (e.g., D, this being a more general term or a Markush group, as in this case), the subset symbol $\subset$ may be used to indicate their selection relationship (i.e., D1 $\subset$ D).

Figure 5: Scopes of independent Claim 1 and dependent Claims 2 to 6

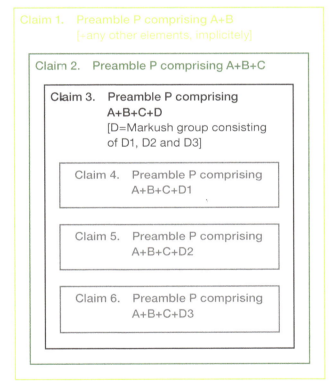

Figure 6 illustrates a different situation from those of Figures 4 and 5. In Figure 6, again Claim 1 is the only independent claim. Claims 2–4 are dependent from Claim 1 and together form a dependency group. Taking into account their respective scopes, Claims 1, 2 and 4 form a dependency chain. Another dependency chain is formed by Claims 1, 3 and 4.

Figure 6 illustrates that Claim 3 depends only from Claim 1 and that Claims 2 and 3 do not have a dependency relationship between them – that is, neither Claim 3 depends from Claim 2 nor Claim 2 depends from Claim 3. Nevertheless, the scopes of Claims 2 and 3 partially overlap, because the scope of Claim 4 is a subset of both the scope of Claim 2 and the scope of Claim 3. From the perspective of claim drafting, Claim 4 can depend from either Claim 2 or Claim 3.

Figure 6: Scopes of independent Claim 1 and dependent Claims 2, 3 and 4

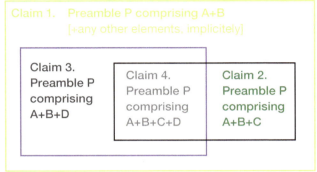

Analysis of claim dependency as an aid for the assessment of validity and infringement

The analysis of dependency relationships among patent claims is very helpful as an aid to patent examiners assessing validity (particularly of novelty and inventive step) during the processing of patent applications and to judges when the validity of claims in granted patents is questioned before the courts. Such analysis of claim dependency is also helpful as an aid for assessing infringement when a case is before the courts.

The analysis starts by separating out the different dependency groups (or a dependency chain), each one being formed of a single independent claim and all the claims that depend from it. Each dependency group is then considered separately. As an illustrative example, let us consider the dependency group formed by the Claims 1–5 whose scopes are depicted schematically in Figure 7a and 7b. Claim 1 is the only independent claim in each. Claims 1–4 are structured as a singular dependency chain: the claim scopes are such that one claim embraces the following claims in the chain, Claim 4 being the narrowest. The scope of Claim 5 does not overlap with the scope of Claim 2 and consequently overlaps with the scopes of neither Claim 3 nor Claim 4.

Let us consider first the assessment of novelty, which involves comparisons between the scope of a claim and a piece of prior art. In Figure 7a and 7b, a piece of prior art reference (P1 and P2, respectively) is represented by a small circle. For example, Figure 7a illustrates the situation in which a prior art reference P1 falls outside the scope of the independent claim (Claim 1). This means that the independent claim is novel with regard to the prior art reference P1. In such a situation, the

Figure 7: (a) Claims 1 to 5 are novel ; (b) Claims 1 to 3 lack novelty, but claims 4 and 5 are novel

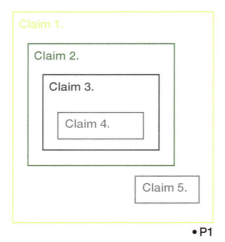
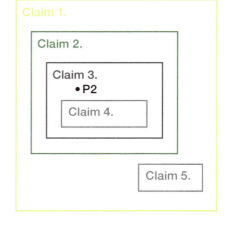

• Relevant piece of prior art

validity assessment of the claims is highly simplified, since, by definition, it can be concluded that the rest of claims in the dependency chains from Claim 1 (Claims 2–5) are also novel with regard to the prior art reference P1. If the same conclusion can be reached with regard to all pieces of prior art found through the prior art search, then it can be concluded that all of Claims 1–5 are novel.

Figure 7b illustrates the situation in which a prior art reference P2 falls inside the scope of Claim 3, which is also within the scopes of Claims 1 and 2, but is outside the scope of Claim 4. This means that Claims 1, 2 and 3 are invalid for lack of novelty with regard to the prior art reference P2, but Claim 4 is not. The prior art reference P2 is also outside the scope of Claim 5 and therefore Claim 5 is also novel. Care must be taken not to conclude (wrongly) that invalidity of an independent claim necessarily implies invalidity of all of the claims dependent from it – a relatively frequent mistake made by nonexperts. Also, Claim 4 is novel does not mean it is valid: other patentability criteria such as inventive step requirements should be also met.

Let us now consider the assessment of literal infringement of a patent having the dependency groups shown in Figure 8a and 8b. Assume that all claims are considered valid. A declaration of infringement of a patent involves making two judgments:

(i) that at least one prohibited act of those contemplated in the legal provision on patent infringement (e.g., making, using or selling the claimed invention without patent owner's consent) has been carried out – a fact that we will assume has been proven in this case; and
(ii) that the "accused embodiment" (e.g., a product sold by the alleged infringer) associated with that prohibited act

falls within the scope of *at least one valid claim* of the patent – a decision that involves comparing the claim scopes with the accused embodiment.

Figure 8a illustrates the situation in which the accused embodiment of an alleged infringer Q1 (represented by the small circle) falls outside the scope of the independent claim, Claim 1. This means that Claim 1 is not infringed. In such a situation, the infringement assessment of other claims is highly simplified, since, by definition, it can be concluded that none of the claims in the dependency chain from Claim 1 is infringed.

Figure 8b illustrates the situation in which the accused embodiment Q2 falls inside the scope of Claim 3. This means that all elements of Claim 3 are found in the accused embodiment Q2. Consequently, all elements of Claims 1 and 2 should be also found in the accused embodiment Q2, and Claims 1, 2 and 3 are infringed. Conversely, since accused embodiment Q2 is outside the scope of Claim 4, meaning that not all elements of Claim 4 are found in the accused embodiment Q2, Claim 4 is not infringed. Similarly, in this example, Claim 5 is also not infringed by Q2. Thus care must be taken not to conclude (wrongly) that infringement of the independent claim implies infringement of all the claims dependent from it – another relatively frequent mistake made by nonexperts.

3.6 Schematic example of drafting a set of claims

The drafting of a set of claims will be strongly influenced by the information and ideas available from inventors, the known prior art, the business interests of the applicant and, last but

Figure 8: (a) No infringement of Claims 1 to 5; (b) Claims 1 to 3 are infringed, but not Claims 4 and 5

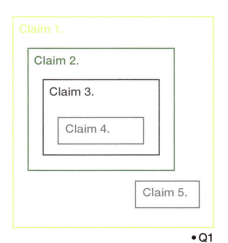
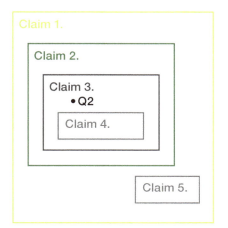

• Questioned embodiment of an alleged infringer

not least, the drafting skills of and the time available to the patent drafter.

The drafting process typically starts with a brainstorming meeting between the patent drafter and the inventor(s), with the initial objectives of (at least tentatively):

- identifying the invention(s);
- selecting a claim type for the first independent claim (which might be later supplemented by other independent claims); and
- choosing a preamble at an appropriate level for the dependency group corresponding to the independent claim.

All this is to be done taking into account the specific embodiments available (examples, drawings, etc.) and the identified closest prior art.

The independent claim will state the *essential elements* of the invention. Those essential elements are necessary for achieving the technical effect underlying the solution of the technical problem with which the application is concerned (the problem usually being derived from the description). The independent claim should therefore contain all of the essential elements explicitly described in the description as necessary for the essential functionality of the invention. To achieve the broadest possible protection, the essential elements will be stretched to their greatest reasonable extent, taking into account the essential functionality and prior art.

For all of the claims (independent and dependent), some argument of – or a strategy for – inventive step should be formulated, for example being nonobvious, or giving rise to an unexpected advantage or effect. A product claim should define the elements or technical features that give rise to that advantage or effect, not the advantage or effect itself. Care must be taken not to draft a claim as a "mere desideratum" (i.e., a statement of a result without saying how this is achieved).

Dependent claims will be concerned with more *particular embodiments* of the invention – that is, a more specific disclosure of the invention than that set out in the independent claim. If the independent claim is novel, every dependent claim will be novel by definition. However, some dependent claims should be drafted as "fallback positions" in case the independent claim is found during prosecution (or litigation) to be not novel or to lack inventive step. Thus, in the brainstorming phase, it is very important to identify the *order of importance* to the applicant of various elements of the invention (both essential and nonessential), considering the patentability requirements, commercial and business settings, and future enforcement possibilities. (In the schematic example that follows, the order of importance of elements is represented by the alphabetical order of their symbols.)

When considering an element defined by a term of a preferred embodiment (e.g., A11), the patent drafter – with the help of the inventor – should think of broader terms that, while less popular, may be useful for drafting broader claims (e.g., $A11 \subset A1 \subset A$). The patent drafter and the inventor should also think of other elements that a person skilled in the art would clearly consider to be technical equivalents in the context of the invention. Sometimes, including alternative elements in a Markush group may help in drafting broader claims – and the possibility of broadening from a structural element to a functional one (e.g., with broader terminology) should always be borne in mind.

In general, one dependent claim is drafted per selected or added element. But there are cases (such as in a Markush formula) in which several elements (such as chemical radical values) are selected simultaneously (see section 2.3 of this module). A dependent claim adding an element selected from among a group or further characterizing an element can depend from only those preceding claims that themselves provide an *antecedent* for that element. A dependent claim adding an extra element does not need an antecedent; it can have dependency from any of the preceding claims in the group and it can (but not necessarily should) have multiple dependency from several or all the preceding claims.

In dependent chains, elements may be added successively in decreasing order of importance.

With these general ideas in mind, let us consider one example (not necessarily the best) of a schematic approach to drafting a single dependency group of claims.

This single dependency group of claims is intended to be included in the first patent application from which priority is claimed in the subsequent PCT application filed with the EPO that enters the national/regional phases in China, Japan, the Republic of Korea, the United States and the EPO itself

Example.

After a brainstorming phase, the inventor and the patent drafter have concluded the following.

(i) "A writing device" is appropriate for the designation of the claimed subject matter.
(ii) Inventors have made a prototype, "a writing device having A11, B11, C1, D, E and F," that will be disclosed in detail in the *description of embodiments* section of the patent application (probably with drawings, if it is an electromechanical invention).
(iii) Only elements A11, B11 and C1 (as such or broadened) of the prototype are considered essential elements of the invention.
(iv) The order of importance of the rest of the elements of the prototype is D > E > F (meaning that D is the most important and the importance decreases through E to F, which is the least important). Although it is not included in the prototype, element G is also interesting, but it is less important than element F.
(v) An element having two mutually exclusive alternatives, H1 and H2, is considered useful to differentiate two market sectors.

(vi) The closest prior art known by inventors and crafter is a document disclosing "a writing device having A11 and B11."
(vii) Of the three essential elements in the prototype, there is *strong* support to broaden the terminology from A11 to A1 and from A1 to A (A11 $\subset$ A1 $\subset$ A).
(viii) There is *very reasonable* support to broaden the terminology from B11 to B1 and from B1 to B (B11 $\subset$ B1 $\subset$ B).
(ix) It is *reasonable* to think that a person skilled in the art would consider element C1 of the prototype to be equivalent to C2, C3 and C4, which makes reasonable the use of a Markush group consisting of the four elements.

From these premises, the following independent claim will be straightforwardly drafted:

[standard format]

Claim 1. A writing device comprising:
  – element A;
  – element B; and
  – element C selected from the group consisting of C1, C2, C3 and C4.

Claim 1 is drafted in standard format.

Depending on the case, an EPO examiner could ask that Claim 1 should be drafted in two-part format. Having in mind that "a writing device having A11 and B11" is part of the prior art, Claim 1 would then read:

[two-part format]

Claim 1. A writing device comprising: element A; and element B; characterized by further comprising element C selected from the group consisting of C1, C2, C3 and C4.

Regardless of which format is used in Claim 1 and before drafting dependent claims that add *extra* elements, the patent drafter recommends adding fallback positions: dependent claims that add selected elements from the broad elements of Claim 1.

In this case, the addition of selected values will follow the order A > B > C (i.e., the order of importance of these elements) , given the different degrees of support in the respective broadening of prototype elements A11, B11 and C1. Thus the first two dependent claims will read:

Claim 2. The writing device according to Claim 1, wherein element A is A1.

Claim 3. The writing device according to Claim 2, wherein element A1 is A11.

So far, Claims 1–3 form a dependency chain with only singular dependency, as is recommended when successive selected elements are added.

However, when, in the following dependent claims, an extra element is added, writing the claim in multiple dependent form is strongly recommended for the EPO, for the reasons explained in section 3.3 of this module. Thus Claims 4–6 will read:

Claim 4. The writing device according to any one of Claims 1–3, wherein element B is B1.
Claim 5. The writing device according to Claim 4, wherein element B1 is B11.
Claim 6. The writing device according to any one of Claims 1–5, wherein element C is C1.

Now, claims adding the rest of the elements in order of importance (D > E > F > G) are drafted, with the two mutually exclusive alternatives H1 and H2 at the end:

Claim 7. The writing device according to any one of Claims 1–6, further comprising element D.
Claim 8. The writing device according to any one of Claims 1–7, further comprising element E.
Claim 9. The writing device according to any one of Claims 1–8, further comprising element F.
Claim 10. The writing device according to any one of Claims 1–9, further comprising element G.
Claim 11. The writing device according to any one of Claims 1–10, further comprising element H1.
Claim 12. The writing device according to any one of Claims 1–10, further comprising element H2.

The claim set has 12 numbered claims (3 below the limit of 15 that, at time of writing, the EPO will allow without requiring an extra claim fee); but a simple calculation shows that the set covers a total of 844 actual claims.

The claim set in this example will be appropriate for the EPO and those patent offices that allow multiple dependencies from multiple dependent claims – something not permitted at the USPTO.

Before the PCT international application with the previous claim set enters a U.S. phase, the applicant should make use of the opportunity offered under the PCT[27] for amending the claims to fit national requirements. Great care should be taken when drafting a claim set appropriate to the USPTO. If this task is not performed by the same person who drafted the PCT application, they should give specific instructions

about the detail underlying the original claim set to a new drafter. In the hands of a different patent expert, there is a risk that all of the multiple dependencies might simply be erased, transforming every claim "according to any one of Claims 1–x" into a claim "according to Claim 1," thus creating a *dependency pyramid* with Claim 1 as its vertex. As we explained in section 3, such a pyramid structure is not generally recommended, because it does not offer good fallback positions in the event that the vertex Claim 1 is found not to be novel.

Let us look at one systematic approach (not necessarily the best) for adapting claims originally drafted in the EPO style (two-part format) to the USPTO-style dependency groups, building on our last example.

Example

In the first instance, original Claims 1–3 are equally appropriate for the USPTO, because they have no multiple dependency.

Original Claims 4 and 6–12 *are* written in multiple dependent form.

To "deconstruct" multiple dependencies into appropriate singular dependencies, the patent drafter will prepare:

(i) dependency chains with the broadest meaning of the elements;
(ii) dependency chains with the narrowest meanings of the elements; and
(iii) claims with intermediate meanings of the elements, in case the total number of claims is still reasonable (ideally no more than 20, to avoid the extra claim fee otherwise payable).

In this particular example, steps (i) and (ii) are enough to draft the following 20 claims appropriate to the USPTO ("US-Claims").

First, step (i):

US-Claims 1–3 = Claims 1–3 in EPO style, in the standard format
US-Claim 4. The writing device *according to Claim 1, wherein element B is B1.*
US-Claim 5. The writing device according to Claim 4, wherein element B is B11.
US-Claim 6. The writing device *according to Claim 1, wherein element C is C1.*
US-Claim 7. The writing device *according to Claim 1, further comprising element D.*
US-Claim 8. The writing device according to Claim 7, further comprising element E.

WIPO Patent Drafting Manual

US-Claim 9.   The writing device according to Claim 8, further comprising element F.
US-Claim 10. The writing device according to Claim 9, further comprising element G.
US-Claim 11. The writing device according to Claim 10, further comprising element H1.
US-Claim 12. The writing device according to Claim 10, further comprising element H2.

Next, step (ii):

US-Claim 13. The writing device *according to Claim 3*, wherein *element B is B11*.
US-Claim 14. The writing device *according to Claim 13*, wherein element C is C1.
US-Claim 15. The writing device according to Claim 14, further comprising element D.
US-Claim 16. The writing device according to Claim 15, further comprising element E.
US-Claim 17. The writing device according to Claim 16, further comprising element F.
US-Claim 18. The writing device according to Claim 17, further comprising element G.
US-Claim 19. The writing device according to Claim 18, further comprising element H1.
US-Claim 20. The writing device according to Claim 18, further comprising element H2.

Note that US-Claim 4 is written as being dependent from the broadest of the first three (Claim 1) and it adds B1, the broadest selected element from B, whereas US-Claim 13 is written as being dependent from the narrowest of the first three (Claim 3) and it adds B11, the narrowest selected element from B. Thus US-Claim 6 is written as being dependent from the broadest claim (Claim 1), whereas US-Claim 14 is written as being dependent from the narrow US-Claim 13, both of them adding selected element C1. US-Claim 7, adding extra element D, is written as being dependent from the broadest claim (Claim 1), so US-Claims 8–12, all hanging from US-Claim 7, are broadly targeted. However, US-Claim 15, adding extra element D, is written as being dependent from narrower US-Claim 14 that refers to Claim 13 depending from the narrowest of the first three claims (Claim 3), so US-Claims 15–20, all hanging from US-Claim 14 are narrowly targeted.

With this set of 20 claims and in light of the U.S. practice regarding amendment and added matter, the USPTO will likely accept, via amendment, any claim with a scope between those of US-Claim 1 (the broadest) and US-Claims 19–20 (the narrowest).

Key words

- Claim
- Invention
- Embodiment
- Broad and narrow claims
- All-element rule
- Preamble
- Transitional phrase
- Body of the claim
- Element
- Limitation
- Claim punctuation
- Antecedent basis
- Two-part claim
- Alternative elements
- Markush claim
- Functional element
- Means-plus-function claim
- Independent claim
- Dependent claim
- Multiple dependent claim

Self-Test

☐ Distinguish between an invention and an embodiment (of the invention).

☐ Which part of the patent defines the scope of protection provided by a patent?

☐ Why might a patent drafter want to include both broad and narrow claims in a patent?

☐ Name the three parts of a claim. Explain each part.

☐ What is the difference between an open-ended transitional phrase and a closed transitional phrase?

☐ A patent claim may be simply a list of parts (of the invention) with no apparent relationship to each other. True or false?

☐ Explain what constitutes proper antecedent basis with respect to a patent claim.

☐ A dependent claim may depend from another claim, which may be either independent or another dependent claim. True or false?

☐ What is a multiple dependent claim?

☐ What is a multiple-multiple dependent claim?

☐ What is a Markush claim?

☐ What is a means-plus-function claim?

Module V
Types of claim

1.	**Basic types of claim**	**67**
1.1	Product claims	67
1.2	Process (or method) claims	68
1.3	Preamble with the purposive expression "for"	68
2.	**Specific types of claim**	**69**
2.1	Product-by-process claims	69
2.2	Parameter claims	70
2.3	General use claims	71
2.4	Medical indication claims	71
2.5	Composition claims	73
2.6	Biotechnology claims	73
2.7	Computer-implemented invention claims	74

Module V. Types of claim

For many inventions, claims in more than one category are needed for comprehensive patent protection. The section explores some of the various types or categories of claim that the patent drafter may prepare for a client seeking the fullest scope of coverage possible.

1. Basic types of claim

It is sometimes said that there are only two basic types of claim: claims to a physical entity (a product, an apparatus) and claims to an activity (a process, a use).

Examples of *product claim* are:

- "A steering mechanism incorporating an automatic feed-back circuit …"
- "A woven garment comprising …"
- "An insecticide consisting of X, Y, Z"
- "A communication system comprising a plurality of transmitting and receiving stations"

Process claims are applicable to all kinds of activity in which the use of some material product for effecting the process is implied; the activity may be performed upon material products, upon energy, upon other processes (as in control processes) or upon living things.

1.1 Product claims

A product claim addresses:

(i) a substance or compositions (e.g., a chemical compound or a mixture of compounds); or
(ii) any physical entities (e.g., an apparatus, an article, an object, a device, a machine or a system in which more than one apparatus cooperate).

In U.S. law, the former is known as *composition of matter* and the latter, *machine* and *manufacture*.

For example, a claim that covers a tripod for a camera or a window crank is a product claim addressing a physical entity. For the sake of convenience, we will call it an *apparatus claim*. When drafting an apparatus claim, the patent drafter will first prepare a preamble that recites what the apparatus is and sometimes also what it does. Next, the patent drafter will list the essential elements of the invention – that is, those required for the inventive device to function in its most basic form (the essence of the invention). The novelty of the invention lies in these essential components.

In general, infringement of a product claim occurs when a third party, not authorized by the patentee, makes, uses, offers for sale, sells or imports for these purposes the product covered by the claim.

Professional tip

Once you believe you have reasonably captured the essence of the invention, review and re-review the claim to see how many words you can remove from it while still preserving the essence of the invention. You may want to involve the inventor(s) in this process, because it may help them to conceptualize their invention more clearly.

1.2 Process (or method) claims

A process claim addresses:

(i) a process that results in a product (e.g., a manufacturing process); or

(ii) a process not yielding a product (e.g., a process of computing data or a process of diagnosing the safety of a system).

In general, the terms *process* and *method* are accepted as synonymous in claims drafting.

A method claim might look like this:

1. A method for making tea, the method comprising:
   - boiling water;
   - adding sugar to the boiling water;
   - adding tea leaves to the boiling water to form a mixture;
   - adding milk to the mixture; and
   - filtering the mixture.

In this example, the series of steps performed in the process of making tea are stated sequentially in the order they are performed. In many jurisdictions, however, the steps performed in a method claim are presumed to occur in any order, unless otherwise stated, for both prior art and infringement purposes. In the example set out above, the step of boiling water must occur before the step of adding sugar to the water, but the step of adding sugar to the water could occur after any other step, for example after adding the milk. From the point of view of infringement, the patent drafter should look for words and limitations that can be removed from claims; here, they should consider whether adding milk and sugar is always necessary when making tea in accordance with their client's invention.

In general, infringement of a process claim occurs where a third party, not authorized by the patentee, uses the claimed process. In addition, if a claimed process results in a product, unauthorized acts of using, offering for sale, selling or importing for these purposes the product obtained directly by that process also constitute infringement of the process claim.

A claim for use of a product in a process, known as a *use claim*, is a particular form of process claim and is accepted in some jurisdictions. For example, in the European Patent Office (EPO), a use claim in a form such as "the use of substance X as an insecticide" will be treated as equivalent to a process claim in the form "a process of killing insects using substance X." Not all jurisdictions allow such claims, however: in the United States, for example, a use claim must be drafted as a process claim.

We will look more closely at use claims in section 2.3.

1.3 Preamble with the purposive expression "for"

If a claim commences with words such as "An apparatus *for* carrying out the process, etc. ...," this may be construed in many jurisdictions as meaning merely an apparatus suitable for carrying out the process. Accordingly, in such jurisdictions, an apparatus that otherwise possesses all of the features specified in the claims but which would be unsuitable for the stated purpose or which would require modification to enable it to be so used should normally not be considered as anticipating the claim or an infringement of the claim. Similar considerations apply to a claim for a product for a particular use. For example, if a claim refers to a "mold for molten steel," this implies certain limitations for the mold; hence a plastic ice cube tray with a melting point much lower than that of steel would not come within the claim.

Similarly, a claim to a substance or composition for a particular use should be construed as meaning a substance or composition that is in fact suitable for the stated use. A known product that, on its face, is the same as the substance or composition defined in the claim but which is in a form that would render it *unsuitable* for the stated use would not deprive the claim of novelty; a known product in a form in which it is in fact *suitable* for the stated use – even if it has never been described for that use – would typically deprive the claim of novelty in many jurisdictions. An exception to this general principle of interpretation exists in some jurisdictions that have special rules for claims for use of a known substance or composition in a surgical, therapeutic or diagnostic method.

Let us now look at a sample apparatus claim.

Example

1. An apparatus for supporting a camera, comprising:
   - a pivotal mounting configured to hold the camera; and
   - a plurality of legs arranged to support the pivotal mounting.

The preamble recites that the claim is for an apparatus for supporting a camera; the body of the claim recites that the essential elements of this apparatus are a pivotal mounting for the camera and legs arranged to support the pivotal mounting.

Remembering that, from the infringement perspective, the patent drafter should always consider whether words might be removed and the claim yet be complete, we might question here whether the adjective "pivotal" is strictly necessary for the mounting of the tripod.

In contrast to an apparatus or product claim, in the case of a method claim commencing with such words as "A method for re-melting galvanic layers," the part "for re-melting" should not be understood as meaning that the process is merely suitable for re-melting galvanic layers but rather as a functional feature concerning the re-melting of galvanic layers and hence as defining one of the steps of the claimed method.

A distinction has to be made where the claim is directed to a process (or a method) that comprises physical steps which result in a product. In that case, mentioning its purpose means that the process merely has to be *suitable* for producing the intended outcome, and is not actually used to deliver the product as an integral method step. Consequently, if prior art discloses a method without indicating the particular product that is its intended outcome, it will anticipate a claim directed to the same method that goes on to recite a particular product.

2. Specific types of claim

2.1 Product-by-process claims

Claims for products defined in terms of a process of manufacture (e.g., "Product X obtainable by process Y") are allowable in some jurisdictions, provided that the products as such fulfill the requirements for patentability – that is, they are novel and inventive, among other things. A product is not typically rendered novel merely because it is made by means of a new process, however, and a claim defining a product in terms of a process will be construed in many jurisdictions as a claim to the product as such. Irrespective of whether the term "obtainable," "obtained," "directly obtained" or an equivalent wording is used in such a *product-by-process claim*, it is still directed to the product and hence confers absolute protection upon that product.

When a product-by-process claim defines a product by its method of manufacture, to meet the novelty requirement the claimed product must not be identical to a known product. The burden of proving allegedly distinguishing product-by-process features lies with the applicant, who has to provide evidence that the modification of the process parameters results in a different product, for example by demonstrating differences in the properties of the products. In jurisdictions such as that of the EPO, the *purpose* of the process will also be taken into consideration when determining the features of a product obtained by a process. This contrasts with evaluation of a method for or process of obtaining a product in which indication of the particular purpose of the process (product preparation) merely implies *suitability* for that purpose.

In most jurisdictions such as the EPO, if the subject matter of a claim is a process of obtaining a product, the protection conferred by the patent extends to the products directly obtained by such process, and this applies both to processes producing products that are completely transformed from their materials and to those processes producing only superficial changes (e.g., painting, polishing).

Some other jurisdictions, however, treat product-by-process claims as method claims. In Japan, the product-by-process claim has been found to be indefinite (unclear); it will be used only in special circumstances, such as when defining the structural or characteristic elements of the claimed product would be impossible or impracticable as of the filing date.

Product-by-process claims are typical for complex chemical entities that are difficult or impossible to define structurally, such as polymers or foods.

Professional tip

Always check whether a product-by-process claim is not only permissible but also the best approach to protecting your client's invention in a given jurisdiction. You might consider such a claim as part of a mix of formats from which you will later elect the proper claims, depending on the jurisdiction, prior art, etc.

Example

This product-by-process claim aims to protect a particular oat drink:

1. A homogeneous and stable cereal suspension having the taste and aroma of natural oats, comprising intact ß-glucans from the starting material, and having a viscosity below 0.5 Pas at room temperature, obtainable by:
   – (a) dry- or wet-grinding rolled oats or otherwise heat- and water-treated oats to meal;
   – (b) suspending the oatmeal in water, if the meal has been produced by dry grinding;
   – (c) treating the suspension with ß-amylase, … ;
   – […]
   – (g) subjecting the suspension to ultra-high temperature (UHT) treatment to obtain a sterile product while inactivating the enzymes added.

2.2 Parameter claims

Parameters are characteristic values of measurable properties (e.g., the melting point of a substance, the flexural strength of steel, the resistance of an electrical conductor) and they may sometimes be defined as mathematical formulae outlining the combination of several variables.

Many jurisdictions allow claims that define products by using parameters such that the invention can either be defined only in such terms or cannot otherwise be defined more precisely without unduly restricting the scope of the claims, and where the result is one that can be directly and positively verified, without undue experimentation, by tests or procedures adequately specified in the description or known to the person skilled in the art.

For example, the claimed invention may be an ashtray in which a smoldering cigarette end will automatically be extinguished because of the shape and relative dimensions of the ashtray. The latter may vary considerably in a manner difficult to define, yet still providing the desired effect. So long as the claim specifies the construction and shape of the ashtray as clearly as possible, it may define the relative dimensions by reference to the result to be achieved, provided that the specification includes adequate directions to enable the person skilled in the art to determine the required dimensions by routine test procedures.

Professional tip

It is crucial that you consider the degree of protection this form of claim provides: even if it is approved, might your client's competitors still defeat it with prior art unknown to you and your client at the time of filing? Remember that your focus is on protecting the invention *and* achieving the applicant's business objectives – two goals that are often significantly more difficult than simply achieving a minimally acceptable claim format in a given jurisdiction.

The EPO, for example, will allow characterization of a product mainly by its parameters in those cases in which the invention cannot be adequately defined in any other way, provided that those parameters can be clearly and reliably determined either by indications in the description or by objective procedures which are usual in the art. The same applies to a process-related feature that is defined by parameters. The EPO suggests that sometimes, however, such claims disguise lack of novelty; accordingly, the patent drafter can expect a patent examiner to scrutinize such claims in detail before allowing them.

Another instance in which a parameter claim may be justified is an invention relating to polymorph. Different polymorphs (crystalline forms) of a chemical compound cannot be claimed by means of their formula; the formula is the same for all of them. It is their crystalline structure that differs, such that polymorphs can be claimed only by means of parameters defining infrared spectra and X-ray diffraction pattern, for example.

2.3 General use claims

Although a product claim aims to protect every use of the product, protection of a new and inventive use of a product may be also sought by a use claim (a subtype of the basic process claim). Every use claim is associated with a particular purpose of the use, that purpose being considered a functional element or technical feature of the claim in some jurisdictions.

In some jurisdictions such as the EPO, a use claim in a form such as "the use of substance X as an insecticide" will be accepted for nonmedical uses (i.e., uses outside therapy, surgery or diagnosis, on humans or animals) and it will be treated as equivalent to a process or method claim in the form "a process of killing insects using substance X." Thus a claim in that form should not be interpreted as a product claim for substance X recognizable, for example by further additives, as intended for use as an insecticide. Similarly, a claim for "the use of a transistor in an amplifying circuit" would be equivalent to a claim for "a process of amplifying using a circuit containing a transistor" and it should neither be interpreted as a product claim directed to "an amplifying circuit in which the transistor is used" nor to a process claim in the form "the process of using the transistor in building such a circuit."

Not all jurisdictions allow such use claims, however, and this includes particularly the United States, where "use" is not one of the statutory classes of claim.

2.4 Medical indication claims

If the essential feature of the invention is a new way of using a known product for a medical purpose (e.g., for treating a particular disease), a patent drafter should pay a particular attention to the applicable national laws and practices, since not only the permissible claim formats but also the patentability of such an invention can be in question. Even if the format is broadly similar or the same, the actual protection conferred by a patent may vary from country to country based on differing interpretations, different judgments of direct or indirect infringement and perhaps exemptions from liability for patent infringement.

In general, such differences have their origin in the exclusion of diagnostic, therapeutic and surgical methods for the treatment of humans or animals as patentable subject matter. In some countries that have implemented this exclusion in law, special claim formats have nonetheless emerged in practice that do not cover the method of treatment but claim an already-known product for a new medical use.

If a substance is found in the state of the art, a claim for "substance X" will not be patentable for lack of novelty. If that previously known substance – until now used for a certain nonmedical purpose (e.g., as an insecticide, a dye, food, a plant protection product, building materials, etc.) – is later found to be effective in the treatment of a disease, a patent application may be filed claiming the known substance specifically for this medical use, which will be labeled its *first medical indication* (also called *first use* or *new use*). In other words, the essential novel and inventive feature of the claim is a medical use of substance X.

If the same situation occurs again, but this time substance X is found to be effective for a wholly different medical use, the subsequent claim on that substance will be for a *second medical indication* (or *second use*).

Such claims, if granted, protect an already-known product for specified medical use.

While the patent laws of some countries specifically rule out the patenting of first, second or any further medical indications of a known product, some allow such claims provided that all of the patentability requirements are met. Typically, one or more of the following claim formats are permissible, depending on the jurisdiction. (The example claims that appear throughout relate to a new use of already-known zidovudine, 3'-azido-3'-deoxythymidine or AZT, for the treatment of AIDS.)

Swiss-type claims   Swiss-type claims typically take the form "use of substance X in the manufacture of a medicament for the treatment of condition Y":

1. Use of 3'-azido-3'-deoxythymidine in the manufacture of a medicament for the treatment or prophylaxis of AIDS.

It was the only format allowed in the EPO between 1985 and 2010 and remains accepted in many countries. It is a process claim, covering the manufacturing process of a known medicine for a novel medical indication. Accordingly, direct infringers of the Swiss-type claims are those who manufacture the patented pharmaceutical.

Purpose-limited product claims   Purpose-limited product claims take the form "substance X for use in the treatment of condition Y":

1. 3'-azido-3'-deoxythymidine for use in the treatment or prophylaxis of AIDS.

This claim format has been compulsory in the EPO since 2011 and it is being introduced by some signatories to the European Patent Convention (EPC) such as in the Spanish Patent Act (Law 24/2015).

Use claims   In countries where the use claim format is accepted for protection of first, second or further medical indication (e.g., Germany, Canada and Australia), it is possible to draft a claim in the form "use of substance X for the treatment of condition Y":

1. Use of 3'-azido-3'-deoxythymidine for the treatment or prophylaxis of AIDS.

Substance when used to treat a particular disease   An example of this claim format may read:

1. 3'-azido-3'-deoxythymidine whenever used or intended to be used in the treatment or prophylaxis of AIDS in a human.

In addition, some countries may allow claims directed to pharmaceutical formulations for a particular purpose.

Method of treatment claims   Method of treatment claims typically take the form "a method of treating a human having [medical condition Y] comprising administration of an effective amount of [substance X]."

1. A method of treating a human having AIDS comprising the oral administration of an effective AIDS treatment amount of 3'-azido-3'-deoxythymidine to said human.

This claim format is accepted in the United States and Australia, in which diagnostic, therapeutic and surgical methods for the treatment of humans or animals are not excluded from patentable subject matter. In the United States, medical practitioners are protected from liability for patent infringement; method of treatment claims are therefore enforced against manufacturers and/or distributors of the patented product, based on indirect infringement of the patent, whether contributory or induced. Australian law does not include a similar provision exempting medical practitioners from patent infringement. However, in practice, the pharmaceutical companies that own such patents don't have any commercial incentive to sue their clients, namely, the doctors who prescribe infringing medicines and the patients who purchase and consume them.

Example

A novel chemical compound, substance X, is prepared by a specific process, process Z. Evidence is provided that supports the specific use of substance X in the treatment of condition Y. In this case, the invention is related to a new product *and* to its first medical use, and hence the patent application to be filed in the EPO should include at least the following types of claim.

Product claim (i.e., the product *as such*)

Claim 1.   Product X.
  – General/first medical use claim:

Claim 2.   Product X for use as an active pharmaceutical ingredient.
  – Specific/second medical use claim:

Claim 3.   Product X for use in the treatment of condition Y.

Depending on the case, it may be worth including in addition a preparation process claim:

Professional tip

To get the best protection available for specific medical uses, you should ensure that the description set out in the first application on which priority is based allows you to select the most appropriate claim format(s) for the jurisdiction(s) in which you may be filing subsequent applications.

Claim 4.   A preparation process of product X, comprising … [steps of process Z].

In this set of claims, if a product claim (Claim 1) is novel and nonobvious, any claim for a use of substance X (Claims 2 and 3) and any claim for a preparation process of substance X (Claim 4) will automatically be considered novel and nonobvious.

In any case, and although a product claim protects any use of the product and any process for preparing the product, it is generally advisable that a patent drafter includes claims of various types in the set not only so that the essential features of the invention can be comprehensively protected but also to mitigate the risk that the product claim is later found invalid.

In doing so, however, the patent drafter must always be mindful that patent laws and practices in this area vary significantly.

2.5 Composition claims

Claims related to compositions are used where the invention to be claimed has to do with the chemical nature of the materials or components used. For example, a claim related to a zinc electroplating solution might read:

1. A copper electroplating solution, comprising:
    (a) an alkaline solution of copper sulfate, 30–50 grams per liter;
    (b) sulfuric acid, 2–4 times the copper acetate solution; and
    (c) an aqueous solution of a pH-modifying substrate in an amount sufficient to adjust the pH to a value of 3.5–5.0.

In preparing claims, it is up to the patent drafter to claim each of the elements as narrowly or as broadly as necessary in view of the prior art, the scope of the invention and other relevant factors. For example, in the claim above, elements (a) and (b) are narrower than element (c) insofar as the claim spells out the exact name of the compound in elements (a) and (b), but element (c) is stated only generically. Thus *any* pH-modifying substrate that performs the function of adjusting the pH of the solution to a value of 3.5–5.0 will fall within the limitation as stated in (c).

2.6 Biotechnology claims

Biotechnology, in general, relates to all practical uses of living organisms. In 1873, Louis Pasteur received U.S. Patent 141,072 claiming "yeast, free from organic germs of disease, as an article of manufacture." This patent is sometimes considered the first patent concerning a microorganism.

Uses for biological and life science inventions may be either commercial or therapeutic. Thus biotechnology inventions may include cDNA, recombinant DNA, DNA fragments, protein, monoclonal antibodies, anti-sense DNA and RNA, recombinant vectors and expression vectors.

A set of sample biotechnology claims to cover an invention related to nucleic acids and encoded proteins may read:

1. An isolated polynucleotide comprising a member selected from the group consisting of:
    (a) a polynucleotide encoding a polypeptide comprising amino acid 1 to amino acid 255 as set forth in SEQ ID NO:2; and
    (b) a polynucleotide which hybridizes to and which is at least 95% complementary to the polynucleotide of (a).

2. The polynucleotide of claim 1 comprising nucleotide 1 to nucleotide 1080 of SEQ ID NO:1.

In this example, note that the gene sequence is referenced in the claim and not spelled out in full.

Many jurisdictions have special requirements for inventions related to biotechnology inventions and for sequence listings and deposit rules. (See also Module VI, section 14, on exclusions from patentability, and Module VI, section 15, on the requirement for industrial application.)

Where an invention involves a biological material and words alone cannot sufficiently describe in a patent application how to make and use the invention in a way that a person skilled in the art could follow, access to the biological material may be necessary to satisfy statutory patentability requirements. To ensure access to the biological material for the purpose of patent procedures, many jurisdictions have introduced a deposit system.

An example of claims involving such biological material may read:

1. A seed of cotton cultivar designated PHY 78 Acala, wherein a representative sample of seed of said cultivar was deposited under ATCC Accession No. PTA-5666.

This example shows that a sample of the claimed seed of the cotton cultivar was deposited with the American Type Culture Collection (ATCC) and given a reference number ("PTA-5666") with which it can be accessed.

The Budapest Treaty on the International Recognition of the Deposit of Microorganisms for the Purposes of Patent Procedure was established in 1977 to facilitate the recognition of deposited biological material in patent applications throughout the world.[28] The Treaty requires a Contracting

Party that allows or requires the deposit of microorganisms for the purposes of patent procedure to recognize, for such purposes, the deposit of a microorganism with any *international depositary authority* (IDA), irrespective of whether that authority is within or outside the territory of the state. An IDA is a scientific institution – typically a "culture collection" – which is backed by an assurance from its government that the institution complies and will continue to comply with the requirements of the Treaty.

2.7 Computer-implemented invention claims

In most jurisdictions, abstract ideas, software or computer programs as such, pure mental acts and methods of doing business as such are not patentable subject matter and are excluded from patent protection. While the patentability of computer-implemented inventions in various jurisdictions is beyond the scope of this manual, patent drafters should be aware of how the subject matter of their clients' inventions may be interpreted in the jurisdiction(s) targeted.

Patent applications related to computer software and/or hardware devices that execute specialized algorithms typically include product claims (i.e., for an apparatus, a device, a system), method claims and use claims.

The first claim (Claim 1) of an application regarding a computer-implemented invention is frequently a method claim. This is because most of these patents include the dynamic aspects (the behavior) of computer programs. In other words, a computer program performs an algorithm, which is essentially a method.

It is also important to include product claims in a patent application for this type of invention. Typically, computer implemented inventions are implemented on general-purpose hardware (e.g., a PC or a handheld electronic device) and hence there is no need to formulate special apparatus features. In many jurisdictions that allow a product claim to refer back to one or more method claim(s) (see Module IV, section 3.4), one way of drafting such a product claim is by simply referring back to both the independent and dependent method claims. This will allow a patent drafter to refer to the full set of method claims in a single product claim.

Example

1. A computer-implemented method for transferring a server from a standby mode to a fully activated mode, the method comprising the steps of:
   - sending, from a client to the server, which is in a standby mode, an activation signal, wherein the activation signal is adapted to transfer the server from the standby mode to the fully activated mode;

   - receiving, by the server, the activation signal; and
   - transferring the server from the standby mode to the fully activated mode in response to the reception of the activation signal.

Claims 2–10 are also method claims and the claims continue:

11. A data-processing system comprising means for carrying out [each of the steps of] the method according to any one of Claims 1–10.

To adapt the claim set to suit a jurisdiction in which such a reference is not allowed, the patent drafter rephrases each method step by using "means for …":

11. A data-processing system comprising:
    - means for sending, from a client to the server, which is in a standby mode, an activation signal, wherein the activation signal is adapted to transfer the server from the standby mode to the fully activated mode;
    - means for receiving, by the server, the activation signal; and
    - means for transferring the server from the standby mode to the fully activated mode in response to the reception of the activation signal.

In jurisdictions such as the United States where claims using the term "means" may not be broadly interpreted, a patent drafter may substitute generic terms, such as "a transmitter for sending" in place of "means for sending."

The acceptable claim formats for such inventions may vary from country to country and may include computer-readable medium claims, data structure claims, propagated signal claims and computer program product claims. In some jurisdictions, some specialized claim formats for computer-implemented inventions are common, including those relating to the software arts. Typically modifications of more basic claim types, these are beyond the scope of this manual.

A *computer-readable medium claim*, also known in the United States as a *Beauregard claim*,[29] attempts to protect an invention when it is embodied in a particular medium (e.g., a CD-ROM). Such claims, which can be in any of several different formats, allow a patent holder to seek damages against not only persons who make or use infringing software but also those who sell such software, including retail sellers and wholesalers.

One of the more common formats for such a claim is to take the body of a method claim for the invention and add a "computer-readable medium" preamble:

1. A computer-readable storage medium storing instructions that when executed by a computer cause the computer to perform a method for using a computer system to [a specified function], the method comprising: …

A *data structure claim*, also known in the United States as a *Lowry claim*,[30] attempts to provide protection for those computerized inventions that include novel computer data structures. Of several possible formats, one of the more common is:

1. A memory for storing data for access by an application program being executed on a data-processing system, comprising:
– a data structure stored in the memory, the data structure including information resident in a database used by the application program and including:
    – a first data object configured to … ;
    – a second data object configured to … ; and
    – a third data object configured to … .

Professional tip

Remember that the practices in each jurisdiction will evolve as technology evolves in the field – which means that you must stay up to date with the latest legal developments in those fields and jurisdictions relevant to you and your clients.

Key words

- Product, apparatus or device claims
- Method or process claims
- Product-by-process claims
- Parameter claims
- Use claims
- Medical indication claims
- Composition claims
- Biotechnology claims
- Sequence listings
- Deposit of biological material
- Computer-implemented invention claims
- Computer-readable medium claims
- Data structure claims

Self-Test

☐ Distinguish between a product (apparatus or device) claim and a method or process claim.

☐ Where the preamble of a claim reads "A mold for molten steel," the claim implies a mold suitable for molten steel in many countries. True or false?

☐ Product X manufactured by process A is already known. An inventor came up with a new manufacturing process B to produce product X. Since process B is new, a claim "Product X obtained by Process B" meets novelty vis-à-vis the prior art in all countries. True or false?

☐ Claims that define the invention by a result to be achieved are easy to draft and provide good protection. True or false?

☐ A claim in the format "The use of substance ABC as a …" would be acceptable in all jurisdictions. True or false?

☐ Substance X has been used as a sweetener for many years. An essential inventive concept of a new invention is use of substance X as an antiseptic compound. What types of claim could you draft, bearing in mind the differences among national patent practices?

☐ How does a computer-readable medium claim resemble a method claim?

☐ What does the Budapest Treaty provide with respect to biotechnology patents?

☐ What is wrong with the formatting of the following claim?

☐ An apparatus for harvesting corn, comprising:
    – a thrasher for cutting corn;
    – moving the cut corn into a hopper; and
    – a rotating pivot attached to the thrasher.

Module VI
Patent claim design

1.	**Prepare the claims first**	**77**
2.	**Broad and narrow claims**	**77**
3.	**Clarity, claim word choice and inconsistencies**	**79**
	3.1 Defining terms	79
	3.2 Distinguishing elements	80
	3.3 Relative terms	80
	3.4 Uncertainty	81
	3.5 "In"	81
	3.6 Inconsistency	82
	3.7 Putting this into practice	82
4.	**Claim variations and modifications of the invention**	**83**
5.	**Avoiding unnecessary limitations**	**84**
6.	**Negative limitations and disclaimers**	**84**
7.	**Claims and competing products**	**85**
8.	**Claims must overcome prior art**	**85**
9.	**Using multiple claim types for the same invention**	**85**
10.	**Ensuring that the description supports the claims**	**86**
11.	**Unity of invention**	**87**
12.	**Claim point of view**	**88**
13.	**Narrowing a patent claim during prosecution**	**91**
14.	**Exclusions from patentability**	**92**
15.	**Requirement for industrial applicability**	**93**
16.	**"Reading on" a patent claim**	**93**
17.	**Claim construction in the courts**	**93**

1. Prepare the claims first

When preparing a patent application, the patent drafter should start with the claims because doing so helps them and the inventor to refine the idea of the invention. The drafting of the description and other parts of a patent application will flow naturally once the invention is clear.

2. Broad and narrow claims

Drafting a combination of broad and narrow claims will help to effectively capture the complete scope of an invention's novelty. An ideal approach is to draft a set of claims that ranges from the broadest to the narrowest in terms of coverage. In practice, it might be easiest to start with a narrow claim and then gradually remove elements and/or replace narrow terms with broader ones to arrive at the broadest. Once the patent drafter is confident they have before them the broadest claim possible, they can draft a set of claims dependent from it.

Example

The client has invented a novel apparatus for turning lead into gold. The physical embodiment of the invention has a box-like metal frame, an electric motor, a bowl for retaining scrap lead and a lead–gold zapper element that causes the matter transition. The client shows the patent drafter the physical embodiment of the invention.

This embodiment is the patent drafter's starting point. The "invention" is really an abstract concept and something broader than the physical embodiment, but the embodiment is what the drafter knows best. They arrive at the following claim:

1. An apparatus for turning lead into gold, comprising:
   – a box-like metal frame;
   – an electric motor mounted inside the box-like metal frame;
   – a bowl for retaining scrap lead housed on a surface of the box-like metal frame; and
   – a lead–gold zapper element attached underneath the bowl and inside the box-like metal frame and configured to receive electric power from the electric motor.

The patent drafter reviews this first draft. It broadly and accurately describes the inventive aspects of the physical embodiment of the client's invention.

In writing even this first draft, the drafter has already omitted some features that they know could not represent patentable novelty for this particular invention, such as the

color of the box, and they now carefully review the claim to see if it could possibly be broader.

First, they note that the "box-like metal frame" would not be an essential feature of this invention and that, since they have used the transition "comprising," they can probably eliminate this element altogether; after all, a competitor could avoid infringement by housing the device in something other than a "box-like metal frame." So the patent drafter rewrites the claim as:

1. An apparatus for turning lead into gold, comprising:
   – *an electric motor*;
   – *a bowl for retaining scrap lead*; and
   – a lead–gold zapper element *operably coupled to the bowl* and configured to receive electric power from the electric motor.

The patent drafter reviews the claim again – still trying to broaden it to fully capture the essence of the invention.

They note that "electric motor" is fairly specific. The patent drafter brainstorms all of the related terms that come to mind, such as "motor," "power source" and "electric power source," and asks: is it essential that the invention is powered by a motor? Should the power source be electric? For various reasons, they agree with the client to use the term "power source." The claim is now set out as:

1. An apparatus for turning lead into gold, comprising:
   – a *power source*;
   – a bowl for retaining scrap lead; and
   – a lead–gold zapper element operably coupled to the bowl and configured to receive *power from the power source*.

The patent drafter reviews the claim once again. They notice that the "bowl" element does not really have to be a *bowl* for the invention to retain lead properly and they also notice that they have referred to the "lead" as "scrap lead" rather than simply "lead." Since they know that the invention will work with any kind of lead, they decide to delete the "scrap" adjective as unnecessarily limiting and they realize that any shape of retainer will work properly in place of a bowl. Consequently, the patent drafter decides to use an abstract term, "lead retainer," to cover *any* vessel for retaining lead, and rewrites the claim as:

1. An apparatus for turning lead into gold, comprising:
   – a power source;
   – a *lead retainer*; and
   – a lead–gold zapper element operably coupled to *the lead retainer* and configured to receive power from the power source.

The patent drafter continues reviewing the claim.

They eventually realize that the "power source" is not novel and does not really work in combination with the other elements to produce a novel apparatus. Consequently, they decide to eliminate this element from their broadest claim. The patent drafter has similar thoughts about the inventive contribution provided by the "lead retainer," no matter how abstract a term they choose – but if the patent drafter deletes both the "power source" and the "lead retainer" from the claim, the only element left will be the "lead–gold zapper," and the patent drafter knows that, in the jurisdictions of interest to their client, patent claims must recite more than one element.

At this point, the patent drafter begins to study the "lead–gold zapper" in greater detail and realizes that such elements themselves do not exist in the prior art at all. Consequently, the patent drafter realizes that the principal claims should focus entirely on the novel elements that comprise the lead–gold zapper.

After drafting their "lead–gold zapper" claims, the patent drafter revisits the apparatus claim directed toward an entire device containing the lead-gold zapper and decides to include it for strategic purposes. Recall that this claim now reads:

1. An apparatus for turning lead into gold, comprising:
   - a power source;
   - a lead retainer; and
   - a lead-gold zapper element operably coupled to the lead retainer and configured to receive power from the power source.

The patent drafter can easily add dependent claims to this apparatus by looking back at the changes they made while trying to arrive at the broadest possible claim. Not every element removed from a draft claim is worth keeping, but the full set of dependent claims that the drafter draws out of the elements removed and/or altered is:

2. The apparatus according to Claim 1, further comprising:
   - a box-like metal frame, wherein the power source and the lead-gold zapper element are retained inside the box-like metal frame.
3. The apparatus according to Claim 1, wherein the power source is an electric motor.
4. The apparatus according to Claim 1, wherein the lead retainer is a bowl.
5. The apparatus according to Claim 4, wherein the lead retainer is configured to receive scrap lead.

The patent drafter has now prepared a complete claim set for an apparatus for turning lead into gold; they have also realized that they should draft a claim set that focuses on only the lead–gold zapper element (e.g., "A lead–gold zapper, comprising …"). This patent application will therefore include two independent claim sets.

The patent drafter adds a third set by drafting a series of method claims that cover the operations of the lead–gold zapper element – and perhaps even another series of claims that covers the entire process of turning lead into gold (e.g., an analog to the apparatus claim).

The patent application now includes four independent claim sets (or dependency groups).

The patent drafter might now decide to take one of the claim sets, such as the apparatus claim, and turn it into two separate sets that each focuses on an alternative point of novelty. Independent Claim 1 might be rewritten, first, to include the elements of dependent Claim 3; next, they might rewrite it to include the elements of dependent Claim 4. This would give the patent drafter two claim sets, each with a slightly different focus. These new claims will read as:

1. An apparatus for turning lead into gold, comprising:
   - an *electric motor*;
   - a lead retainer; and
   - a lead–gold zapper element operable coupled to the lead retainer and configured to receive electrical power from the electric motor.

1. An apparatus for turning lead into gold, comprising:
   - a power source;
   - a lead-retaining *bowl*; and
   - a lead–gold zapper element operable coupled to the lead-retaining bowl and configured to receive power from the power source.

In practice, however, a patent drafter should pursue alternative paths such as these only when each truly represents independent novelty of commercial significance or when the prior art is unclear or ambiguous.

Before drafting the broadest possible claims, the patent drafter must check whether the inventor envisioned a viable scope for the invention significantly narrower than that of the claims proposed. If the patent application is for a car with three wheels and the client absolutely does not see their invention being adaptable to any other kind of vehicle, for example, the claims should be narrowly drafted and remain specific to cars, not unnecessarily extend protection to all vehicles or moving objects. If the inventor thinks that the invention is adaptable or if the patent drafter can foresee potential infringers adapting this invention to other vehicles, it will be prudent to draft the claims broadly enough to cover any vehicle and not only cars. In this way, the patent drafter will sometimes help their client to recognize the potential of their invention. Many inventors are extremely focused on solving a particular problem and fail to see the full reach of their invention. For example, spread-spectrum communications – one of the most pioneering communications technologies of the 20th century – were originally conceived as merely a solution to the signal jamming of radio-controlled torpedoes. This technology was later used to develop CDMA (2G) cellular telephones: an application far removed from torpedoes.

The patent drafter should note that some jurisdictions have requirements that claims must be "concise." Such requirements may refer both the individual claims and to the claims in their entirety. In these instances, undue repetition of wording between one claim and another, for example, can be avoided by drafting claims in dependent form.

While most jurisdictions have no objection to a reasonable number of such claims directed to particular preferred features of the invention, some patent examiners may object to multiple claims of a trivial nature. What is or what is not a reasonable number of claims depends on the facts and circumstances of each particular case, while the drafting and structure of the claims should not allow the examiner to readily recognize the matter for which protection is sought. The patent examiner may also raise objections where multiple alternatives are presented within a single claim if this obscures its scope.

Limitations on the number of claims are not found in every jurisdiction, but where a patent office has established such, it will have done so not to generate income in the form of additional fees for excess claims but for reasons of administrative efficiency. If an examiner raises an objection with which the patent drafter disagrees, the drafter has a duty to push for the most appropriate scope of protection for their client. There will, of course, always be a point in any jurisdiction at which additional claims will not be in the best interests of the client and the more familiar with a jurisdiction's requirements the patent drafter becomes, the more easily they will recognize this point and be able to advise their client accordingly.

3. Clarity, claim word choice and inconsistencies

The words used to describe the invention must be chosen with care. They should capture not only the invention in its most specific form but also variants with which a competitor might attempt to skirt around a patent to reap some the benefits of the invention without being prosecuted for infringement or required to pay for a license. In some ways, the patent drafter needs to imagine themselves a potential infringer and draft the claims accordingly.

3.1 Defining terms

The clarity of patent claims is of the utmost importance given that they define the matter for which protection is sought. The patent drafter must ensure that the claims are worded so that their category is clear and hence, with it, the scope of the protection sought, which varies across categories. The words selected must convey the meaning the patent drafter wants them to convey and they must adequately cover the invention.

Professional tip

As a patent drafter, always ask yourself questions: *What are the goals of this invention? What is the inventor trying to protect? Who/what is likely to infringe? To whom could the patent be licensed? For what? Am I adequately protecting the invention by drafting the claims this way or that way?*

As a patent drafter, you need to be very creative and try in your claim set to get the maximum possible protection for the invention, while also building in fallback positions.

The meaning of the terms used in a claim should typically be clear to the person skilled in the art – or, at the very least, not entirely alien to them. If some terms may be unfamiliar or used in an unfamiliar way, the patent drafter will do well to define them in the description. They will then need to ensure that any such new or alternative meaning is clear in the claims – because claims are required to be self-contained (i.e., understandable without reference to the description, even though the description may guide their interpretation).

On occasion, such definitions may depart from a literal meaning of the words; it should not, however, depart from any established meaning in the relevant art and the patent drafter should ensure that all meanings are appropriate in the specific circumstances in which they seek to use the term.

In this case, as well as more generally, the patent drafter will do well to read through each claim, as drafted, looking not only at its technical sense but also at the meaning and scope its wording would normally be given both literally and in the relevant art, because this is how an examiner – or the courts – may interpret the claim. In particular, the patent drafter should take care to avoid ambiguity that might lead to interpretations or characterizations other than those intended.

For instance, a patent drafter might have chosen to use the term "board" in the claims – but the word "board" can have different meanings. If the patent drafter chooses the word "board" without clarifying whether they mean a "circuit board" or a "wooden board," for example, the claims may be ambiguous. While any selected word must be as broad as necessary to provide the appropriate scope of protection, there are instances in which a word with clearer, more specific meaning might be more appropriate, and in any such case that meaning should be defined in the description so that there is no room for confusion.

3.2 Distinguishing elements

When drafting claims, adhering to the rule "same element – same term – same numeral" will support clarity, ensuring that a single particular element is named and numbered consistently throughout the patent application and that the same term or number is not attributed to any other element. In the event that several synonymous terms are commonly used in practice to designate a given element, the drafter should cite all synonymous terms on the first mention of the element and confirm which of these will be used in the application. Similarly, any abbreviations should be defined in full on their first instance in the description and the same abbreviation then used consistently throughout the rest of that part. Because claims are required to be self-contained, the same will be true if the abbreviation appears again there.

For distinguishing different elements that share the same label, "X," different phrases may be formed using the common label with different words that function as adjectives. The simplest example might be ordinals, for example "first X," "second X," "third X," etc. Where the labeled elements relate to a point of reference, the patent drafter might use "forward X," then "reverse X" or "proximal X" and, later, "distal X." Ordinal labels can also be used to exclude a number of components. For example, to claim an apparatus with three or more antennas (perhaps because the apparatus with fewer than three antennas is prior art), the drafter might write:

An apparatus comprising a first, a second and a third antenna, …

When multiple pairs of elements are related, "each" and "respective" can be used (e.g., "each emitter comprising a respective receiver").

3.3 Relative terms

Be precise in drafting claims and avoid relative adjectives – that is, words such as "long," "short," "tall," "wide," "fast," "slow," "perfect," etc. Such words are often subjective measures and cannot provide clear limitations unless they are used with reference to another claim element. For example, "a long piece of wood" becomes meaningful only when framed as:

– a first piece of wood;
– a second piece of wood, wherein the first piece of wood *is longer than* the second piece of wood.

If a patent drafter does use such a bare term, the patent examiner is likely either to object to it or simply to read it out – in other words, to read "a long piece of wood" as nothing more than "a piece of wood" and, in fact, no different from "a tiny piece of wood." Even worse, should such a claim end up in an issued patent and brought to the courts, an accused infringer may easily argue, "We use pieces of wood – but we don't use *long* pieces."[31]

Similarly, relative terms such as "thin," "strong" or "high" ought not to appear in a claim unless the term has a well-recognized meaning in the particular art (e.g., "high-frequency" in relation to an amplifier) and this is the meaning intended. Where the term has no such well-recognized meaning and an examiner objects, the patent drafter should try to substitute more precise wording found elsewhere in the original disclosure as of the filing or priority date. (Adding a definition that has no basis in the original disclosure might impermissibly extend the subject matter.) Where there is no basis in the original disclosure for a clear definition and the term is not essential to the invention, the patent drafter may even consider deleting it entirely; after all, if the term is essential, it should not be unclear.

Equally, the applicant cannot use an unclear term to distinguish their invention from the prior art.

3.4 Uncertainty

Particular attention is required whenever the adverbs "about" or "approximately" are used. Such a word may be applied, for example, to a particular value (e.g., "about 200C°") or to a range (e.g., "about x to about y"). Patent examiners will often permit such words only if their presence does not prevent the invention from being unambiguously distinguished from the prior art in terms of novelty and inventive step. Even when a patent examiner accepts such a term, the patent drafter should still be wary that a court may later find it to be uncertain.

Terms related to "optional features" – that is, expressions such as "preferably," "for example," "such as" or "more particularly" – should be looked at carefully to ensure that they do not introduce ambiguity. In some jurisdictions such as that of the European Patent Office (EPO), expressions of this kind may have no limiting effect on the scope of a claim: the feature following any such expression will be interpreted as entirely optional. But this is not necessarily true in all jurisdictions. Some may be stricter than the EPO, holding that the use of such terms renders the claim impermissibly indefinite. More importantly, a defendant in a patent litigation is likely to argue that such expressions *do* have a limiting effect because otherwise they would (indeed, should) not have been recited in the claim. While the patent owner may ultimately win this battle, it is the patent drafter's responsibility to prepare claims that minimize the possibility of such litigation (and the costs that accompany it).

3.5 "In"

In many jurisdictions, it is worth taking particular care when drafting claims that employ the word "in" (and other prepositions) to define a relationship between different physical entities (i.e., a product, an apparatus), or between entities and activities (i.e., a process, a use), or between different activities. Examples might include:

(i) "A cylinder head *in* a four-stroke engine"
(ii) "*In* a telephone apparatus with an automatic dialer, dial-tone detector and feature controller, the dial-tone detector comprising …"
(iii) "*In* a process using an electrode feeding means of an arc-welding apparatus, a method for controlling the arc-welding current and voltage comprising the following steps: …"
(iv) "*In* a process/system/apparatus, etc. … the improvement consisting of …"

In examples (i)–(iii), the emphasis is on the fully functioning subunits (the cylinder head, the dial-tone detector, the method for controlling the arc-welding current and voltage) rather than the complete unit within which the subunit is contained (the four-stroke engine, the telephone, the process).

Many jurisdictions will find it unclear whether the claim protection sought is limited to the subunit as such or whether the unit as a whole is to be protected. For the sake of clarity, claims of this kind should therefore typically be directed either to "a

Professional tip

It might also be argued that the "in" claims unnecessarily limit the client's scope of protection: was the patent drafter positive that the claimed "cylinder head" would work only in a four-stroke engine? Make sure that you seriously consider whether a prepositional ("in") word or phrase is even necessary for protecting your client's invention before using it.

unit *with* (or comprising) a subunit" (e.g., "four-stroke engine *with* a cylinder head"), or to the subunit as such, specifying its purpose (e.g., "cylinder head *for* a four-stroke engine").

With claims of the type indicated by example (iv), the use of the word "in" sometimes makes it unclear whether protection is sought for the improvement only or for all of the features defined in the claim. Here, too, it is essential to ensure that the wording is clear – although claims such as "use of a substance … as an anticorrosive ingredient in a paint or lacquer composition" may be acceptable on the basis of second non-medical use in jurisdictions such as the EPO (see Module V, section 2.4).

3.6 Inconsistency

Any inconsistency between the description and the claims may throw doubt on the extent of protection, rendering the claim unclear or unsupported and consequently objectionable.

Let us look at some examples of inconsistencies.

Simple verbal inconsistency   A statement in the description suggests that the invention is limited to a particular feature, but the claims are not thus limited nor does the description place any particular emphasis on this feature and there is no reason to believe the feature to be essential for performance of the invention.

In such a case, the inconsistency can be removed either by broadening the description or by limiting the claims. Similarly, if the claims are more limited than the description, they may be broadened or the description may be limited. (Remember, however, that a description cannot be broadened after the application's filing in many jurisdictions – even when "broadening" means not adding to but *deleting* material from the description.)

Inconsistency regarding apparently essential features   It appears to the examiner, either from general technical knowledge or from what is stated or implied in the description, that a certain described technical feature not mentioned in an independent claim is essential to the performance of the invention – that is, it is necessary for the solution of the problem to which the invention relates. Alternatively, the independent claim may include features that do not seem essential for the performance of the invention.

The examiner will not suggest that a claim be broadened by the omission of apparently inessential features. It is the essence of the patent drafter's duty to obtain broad claim protection; the government examiner has only a duty to say when a claim is "too broad" and no

such duty to draw it to an applicant's attention when a claim is unduly narrow.

Part of the subject matter of the description and/or drawings is not covered by the claims   The claims all specify an electric circuit employing semi-conductor devices, but one of the embodiments in the description and drawings employs electronic tubes instead.

In such a case, the inconsistency can normally be removed either by broadening the claims (assuming that the description and drawings as a whole provide adequate support for such broadening) or by removing the "excess" subject matter from the description and drawings.

As a separate matter, if examples in the description and/or drawings that are not covered by the claims are presented not as embodiments of the invention but as background art or examples that are useful for understanding the invention, these examples may be permissible. In some jurisdictions, such as the United States, the inclusion of subject matter in the description that is not found in the claims will not ordinarily give rise to an objection – but the unclaimed subject matter may be regarded as being dedicated to the public (i.e., in the public domain).

These examples reiterate the requirement that the description must support the claims (see also section 10 of this module).

3.7 Putting this into practice

Actual practice in enforcing the clarity requirement may vary from jurisdiction to jurisdiction.

In the United States, claims are most frequently objected to as indefinite (not clear) when there is a lack of antecedent basis, assessed literally on the basis that a certain claimed term that is recited for the second or further time in the claims follows "a" or "an" rather than "the."

Under the European Patent Convention (EPC), claims are required to recite the technical features of the invention. For an independent claim, this means that *all* of the essential features necessary to define the invention must be recited. The EPO examiner may object to an independent claim on the basis of the clarity requirement by requiring that a claim include a feature disclosed elsewhere, but unclaimed, once that feature is determined to be "essential" to the invention.

In addition, in Europe under the EPC, the description is required to disclose the technical problem to be solved, the solution to the problem and the advantageous effect of the invention over the prior art. The absence of any of these will see the application objected to for lack of clarity, as will excessive numbers of claims or a lack of reference signs in the claims, which will tend to impede an examiner's progress.

In Japan, the product-by-process claim is found to be unclear in principle, unless defining the claimed product by means of structural or characteristic elements would have been impossible or impracticable to define as of the filing date.

Finally it is worth noting that when a claim is directed to a further therapeutic application of a medicament and the condition to be treated is defined in functional terms (e.g., "any condition susceptible of being improved or prevented by selective occupation of a specific receptor"), the claim can be regarded as satisfying the clarity requirement in many jurisdictions (such as the EPO) only if instructions, in the form of experimental tests or testable criteria that are available from the patent documents or from the common general knowledge, would allow the skilled person to recognize which conditions fall within the functional definition and accordingly within the scope of the claim.

Example

Patent applications should be drafted with clarity and brevity. Patent drafting is one of many areas in which the familiar aphorism "keep it short and simple" (KISS) applies, meaning:

- using plain language wherever plain language will do the job;
- writing short sentences without altering the usual order of words; and
- avoiding long-winded redundant expressions.

Compare the following:

[As originally drafted]

Claim 1. An optoelectronic modulable light-emitting device, comprising: a dielectric (1) with embedded nanocrystals (2), characterized in that the optoelectronic modulable light-emitting device further comprises: first charge injection means (3) to inject charges into the dielectric (1) in such a way that these first charge injection means (3) are able to inject charges comprising …; second charge injection means (4), different from the first charge injection means (3), wherein these second charge injection means (4) are able to … , and wherein these second charge injection means (4) are able to …

[As revised]

Claim 1. An optoelectronic modulable light-emitting device, comprising: a dielectric (1) with embedded nanocrystals (2); first charge injection means (3) that are able to inject charges into the dielectric (1), the charges comprising … ; second charge injection means (4) that are to … , and are able to …

Is the expression "characterized in that the optoelectronic modulable light-emitting device further comprises" in the original draft really necessary? Or is it unnecessarily verbose?

Moreover, if the terms "first" and "second" are being used as labels to differentiate between two different elements sharing the same phrase ("charge injection means") and are referenced in the drawings by two different numerals (3 and 4), what is the purpose of the phrase "second charge injection means (4), different from the first charge injection means (3)" in the original draft? Is it not clear enough that the use of the words "first" and "second," coupled with the reference numerals (3) and (4), shows that these charge injection means are different?

4. Claim variations and modifications of the invention

While drafting claims, it is important to think constantly about variations of the invention. In legal terms, these variations are known as *embodiments*. A patent drafter should imagine themselves a would-be infringer: how might they work around the claims? What variations might a competitor introduce that would allow them to escape infringement? The variations or alternative embodiments that emerge are those that should be included in the description and draft claims. It is important too not to overlook alternative embodiments that can perform the same function: claims relating to these are critical in providing a broad scope of protection.

Example

An inventor has developed a device that covers a pencil with an eraser attached to the pencil. Claims directed to the main (or preferred) embodiment might be drafted as:

1. A device, comprising:
   - a pencil; and
   - an eraser attached to the pencil.
2. The device according to Claim 1, wherein said eraser is detachably attached to the pencil.
3. The device according to Claim 2, wherein the pencil is red in color.

WIPO Patent Drafting Manual

For the same invention, claims directed to an alternative embodiment might read:

1. A device, comprising:
   – a crayon; and
   – an eraser attached to the crayon.
2. The device according to Claim 1, wherein said eraser is attached detachably to the crayon.
3. The device according to Claim 2, wherein the crayon is red in color.

Comparison of the "crayon" claim set with the "pencil" claim set suggests that the patent drafter might go on to draft an even broader claim set directed to "a writing implement," and then draft dependent claims directed toward a crayon and a pencil.

Professional tip

In conceiving of these alternative embodiments, remember always to be mindful of the client's budget and not to exceed the inventor's own scope.

5. Avoiding unnecessary limitations

A basic rule when drafting claims is to continually review the claims and delete unnecessary elements (i.e., limitations). We noted elsewhere one technique – that is, to draft a claim as a single extended sentence and include all reasonable elements to an embodiment of the invention, then review the sentence and eliminate all elements that are inessential to the invention to arrive at its essence. In this way, the patent drafter can construct a claim that captures the invention in its broadest form and avoids any unnecessary limitations. This single claim can be supplemented with sets of claims that have a different scope and which reintroduce some of those other elements. The resulting set of claims for the invention will be broad and the scope of the patent protection, if granted, equally so.

Another rule is that claims must not rely on references to the description or drawings to explain the invention's technical features, except where absolutely necessary. So-called *omnibus claims* that refer to the description or the drawings without providing any specific limitations (e.g., "An apparatus for harvesting corn as described in the description" or "A juice machine as shown in Figure 4") are not accepted in most jurisdictions.

In any case, the onus is upon the applicant to show that it is "absolutely necessary" to rely on reference to the description or drawings. An allowable exception might be where the claim is for an invention of a peculiar shape that is well illustrated in the drawings but cannot be readily reduced to words or represented by a simple mathematical formula. Another special case may be claims for an invention relating to chemical products, some of the features of which can be defined only by means of graphs or diagrams.

6. Negative limitations and disclaimers

A claim's subject matter is normally defined in terms of positive features indicating that certain technical elements are present. On rare occasion, the patent drafter may restrict the subject matter using a negative element expressly stating that a particular feature is absent (e.g., "*non*wooden"). Such negative elements may be recited, for example, to remove nonpatentable embodiments disclosed in the application as filed or if the absence of a feature can be deduced from the application as filed.

Furthermore, in some jurisdictions such as the EPO, a prior-art disclosure may be excluded by using a "disclaimer" to re-establish the novelty of an inventive step that accidentally overlaps with the disclosure. A disclaimer with no basis in the application as filed can only re-establish novelty; it cannot make an obvious step inventive. It is also crucial that the wording of the disclaimer does not extend beyond the content of the application as filed (see also Module IX, section 3).

More generally, negative elements or disclaimers may be used only when adding positive features to the claim:

(i) would not define more clearly and concisely the subject matter that is still protectable; or

(ii) would unduly limit the scope of the claim.

For example, a chemical process that could utilize every known metal except "copper" (and the inventor themselves does not really know why copper cannot be used) could be expressed in the form "a metal, excluding copper …" – although, even then, the patent drafter may eventually land upon a suitable word that expresses the element more positively.

Some also argue that a patent drafter should avoid negative elements and disclaimers because the spirit of claims as providing protection for inventions is best captured in elegant and artful language.

7. Claims and competing products

A patent drafter should ask their client about competing products. This background knowledge can be put to good use in drafting claims that cover competing products in the market – provided that the competing products are not prior art.

Because prosecution of the patent application may take several years, the patent drafter should keep abreast of competing products in the field of invention emerging during that time. If the patent drafter learns of a new competing product while the patent application is pending, they may wish to amend the pending claims so that they read better on both the client's invention *and* the competing product (assuming that the competing product is definitely not prior art). In this way, the scope of the issued patent claims may cover the competitor's product and the competitor will have no option but take a license from the client.

Amendments of claims and a patent application during the patent prosecution are explained in Module IX, section 3.

8. Claims must overcome prior art

The patent drafter must prepare claims that overcome any prior art related to the invention that they already know about;

otherwise, the patent will be invalid. The ideal strategy is to draft a claim that is narrower than the presently known prior art but broader than competing products.

Bear in mind too that some jurisdictions, such as the United States, require the patent drafter, the inventor and any other parties associated with the patent application to disclose to the patent office all pertinent prior art of which they are aware. Failure to comply with this requirement can, in some circumstances, render the resulting patent invalid and end the patent drafter's license to practice.

9. Using multiple claim types for the same invention

If the same invention can be claimed as both a method and as an apparatus, the patent drafter should not hesitate to do so. It is not the case that an invention can be captured in only one form; in fact, to get the broadest possible protection for the invention, it is advisable to claim the invention in different forms.

Let us look at some sample claims.

Example

An invention pertains to software for searching the Internet.

A system claim for the invention might read:

1. A system for searching the Internet, said system comprising:
   – a software module configured to perform a search;
   – a database configured to store results produced by the search; and
   – a user interface configured to present the search results to a user.

Note that, in Claim 1, we have enumerated the different components of the invention and the way in which they interact with one another. We identified the three elements and recited the function performed by each. We stated that the software module performs the search, the database stores the search and the interface makes the search available to a user.

A method claim for the same invention may read:

2. A method for performing an Internet search, the method comprising:
   – transmitting a search request over the Internet from a software module;
   – receiving search results over the Internet from the search request by the software module;

WIPO Patent Drafting Manual

- storing the search results in a database; and
- presenting the search results to a user through a user interface.

Notice that, in Claim 2, we have introduced the different steps involved in performing this search and, at the same time, we have introduced the components that perform each of the functions stated. For example, the first step is stated as being performing the Internet search by means of the software module.

10. Ensuring that the description supports the claims

As has been noted elsewhere, the description and drawings must support the claims. This means that there must be a basis in the description for the subject matter of every claim. The support requirement does not mean that the patent drafter must draft the description and the claims in identical terms, but the scope of the claims will typically not be interpreted more broadly than the descript on and drawings and, in some jurisdictions, the contribution to the art warrant.

Most claims are generalizations from one or more particular examples. When drafting a patent application, the patent drafter will try to generalize in the claims particular embodiments disclosed in the description and drawings; the patent examiner will judge the extent of generalization in each particular case in light of the relevant prior art. The admissible degree of generalization claimed may vary, depending on the field of technologies and related prior art. Claims for an invention that opens up a whole new field may typically be more extensively generalized than those of one that is an improvement in a well-known field. A fair statement of a claim is one that is neither so broad that it goes beyond the invention nor yet so narrow as to deprive the applicant of a just reward for the disclosure of their invention. The applicant is typically allowed to cover all obvious modifications of, equivalents to and uses of what is described. In particular, if it is reasonable that all of the variants covered by the claims will indeed have the properties or uses the applicant ascribes to them in the description, then the claims may be drafted accordingly.

More insight into the examiner's prosecution of patent applications can be found in Module IX, section 1.

Let us look at some examples of instances in which claims might be found to be supported or unsupported.

Example 1

A claim relates to a process for treating all kinds of "plant seedling" by subjecting them to a controlled cold shock to produce specified results; the description discloses the process applied to one kind of plant only.

Since plant properties vary widely, the patent examiner has reason to believe that the process is *not* applicable to all plant seedlings. Unless the applicant can provide convincing evidence otherwise, they must restrict their claim to the particular kind of plant referred to in the description. A mere assertion that the process is applicable to all plant seedlings will not be sufficient.

Professional tip

You should bear in mind that the only reasonable restrictions on the breadth of claims relate to the prior art (novelty and inventive step) and whether or not the disclosure is supported, not to any individual patent examiner's subjective judgement of the significance of your client's invention.

Professional tip

We have reiterated throughout this manual that you must always provide adequate support in the description for your client's claims. Remember that you cannot add wholly new material in response to an examiner's objections and try to anticipate any narrower elements that you may later need to add to the claims: try to ensure that you embed support for these in the description at the outset.

86

Example 2

A claim relates to a specified method of treating "synthetic resin moldings" to obtain certain changes in physical characteristics. All of the examples described relate to thermoplastic resins and the method is such as to appear inappropriate to thermosetting resins.

Unless the applicant can provide evidence that the method is applicable to thermosetting resins, they must restrict their claim to thermoplastic resins.

Example 3

A claim relates to improved fuel oil compositions that have a given desired property. The description provides support for one way of obtaining such fuel oils, which is when defined amounts of a certain additive are present. No other ways of obtaining fuel oils with the desired property are disclosed.

The claim makes no mention of the additive. The claim is not supported over the whole of its breadth and the patent examiner objects.

A patent drafter should not attempt to claim something they do not know for certain falls within the scope of the invention. They must seek valid patents for their clients. Not only does the support requirement fairly protect the public from patent claims that are much broader than the applicant can justify, but also it protects the applicant from the consequences of attempting to patent something that is not supported by its description.

To what extent the invention should be disclosed in the patent application is relative and depends on the scope of the protection desired. For broader patent protection, a more extensive disclosure of the invention is required in principle, and the supportive disclosure requirement functions to prevent the claims from being *too* broad compared with what is disclosed in the description and drawings. Conversely, for narrow patent protection, less extensive disclosure of the invention – in some cases, a single embodiment – may suffice. In either case, an unnecessarily extensive disclosure of the invention in the claims is not prohibited as such. It will, however, increase the burden on – and the costs to – the applicant and share more of the invention with the public than is protected under law.

11. Unity of invention

Unity of invention refers to a requirement that a patent application must typically relate to one invention only or to a group of inventions so linked as to form a single general inventive concept. The second of these alternatives – that is, the group linked to a single concept – may give rise to multiple independent claims in the same category; the more usual case is multiple independent claims in different categories. In the United States, the phrase *restriction requirement* is used to express a similar concept.

The requirement is in place essentially to ensure that fee structures are fair and equitable: it prevents a patent applicant from filing a patent application containing a plethora of separate inventions and paying only a single filing fee. Thus the finding of a lack of unity of invention is not typically a fatal flaw for a patent application. If a patent examiner determines that the claims in a patent application lack unity of invention, the patent drafter will typically be required to elect certain claims and cancel or remove the others. The patent drafter will, however, typically be allowed to file another patent application for the unelected claims from the first, known as a *divisional application*. In practice, this means that failing to meet the requirement has time and cost consequences for the client, resulting in additional fees and a delay in obtaining patent protection.

What follows is intended to help the patent drafter to understand where a patent examiner may find a lack of unity of invention. The examples primarily pertain to chemical inventions, but the concepts may be extended to applications in all technical domains.

In some jurisdictions, such as the EPO, unity of invention is considered to be present between intermediate and final products that:

(i) have the same essential structural element – that is, their basic chemical structures are the same or their chemical structures are technically closely interrelated, the intermediate incorporating an essential structural element into the final product; and

(ii) are technically interrelated – that is, the final product is manufactured directly from the intermediate or is separated from it by a small number of intermediates all containing the same essential structural element.

Unity of invention may also be present between intermediate and final products the structures of which are not known, such as an intermediate with a known structure and a final product with an unknown structure or an intermediate of unknown structure and a final product of unknown structure. In such cases, there should be sufficient evidence to lead a person reasonably skilled in the art to conclude that the intermediate and final products are technically closely interrelated, such as when the intermediate contains the same essential element as the final product or incorporates an essential element into the final product.

WIPO Patent Drafting Manual

An application may claim for different intermediate products used in different processes for the preparation of the final product, provided that the intermediate products share the same essential structural element. A new intermediate should not separate the process that leads from the intermediate to the final products. Where different intermediates are claimed for different structural parts of the final product, there will be no unity between the intermediates. If the intermediate and final products are each families of compounds, each intermediate compound should correspond to one of those claimed in the family of the final products; conversely, some of the final products may have *no* corresponding compound in the family of the intermediate products, so that the two families need not be absolutely congruent. The mere fact that the intermediates might have effects or potential applications other than as contributing to the final products should not prejudice unity of invention.

Where a single claim defines (chemical or nonchemical) alternatives – that is, a Markush group (see Module IV, section 2.3) – unity of invention should be considered to be present if the alternatives are of a similar nature and can fairly be substituted for one another. Under the Patent Cooperation Treaty (PCT), when the Markush group is for alternatives of chemical compounds, they are "of a similar nature" where:

(A) all alternatives have a common property or activity, and
(B)(1) a common structure is present, that is, a significant structural element is shared by all of the alternatives, or
(B)(2) in cases where the common structure cannot be the unifying criteria, all alternatives belong to a recognized class of chemical compounds in the art to which the invention pertains.[32]

Professional tip

Remember that the absence of unity of invention is not a fatal flaw. You will typically be able to file a divisional application for the claims that have been restricted out of the application (see Module IX, section 4.6).

The characterization that "a significant structural element is shared by all the alternatives" in B(1) refers to cases in which the compounds share in large part a common chemical structure or, where the compounds have in common only a small portion of their structures, the commonly shared part of the structure is structurally distinctive in light of the prior art and the common structure is essential to the common property or activity. The structural element may be a single component or a combination of linked individual components. The alternative in B(2), "a recognized class of chemical compounds," means that the person skilled in the art would expect members of the class to behave in the same way in the context of the claimed invention – that is, that any member could be substituted for another yet still achieve the same intended result. If it can be shown that at least one Markush alternative is not novel, the patent drafter should look again at whether the claims represent unity of invention.

In some jurisdictions such as the EPO, a lack of unity may be evident *a priori* (i.e., before the examiner considers the claims in relation to the prior art) or may become apparent only *a posteriori*, for example should a document within the state of the art show a lack of novelty or inventive step in an independent claim, thus leaving two or more dependent claims without a common inventive concept.

12. Claim point of view

All of the limitations or elements set out in a single patent claim should have a consistent "point of view." For example, all of the steps recited in a method claim must be performed by the same party. The consistent point of view is important since it sets parties that could directly infringe a patent claim. While this may seem like common sense, it can sometimes be difficult in practice to sustain where an invention is such that inventive components are spread across a range of physical components or activities. The single, consistent point of view is also important when the commercial activity associated with the invention is divided among multiple parties.

Proving direct patent infringement before a court is generally easier than proving indirect infringement (i.e., contributory infringement or by active inducement to infringe), because evidence for the former is typically more readily available than that of the latter. Consequently, for a claim to have deterrent effect, it should be set out such that any attempt to imitate the protected subject matter will be considered an act of direct infringement. In cases in which this is impossible (e.g., because only those who generally should not be sued, such as the general public or business customers, would be likely to directly infringe the patent), claims should anticipate the need to detect and evidence indirect infringement.

As we will discuss later, detecting and proving both direct and indirect infringement is generally easier for product claims than it is for process or method claims.

Let us look at an example of a product claim.

Example

An invention relates to a new compartment for holding the batteries used to power a flashlight. The inventor has discovered that if a small periwinkle-shaped piece of copper having a male receptacle is snapped onto a conventional D-cell battery, when the combined unit is inserted into a flashlight also having a small periwinkle-shaped piece of copper but with a female receptacle, the D-cell battery's operational life lasts three times longer than normal.

A patent drafter could write the following claim:

1. An apparatus for extending flashlight battery life, comprising:
   - a periwinkle-shaped copper piece having a male receptacle and adapted for being operably coupled to a battery;
   - a battery-operated flashlight having electrical wiring; and
   - a periwinkle-shaped copper piece having a female receptacle, the periwinkle-shaped copper piece fastened to the electrical wiring of the battery-operated flashlight,
   - wherein the periwinkle-shaped copper piece having a male receptacle is adapted for operable coupling to the periwinkle-shaped piece having the female receptacle.

While this claim may adequately define the essential inventive concept of the invention, it has no consistent point of view. Some portions of the claim pertain to components related to the battery and others, to components related to the flashlight. (If the battery were to last for the flashlight's lifetime, there would be fewer problems with the claim's point of view.)

But what if the person or entity who markets the battery is not the same person or entity who provides the flashlight? What if one company sells only batteries and another company sells only flashlights? As drafted, this claim would mean that neither the person selling the battery nor the person selling the flashlight would directly infringe it.

Direct infringement by one entity is often a precondition to any type of infringement, such as contributory infringement or inducement, by another entity. Many legal systems require that, to assert patent infringement, a patentee shall prove that at least one entity has committed the direct infringement. While, in some jurisdictions, skilled litigators can often argue direct infringement even of claims like that set out in the example, a patent drafter should still aim to draft claims such that their client will not need to spend considerable amounts of money and time on such argument.

Moreover, the patent drafter must also think about preparing claims such that they support licensing rights. In the commercial world, one company might sell flashlights and another, batteries: neither of these parties is likely to feel pressure to apply for a license in the context of the claim as drafted in the example. Each may genuinely believe that it has sufficient legal grounds to avoid infringing the claim because it practices only a portion of it (see the "all element rule" in Module IV, section 1.3).

Example

Suppose that the patent drafter has drafted three more sets of claims:

- one directed only toward the flashlight portion of the system;
- one directed only toward the battery part of the system; and
- another directed toward the combination of the periwinkle-shaped copper pieces.

While they would still be prudent to keep the original claim, these three additional claims might read:

[*Flashlight claim*]
2. An apparatus for extending flashlight battery life, comprising:
   - a battery-operated flashlight having electrical wiring; and

WIPO Patent Drafting Manual

  – a periwinkle-shaped copper piece having a female receptacle, the periwinkle-shaped copper piece fastened to the electrical wiring of the battery-operated flashlight,
  – wherein the periwinkle-shaped copper piece having a female receptacle is adapted for operable coupling to a periwinkle-shaped piece having a male receptacle fastened to a battery.

[*Battery claim*]
3. An apparatus for extending flashlight battery life, comprising:

  – a battery; and
  – a periwinkle-shaped copper piece having a male receptacle, the periwinkle-shaped copper piece operably coupled to the battery,
  – wherein the periwinkle-shaped copper piece having a male receptacle is adapted for operable coupling to a periwinkle-shaped piece having a female receptacle that is connected to electrical wiring in a flashlight.

[*The connector pieces*]
4. An apparatus for extending flashlight battery life, comprising:

  – a periwinkle-shaped copper piece having a male receptacle and adapted for being electrically coupled to a battery; and
  – a periwinkle-shaped copper piece having a female receptacle, the periwinkle-shaped copper piece being adapted for operable coupling to electrical wiring of a battery-operated flashlight,
  – wherein the periwinkle-shaped copper piece having a male receptacle is adapted for operable coupling to the periwinkle-shaped piece having the female receptacle.

Notice that while Claims 2–3 mention both the battery and the flashlight, the "point of view" in each claim has been shifted exclusively to either the battery or the flashlight or the combination of the two connector pieces. Thus Claim 2 should be easier to license or assert against an infringing provider of flashlights than Claim 1, while Claim 3 should be easier to license or assert against an infringing provider of batteries than Claim 1. Claim 4 focuses on the two periwinkle pieces themselves and could be used against a company that makes the periwinkle parts for later assembly by either battery or flashlight manufacturers.

Professional tip

Drafting patent claims is an iterative process of review and editing. Rarely will you draft an excellent patent claim on your first try – even after years of experience. But what you will learn is that this process ultimately results in patent claims that capture the full scope of your client's invention and deliver solid protection.

Let us now turn to an example of point of view in a process or method claim.

Example

An invention relates to a client-and-server computing system. The invention is a novel way of ordering candy over the Internet in which the customer can use a camera and a robotic arm to fill a candy bag, which is then mailed to them. A client computer (e.g., a home personal computer) makes a request to a server computer (e.g., a computing system of an Internet service provider) and the server computer finds the information, processes it and sends the results to the client.

A patent drafter could write the following claim:

1. A method for dispensing candy, comprising:
  – sending a request from a client computer to a server computer for candy located in a candy store;

Module VI. Patent claim design

- sending candy store video data from the server computer to the client computer;
- displaying the candy store video data on the client computer, wherein the displayed candy store video data provide a visual representation of the candy store to enable a user of the client computer to provide directions for a robotic arm located in the candy store;
- sending robotic arm direction instructions from the client computer to the server computer;
- converting the robotic arm direction instructions into native machine robotic arm direction instructions for the robotic arm at the candy store, wherein the native machine robotic arm direction instructions actuate the robotic arm to fill a candy bag with candy;
- sending a shipping instruction from the client computer to the server computer; and
- converting the shipping instruction into a native machine robotic arm shipping instruction for the robotic arm, wherein the native machine robotic arm shipping instruction actuates the robotic arm to place the candy bag in an open box and seal it for shipping.

Notice that the claim does not have a consistent point of view. Some steps are performed by the client computer and others, by the server computer. This means that neither the person controlling the client computer nor the person controlling the server computer directly infringe the claim.

Likewise, in the commercial world, one company may provide the candy store and the robotic arm, another company may provide the server computer and a third may provide the client computer software. While the candy store and the server computer company will have a commercial arrangement with each other, the client computer software company may have no contract with either party and the server computer will be available to anyone who provides a credit card number for payment for services. In this situation, since not one of these parties completely practices the entire claim and hence not one of them directly infringes the claim, not one of these parties is likely to feel the need to obtain a license from the patentee.

The patent drafter can therefore draft two more sets of claims: one directed only toward the client portion of the system and another directed only toward the server part of the system. (Again, the patent drafter will be prudent also to keep the original claim.)

The two new claims read:

[*Client computer claim*]
2. A method for dispensing candy, comprising:
- receiving at a client computer candy store video data;

- displaying the candy store video data on the client computer, wherein the displayed candy store video data provide a visual representation of a candy store to enable a user of the client computer to provide directions for a robotic arm located in the candy store;
- sending robotic arm direction instructions from the client computer, wherein the robotic arm direction instructions cause the robotic arm at the candy store to fill a candy bag with candy; and
- sending a shipping instruction from the client computer, wherein the shipping instruction causes the robotic arm to place the candy bag in an open box and seal it for shipping.

[*Server computer claim*]
3. A method for dispensing candy, comprising:
- sending candy store video data from a server computer to a client computer, wherein the candy store video data provide a visual representation of a candy store to enable a user of the client computer to provide directions for a robotic arm located in the candy store;
- receiving robotic arm direction instructions at the server computer from the client computer;
- converting the robotic arm direction instructions into native machine robotic arm direction instructions for the robotic arm at the candy store, wherein the native machine robotic arm direction instructions actuate the robotic arm to fill a candy bag with candy;
- receiving a shipping instruction at the server computer from the client computer; and
- converting the shipping instruction into a native machine robotic arm shipping instruction for the robotic arm, wherein the native machine robotic arm shipping instruction actuates the robotic arm to place the candy bag in an open box and seal it for shipping.

Notice that while Claims 2 and 3 mention both the server and the client computer, the action in each has been shifted exclusively to either the client or the server. Thus Claim 2 should be easier to license or assert against an infringer providing client software than Claim 1, while Claim 3 should be easier to license or assert against an infringer operating server software than Claim 1.

13. Narrowing a patent claim during prosecution

There are several reasons why a patent drafter might need to narrow a patent claim during its prosecution, including that it is necessary to do so to render the claims patentable.

91

A claim may be narrowed by:

(i) adding new elements;
(ii) adding a limitation to a previously recited element; and/or
(iii) further defining how the previously recited elements interoperate.

Let us look again at our pencil example.

Example

A claim may be narrowed by adding an extra element, such as a cap for the pencil. The claim might read:

1. An apparatus, comprising:
   – a pencil having an elongated structure including two ends and a center between the ends;
   – an eraser attached to one end of the pencil;
   – a light attached to the center of the pencil; and
   – a removable cap attached to one end of the pencil.

The additional element of the cap narrows the claim. Thus the claim no longer reads on a pencil with only a light attached and an eraser; all three elements must be present in an infringing device for the claim to read on it.

Most patent offices require the patent drafter to clearly show any changes being made to amend a claim during the examiner's prosecution of it. Thus, depending on local patent rules, the amendment to a claim such as that above might be submitted to the patent office as:

1. [Amended] An apparatus, comprising:
   – a pencil having an elongated structure including two ends and a center between the ends;
   – an eraser attached to one end of the pencil;
   – a light attached to the center of the pencil; and
   – a removable cap attached to one end of the pencil.

Here, the words in square brackets explain the editorial intervention (i.e., the claim has been "amended"), strike-through indicates deleted words and underlining indicates newly added words.

When narrowing a claim by adding a new element, the new element should further define either an existing structural/functional element or be a relational element (i.e., define the relationship between existing elements). The new element must, however, be new only to the claim; it must already be found in the description – because it is impermissible to create new relationships between parts that were not disclosed in the description as of the filing date. Moreover, the patent drafter should not add elements that will significantly reduce the breadth of a claim without first considering alternative possible amendments and without counseling the client about the likely impact of such amendments.

A patent drafter can often overcome the prior art not by adding a completely new limitation to a claim but by further defining the elements already recited – or by further interrelating those elements, such as by amending a claim to add that "A receives the output of B."

Example

The pencil claim could alternatively be narrowed further by defining the light element:

1. An apparatus, comprising:
   – a pencil having an elongated structure including two ends and a center between the ends;
   – an eraser attached to one end of the pencil; and
   – a light attached to the center of the pencil, wherein the light is directed to shine away from the end of the pencil having the eraser.

More details regarding amendment of claims and applications in general during the patent prosecution are outlined in Module IX, section 3.

14. Exclusions from patentability

Most jurisdictions exclude certain subject matter from patent protection. Some jurisdictions have substantially longer lists of exclusions than others. In the United States, for example, several judicial exceptions to subject-matter eligibility have emerged in case law. For more on patentable subject matter, see Module II, section 2.4.

From time to time, the patent drafter will find that their claims have been rejected on the grounds of some exclusion from patentability. In some cases, they may still obtain patent protection for the subject invention by redrafting the patent claims – another example of where the patent drafter must be diligent and creative in achieving their client's goals.

In the case of software-related inventions, some rejections are matters of "form over substance." Sometimes, the patent drafter will need only to (re)word their claims in a particular way to avoid an exclusion on patentability grounds – even though the description remains substantively the same.

The patent drafter will often find that they must exercise particular care with respect to biotechnology inventions. Issues may arise here because some biotechnology "inventions" are unprotectable as scientific discoveries or inventions the exploitation of which is contrary to order public or morality (e.g., the use of embryos for commercial purposes in some jurisdictions). National and regional laws concerning exclusions from patentable subject matter vary significantly and a patent drafter involved in the biotechnology field will need to stay up to date with legal developments and emerging technologies in the jurisdictions with which they (and their clients) are involved.

As noted earlier in Module II, section 2.4, many jurisdictions exclude methods of treating a human or animal body from patent eligibility. For many of these inventions, however, reformatting the claims may yet allow an applicant to seek protection. For example, methods of testing are generally regarded as industrially applicable inventions, at least by the EPO, and are therefore patentable if the test is applicable to the improvement or control of a product, apparatus or process that is itself industrially applicable. In particular, the use of certain animals for purposes such as for testing industrial products (e.g., to ascertain any pyrogenic or allergic effects) or phenomena (e.g., to determine water or air pollution) may be patentable.

Remember too that, despite the general exclusion of treatment or diagnostic methods, new products for use in these methods of treatment or diagnosis – particularly substances or compositions – may be patentable. Similarly, the manufacture of prostheses or artificial limbs may be patentable even under the general exclusion, for instance a method of manufacturing insoles to correct posture or a method of manufacturing an artificial limb. Taking the imprint of the footplate or a molding of the residuum for the socket of an artificial limb is clearly not of a surgical nature and does not require the presence of a medically qualified person. Furthermore, both the insoles and the artificial limb are manufactured outside the body. By contrast, a method of manufacturing an endoprosthesis that requires a surgical step when taking measurements may not be patentable.

15. Requirement for industrial applicability

From time to time, a patent drafter may need to revise their client's claims to satisfy the requirement for industrial applicability (see Module II, section 2.3). For example, a device for dispensing fashion advice may be found to lack industrial applicability according in a given jurisdiction. In such a situation, the patent drafter may be able to satisfy the requirement by recasting the claims, perhaps as a device for maintaining inventory levels in a clothing warehouse.

In general, the EPO requires that the description of a patent application shall, where this is not self-evident, indicate the way in which the invention is capable of exploitation in

industry. In relation to sequences and partial sequences of genes, this general requirement is given specific form in that the industrial application of a sequence or a partial sequence of a gene must be disclosed in the patent application; a mere nucleic acid sequence without indication of a function is not a patentable invention. In cases in which a sequence or partial sequence of a gene is used to produce a protein or a part of a protein, it is necessary to specify which protein or part of a protein is produced and what function it performs. Alternatively, when a nucleotide sequence is not used to produce a protein or part of a protein, the function to be indicated could be, for example, that the sequence exhibits a certain transcription promoter activity.

16. "Reading on" a patent claim

A claim may *read on* prior art or on an allegedly patent-infringing embodiment (i.e., a product or process alleged to infringe an existing patent). Claims are read on prior art to evaluate their novelty. During patent infringement litigation, claims are read on an accused product or process to evaluate whether or not a patent was infringed.

For a claim to read on an accused product or a process, every element of the claim must be present in the accused product or process (see more on the all-elements rule in Module IV, section 1.3). The patent drafter should therefore make sure that at least one claim (if not all of the claims) in their patent application reads on the embodiments of the invention made, used and sold by their client. Among other things, if the claims do not read on the client's embodiment of the invention, then the patent drafter may have misunderstood the invention (or the client's design or practice may have changed). Additionally, once the patent is issued, the client cannot in good faith use marks to proclaim that the product is protected by patent if it does not satisfy all of the elements of a claim. Worse still, the client may have difficulty collecting lost profit damages against an infringer; even though they may still be able to collect a reasonable royalty, the difference between reasonable royalty and lost profits can be substantial.

17. Claim construction in the courts

The greatest test of a patent drafter's claims will likely come not before the patent examiner but before the courts in the event that the patent is litigated. In patent litigation, the interpretation of the claims is typically the most critical factor in determining whether the patent has been infringed or is even valid over the prior art. The process of interpreting the claims is known as *claims construction*. The scope of protection provided by a given patent is often determined by the meaning of only a few specific terms used in a claim.

WIPO Patent Drafting Manual

Courts will generally interpret patents by reading the claims and the description. If the claims and description do not clearly communicate a specific meaning, courts will refer to the general meaning of the terms to a person skilled in the art. Particularly in the United States, courts increasingly use dictionaries when construing claims and interpret ordinary terms accordingly. The United States, however, begins by giving terms in the claims their ordinary meaning; only then do they review the description and prosecution history to see whether terms have been given some different or special meaning. In such instances, technical dictionaries, encyclopedias and treatises may also be used in court to establish the meanings of terms specific to a particular field of the invention.

A court will generally give a claim term the full range of its ordinary meaning as understood by a person skilled in the art. For instance, if the invention is a chemical invention and the term "amorphous" needs to be construed, the court will likely be persuaded to take into account the ordinary meaning of the term as understood by an average chemist and may turn to a specialized dictionary recognized by practitioners in the chemical field. Likewise, if an invention relates to software and the claim term to be construed by the courts is "cache," then the court may be persuaded to take into account the ordinary meaning of the term to an average software programmer. Indeed, when issues claim validity and infringement are before a court, expert witness testimony may be used as an aid to claim interpretation.

Where a patent application creates a new term, when several different meanings for a term are possible and only one is meant or when the meaning of a term may be ambiguous, it will sensibly be defined in the description section of the patent application. The description can act as a glossary of special claim terminology, and while examiners and courts may subsequently draw on dictionaries, handbooks, treatises, encyclopedias and, sometimes, their own common general knowledge to interpret a claim, it is better to aim for a patent application that is self-contained (i.e., can be understood without external context).

Professional tip

Claims interpretation under the doctrine of equivalents can be unpredictable. If your claims are to deter would-be imitators or successfully litigate against an infringer effectively, you will do well to draft them as though no such regime exists – in other words, literally, giving terms only their ordinary and customary meaning to a person skilled in the relevant art.

It is common to find that words used in claims have multiple dictionary meanings. Some of the meanings have no relevance to the claimed invention. If a particular term has more than one possible meaning and in the absence of any other factors, courts will more likely be persuaded by the customary meaning of a term in a specific art rather than by its ordinary meaning. In construing claims, the court may even examine the intrinsic evidence – that is, the evidence found within the patent, such as the claims, description, drawings, etc., as well as the prosecution file or history of the patent – aiming to ascertain the meaning of the term most consistent with the patent drafter's intention. The patent drafter must always be extremely careful to consider any potential ambiguity in what they write in the patent application and in responses to office actions (see Module IX) – known as written opinions or examination reports in some jurisdictions – received during patent prosecution.

The laws of some jurisdictions provide legal protection beyond the literal scope of the words used in a patent claim. This additional protection is provided via a principle known as the *doctrine of equivalents*. The doctrine of equivalents does not necessarily provide the same scope of protection from one jurisdiction to the next.

Example

A patent claim recites that a "nail" holds Widget A to Widget B. An accused infringer literally infringes the patent claim except that the accused infringer uses a "screw" to hold Widget A to Widget B instead of a nail.

94

Under the doctrine of equivalents, the patentee may be able to argue that a screw was equivalent to a nail for the purposes of the patented invention. If the court were to accept the patentee's arguments, then it would find infringement.

In some countries, the doctrine of equivalents is broad, based on a belief that it can be nearly impossible to find words that adequately describe the full scope of a complicated invention. In these circumstances, the patentee in the example might even be able to argue that "glue" is equivalent to a nail for purposes of the invention.

By contrast, some jurisdictions leave it entirely up to the inventor and patent drafter to set forth in their claims what they consider their invention to be and maintain no doctrine of equivalents. In this case, a judge would hold that the patentee could have simply drafted the patent claims using a term that encompassed both nails and screws, such as a "metal fastener," and find no infringement of the patent in the above example.

The doctrine of equivalents is a complicated legal topic and standards for determining equivalents vary significantly from country to country. It is the patent drafter's responsibility to find out what regime applies in the jurisdictions in which they submit patent applications, including whether the patent drafter's communications during patent prosecution can be used to foreclose application of the doctrine of equivalents. In the jurisdictions where such "prosecution history estoppel" is applied, if, in our example, the drafter had responded to an office action that "only" nails are used in the invention, it would be difficult for the patentee to later argue otherwise – that is, that "glue" or "screws" are equivalent to nails

Key words

- Claim preparation
- Set of claims
- Clarity of claims
- Unnecessary limitations
- Disclaimers
- Overcoming prior art
- Unity of invention
- Claim point of view
- Reading on claims
- Claim construction
- Doctrine of equivalents

Self-Test

☐ Why should the patent drafter prepare the claims before all other parts of the patent application?

☐ Give examples of how a patent drafter might broaden a patent claim.

☐ When drafting claims, the patent drafter should avoid relative words such as "short," "tall," "fast," "slow" and "perfect." True or false?

☐ A patent drafter may define words in the patent differently from their usual definition in dictionaries. True or false?

☐ Why is it important to avoid unnecessary elements when drafting claims?

☐ What is unity of invention?

☐ Explain how a claim can "read on" prior art.

☐ What is claim construction? What is the point of view or reference point used in claim construction?

☐ Why is it important that a claim has a single point of view?

☐ Inventor X states that their invention is a door with a software-implemented door lock using a face recognition system. A patent drafter only needs to draft a product claim reciting a door. True or false?

Module VII
Drafting a description, drawings and an abstract

1.	**Key audiences of patent applications**	**97**
2.	**Order in which to draft a patent application**	**97**
3.	**Drafting parts of a description**	**98**
3.1	Title of invention	98
3.2	Technical field	98
3.3	Background art	98
3.4	Summary of invention	100
3.5	Brief description of drawings	101
3.6	Description of embodiments	101
4.	**Drafting drawings**	**105**
4.1	Types of drawing	105
4.2	Reference indicators	105
4.3	Level of detail	106
4.4	Drawings provided by the inventor	106
5.	**Drafting an abstract**	**106**

In the previous modules, we explored how to draft the claims of a patent application; in this module, we will address how to draft the description, drawings and abstract of a patent application.

1. Key audiences of patent applications

When preparing a patent application, always remember who its audiences will be. Patent examiners and judges are the most obvious, but also the client and the inventor are themselves audiences: the patent drafter must make sure the inventor understands their own patent application. Other potential audiences include competitors, potential infringers and investors. Many investors will scrutinize a technology company's patent portfolio carefully before making an investment decision.

As we explained in Module III, section 2.2, the description part of the application is typically divided into several sections. Since the title of each differs slightly from one jurisdiction to another, the patent drafter should check the format required by that in which protection is sought before preparing the description. For example, the descriptions in international applications under the Patent Cooperation Treaty (PCT) are to be headed thus:

(i)   "Title of invention"
(ii)   "Technical field"
(iii)   "Background art"
(iv)   "Summary of invention" or "Disclosure of invention"
(v)   " Brief description of drawings"
(vi)   " Best mode for carrying out the invention," "Mode(s) for carrying out the invention" or "Description of embodiments"
(vii)   " Industrial applicability" (if relevant)
(viii) " Sequence listing" (if relevant)
(ix)   "Sequence listing free text" (if relevant)

International applications under the PCT are expected to be set out in this way other than when the invention is such that a different approach will support construction or present the substance more economically.

> **Professional tip**
>
> Remember that how you draft a description or any of its parts could affect how the claims are interpreted. Remember too that the rules of its presentation are not the same in all jurisdictions: take care to investigate the precise requirements and customary practice applicable to each section of the description in the jurisdiction(s) of interest to your client(s).

2. Order in which to draft a patent application

Before drafting a patent application, the patent drafter should have identified the invention and be clear about what its inventive features are in comparison with the prior art. Only then will the patent drafter have a complete picture of what embodiments, examples and/or drawings may be needed to sufficiently support the claimed invention. A holistic approach will ensure consistency across the application, which will be key to its interpretation. For example, if a term is used in the claims and the same term appears in the detailed description, someone reading the patent application will clearly understand the term to mean the same technical concept in each instance.

There is no one "correct" way of drafting or order to a patent application and while jurisdictions may prescribe variations on the order set out in the last section, the application is rarely drafted sequentially as such. What follows reflects the preferences of experienced patent drafters; other approaches may be equally effective in a given context. Some practitioners may, for example, prefer to switch the order of items (ii) and (iii).

(i) Drafting first the broadest main claim(s) reciting the inventive features is an efficient way of formulating the essential inventive concept (see also Module VI, section 1). Although it can be tempting to do so, drafting the background art section first may not be the best approach because there is a risk that it will end up being far too long and detailed; instead, the patent drafter should spend their (necessarily limited) time on other, more important, parts of the patent application that provide sufficient disclosure of the claimed invention, such as the detailed description of embodiments, drawings and a summary of the invention.

(ii) After drafting the claims, it is logical to draft the first part of the description – that is, the title, technical field, background art and summary of invention – although the last of these may equally effectively be drafted later, when the patent drafter has completed the description of embodiments and revised the claims.

(iii) Next will be the second part of the description – that is, the brief description of figures, the detailed description of embodiments and the drawings. Since these sections are interrelated, they are drafted as a group.

(iv) Once they have drafted the description and drawings, the patent drafter should revisit the claims: it is likely that writing the description has brought them to a clearer understanding of the invention. For example, they will now be in a better position to spot extraneous elements in the claims that could be a barrier to the broadest possible claim coverage. The patent drafter may now see that the claims do not describe the invention as accurately as they could or may even have had new ideas for claims.

(v) Once the claims are completed, the patent drafter needs to check the drawings and description to verify that the claim terms have been appropriately disclosed and supported, as well as that there is consistency of terms and meaning. Suppose the patent drafter has used a highly abstract term such as "floor-engaging member" to mean a chair leg. The patent drafter may then opt to define this abstract term in the description, for example "The seat piece is attached to the first chair leg, which is but one example of a floor-engaging member suitable for use in an embodiment of the invention."

3. Drafting parts of a description

In this subsection, we will offer more detail on drafting each section of a description. While we follow here the order set out in section 1, section 2 has demonstrated that this may not be the order in which the patent drafter prepares the application.

3.1 Title of invention

The *title*, or *title of invention*, should describe the subject matter of the invention broadly, yet concisely. In some jurisdictions (e.g., the United Kingdom), the title is published shortly after an application is filed, while the remainder of a patent specification is typically published 18 months from the filing (or priority) date. As a result, many patent drafters elect to adopt a broad title.

While it is prudent to avoid being overly narrow in the title of the invention so as not to unduly limit its implied scope, the title should nonetheless sufficiently indicate the subject matter of the invention. Occasionally, a patent examiner may object on the basis that a title is not sufficiently descriptive of the invention.

Conversely, while the title of invention should be appropriately descriptive of the claimed invention, it should not – and usually cannot within the permissible word count – fully characterize the claimed invention itself. For example, if a claimed invention is directed to "a semiconductor device" and "a method for fabricating a semiconductor device" including novel features, the title may typically read "SEMICONDUCTOR DEVICE AND METHOD FOR FABRICATING THEREOF."

In some jurisdictions, such as the United States, the heading "title" is preferred to "title of invention" because heading the section to include the word "invention" risks narrowing claim interpretation.

3.2 Technical field

The *technical field* section recites the technical field to which the invention pertains. This part is normally not more than a single paragraph of two or three sentences simply stating the general technical field in which the person reading the patent is expected to have some expertise (i.e., the art in which the person following the claims is expected to be skilled). This part will indicate a general classification with which the invention might be identified. Should an invention pertain to an improvement of a fuel system for an internal combustion engine, for example, then it might read: "The present invention relates to a fuel system for an internal combustion engine. More particularly, it relates to an electronically controlled fuel injection system for use with the internal combustion engine."

As is the case of the title, the technical field should not identify the claimed invention itself – that is, it should not state the inventive concept or the features of the invention.

3.3 Background art

The *background art* is a section establishing the context of the invention. It sets out briefly the state of the art, in general terms, in the field to which the invention pertains. More importantly, it goes on to identify the problem that the invention sets out to solve – that is, the ways in which existing technology falls short. The state of the art to be included here should be the closest prior art recognizable by the inventor prior to the filing date.

In drafting the section, the patent drafter should double-check that the inventor is indeed citing prior art accessible to the public before the filing date. It is not unusual for an inventor to present would-be prior art that is, in fact, not prior art under patent law, perhaps because an inventor has wrongly assumed that a certain idea or technology obvious to them must be prior art. The prior art included in the description should be only that which has been published and only that which is directly relevant in understanding the invention and the problem it solves.

In some jurisdictions such as the United States, what is disclosed in the background art section may include the inventor's own prior art, which the examiner will refer to as *applicant admitted prior art*. Although it is possible to successfully argue against such a characterization, it is safer to try to avoid such discussions with examiners. If something is wrongly characterized as prior art, that characterization may not be easily remedied by amendment or deletion and the patent examiner may lawfully reject the applicant's claims.

Another caveat about the background art section is that, sometimes, the invention itself is inextricably linked with a "new understanding" of the prior art – but if this new understanding is described in the background section, some of the novel element(s) of the invention may be regarded as present in the prior art. The background art section must be written so that it discloses only the problem and not the solution that the invention represents. (The solution should appear later in the description.)

If the invention resides in recognition of a problem (i.e., if the problem itself is considered to be new), then instead of identifying only the problem, the background art section should reflect its absence in the prior art.

A good background section should be fairly short and merely set the stage for the technical disclosure to be provided in the detailed description section. The background section may conclude with a pithy statement about the shortcomings of the prior art and it should be written to entice its reader into wondering how anyone could ever solve the problem it sets out.

In some jurisdictions, however, it is not generally helpful to mention specific prior art.

Some older patent applications include "objects of the invention" paragraphs in either the background or summary sections. If possible, avoid making any such statement. If it is required by law in the jurisdiction in which the application(s) will be filed, take care to make it no more than a statement of the problem that the invention seeks to overcome or alleviate, as cited in the background prior art. Any such statement risks limiting the invention – for example a statement "the object of the invention is to provide improved safety" when lower cost is also an object – and in some jurisdictions, such as the United States, if a competitor can then argue that its product does not aim to improve safety but instead serves another goal, the competitor may avoid infringement. Another risk is that such statements have a tendency to fuel "fraud" arguments, for example "an object of the invention is to cure cancer" when it would be more accurate to say that it aims to alleviate the symptoms of a particular kind of cancer.

Professional tip

Understanding the problem that the invention solves can help you to draft a focused introduction to the background art that avoids lengthy history of the relevant technology. Take care to avoid modifiers such as "well-known" or "common" that make assumptions about the prior art and your audience's knowledge of it.

Professional tip

Do not spend too much time preparing the background section. It is commonplace in modern patent drafting to include only a brief acknowledgement, describing the prior art at a very high level.

WIPO Patent Drafting Manual

Citation of prior art references

Although, in some jurisdictions, it is not generally required to describe and list the specific prior art references in the background section, other jurisdictions, such as Japan, require applicants to describe and list *at least one* prior art reference known to the inventor or the applicant prior to the filing. According to the common application format (CAF) (see Module III, section 2.6), a list citing specific prior art documents need not be positioned as part of the background art but in the description.

3.4 Summary of invention

The *summary of invention* section should outline what has been invented, in its full scope, and explain how the inventor has overcome the problem(s) set out in the background art section. The function of the summary of invention is to define, in context, the invention in a way that lays the foundation for the broad claims that follow.

Novice patent drafters can be lured by the title of this section into making a range of errors. Many can be avoided by simply summarizing the claims. In fact, some patent drafters prepare the summary section by turning each of the independent claims in the application into paragraphs – an approach that ensures that the precise words used in the claims will appear the description. This is true of both independent and dependent claims, with the two respectively representing essential and optional features that solve the problem.

> **Professional tip**
>
> In drafting advantageous effect, avoid absolute expressions that may be subject to argument or objection ("According to the present invention, noise can be fully eliminated") and instead use relative expressions ("According to the present invention, noise can be reduced" or "According to the present invention, lower noise can be achieved").

Typically included are the advantageous effects of the invention, which help to demonstrate inventive step or nonobviousness in comparison with the prior art. Any such advantages should accompany discussion of the broadest (independent) claim of which they are a feature. As we saw in relation to the background art (see section 3.3), however, there are risks to overexplaining these effects and hence narrowing interpretation of the claimed invention: a potential infringer might argue that their own product has no or few of the advantageous effects claimed for the invention, as affirmed in the patent.

In some jurisdictions, the summary section is further divided into subsections headed "Technical problem," "Solution to problem" and "Advantageous effect." The way in which the problems to be solved are drafted will affect the degree of inventiveness (inventive concept) apparent to the examiner or the courts. The patent drafter must take care to draft the technical problems in the summary of invention such that the solution set out appears to be inventive over the prior art (i.e., nonobvious).

The patent drafter must also take care not to deliver a broad "meta" summary that goes beyond the claims in any way. First, such a summary will invariably suggest additional prior art that can be applied against the invention. By explicitly linking the invention in writing to a broader subject, it will be difficult, if not impossible, to argue later that the prior art does not anticipate the claimed invention. Second, a broad, big-picture summary often includes, in a seemingly minor or insignificant way, another concept that is otherwise not well explained in the application. This provides an entry point for someone who may seek, especially during litigation, to invalidate the patent on the basis that the inventor's disclosure was incomplete because the issues mentioned in the summary are not disclosed elsewhere in the application. Similarly, a broad summary of this sort may imply that the claims are not directed to the fullest scope of the invention.

In some jurisdictions such as the United States, the heading "summary" is preferred to "summary of invention," because heading the section with the word "invention" risks narrowing claim interpretation.

3.5 Brief description of drawings

A *brief description of the drawings* is often positioned just before the detailed description of the embodiment(s). Applications in the mechanical, electrical and electronic fields almost invariably include drawings, while those in the chemical and biotechnology fields may or may not. Most commonly, drawings illustrate specific working examples of the apparatus or device, rather than general principles, and thus provide an appropriate introduction to the embodiments.

When drawings form part of the patent application, the brief description of drawings should state what each drawing figure represents and how the various individual drawings relate to one another. The drawings form an important part of the disclosure, helping to fulfill the requirement of complete description of the invention. The brief section merely states in general terms what the drawings are and what they show; their more detailed description comes later.

Each brief description should define the type of drawing (photograph, line drawing, graph, schematic representation, flowchart, etc.) and any visual perspective (e.g., top-down view, side-on view, perspective view, exploded view, etc.), and add a brief note of what the figure actually depicts (e.g., a device, a chart illustrating data, etc.).

In some jurisdictions, to avoid the narrower interpretation that limits the claims to those illustrated in the drawings, the brief description of drawings should begin with a statement confirming that the drawings are illustrative of one or more embodiments of the invention only and not illustrative of the "invention" itself.

Example

An exemplary embodiment of the present invention is illustrated by way of example in the accompanying drawings in which like reference numbers indicate the same or similar elements and in which:

- Figure 1 is a diagrammatic representation of an exemplary widget within which the present embodiment is deployed;
- Figure 2 is a cross-sectional view of the widget of Figure 1.

3.6 Description of embodiments

The *description of embodiments* section broadly explains various embodiments or examples of the claimed invention. Embodiments therefore have narrower scopes compared to the summary of invention, which represents only the new inventive concept. The earlier sections of the description, such as the title, technical field, background and summary of invention, as well as the claims, discuss the invention in general; this section expands adds depth with one or more examples of the invention (e.g., a specific prototype device). In other words, the description of embodiments breathes life into the claims and provides a sufficient explanation of the claimed invention that a person skilled in the art could reproduce, use and understand it.

Professional tip

In any case, do *not* make a habit out of trying to fix patent applications after they have been filed: eventually, you will make a mistake that cannot be fixed without refiling a completely new application that deprives the client of the original filing date.

If the application contains any drawings, the description of embodiments section must be closely tied to them. For example, to explain each element of an exemplary device and connections between these elements, a patent drafter should refer to each element shown in the drawing. (See Module IV, section 2.2, for more on reference numerals in this context.)

The description of embodiments cannot be substantively amended after the filing date because a patent application cannot be amended during prosecution to include new technical disclosure. Consequently, the patent drafter must make sure that the section is sufficient and complete on the day that the patent application is filed. See Module IX, section 3, for more on the amendment of an application during patent prosecution.

The patent drafter therefore should make sure that the patent application:

(i) reflects the disclosure material provided by the inventor;
(ii) provides sufficient information to enable those skilled in the art to reproduce the invention; and
(iii) provides sufficient depth and detail so that the claims can, if necessary, be narrowed during patent prosecution to avoid any prior art cited by an examiner.

Example

The inventor believes their invention to be new and extraordinary, and hence broadly patentable. They build a working model of the invention before filing a patent application and this working model becomes the prototype for an entire generation of their successful products. In the prototype, the inventor used Widget A connected to Widget B with copper wires. In abstract terms, this widget combination represents an example of a subcomponent X. The other abstract subcomponents in the invention are subcomponent Y and subcomponent Z.

The claim, as filed, reads:

A machine, comprising:

– a subcomponent X;
– a subcomponent Y operably coupled to the subcomponent X; and
– a subcomponent Z operably coupled to both the subcomponent X and the subcomponent Y.

The inventor convinces the patent drafter that the combination of X, Y and Z is so novel that the application does not need to provide any more details about the invention than necessary to support the broadest possible claims, because the inventor wants to save costs and file the application quickly. Thus the application makes no mention of Widget A or Widget B.

The patent examiner finds prior art published by Dr Q at Acme Corp. that discloses subcomponents X, Y and Z. This prior art anticipates the invention claimed in the application.

In reviewing the office action and the cited prior art, the patent drafter finds that absolutely every detail of their client's invention was disclosed by the prior art of Dr Q – except for the fact that the prior art to Dr Q discloses that subcomponent X should be made from Widget C and Widget D, and Dr Q (like so many others) discloses that this is the only known way to make a satisfactory subcomponent X.

Consequently, the patent drafter could overcome the prior art cited by the examiner and obtain a patent for their client if they were to amend the claims to recite:

A machine, comprising:

– a subcomponent X formed by combining Widget A and Widget B;
– a subcomponent Y operably coupled to the subcomponent X; and
– a subcomponent Z operably coupled to both the subcomponent X and the subcomponent Y.

The patent drafter further suspects not only that would this claim be patentable but also that a claim solely directed to forming subcomponent X from Widgets A and B might be patentable – and might actually constitute the client's real invention.

Unfortunately, the client insists that the patent application must not disclose that subcomponent X could be formed from Widgets A and B. Therefore the patent drafter can neither amend the claims to overcome the prior art reference nor amend the claims to recite the highly novel combination conceived by their client.

In this case, the patent application will likely be abandoned – unless the patent drafter can think of another way to amend the claims. The patent drafter might write a new patent application that makes the proper technical disclosure, provided that they are not barred from protection by, among other things, the inventor's own activities or publication of the inventor's original application.

We will look now at some further considerations about the scope and importance of the description of embodiments.

Terminology and choice of words

If the patent drafter uses a highly abstract term in the claims, they should consider using the same term in the description of embodiments section but in a way that ties the term to a specific embodiment of the invention. There must be consistency throughout the patent application, both at the general and specific levels. For example, if the claims use the term "warning device" for an automobile horn, the description of embodiments could either say, "One example of warning device 102 is an automobile horn. Other warning devices may be used, consistent with the spirit of the invention,"[33] or "Automobile horn 102 constitutes a warning device. Many other such warning devices may be used consistent with the spirit of the invention." Providing alternative examples of a warning device (e.g., a siren, a buzzer) can be even more helpful as a foundation for a broader interpretation of the term.

The patent drafter should use simple technical language rather than jargon or special and complex terminology. Plain language makes it easier for competitors or judges to understand the terms and reduces the risk of seeding another meaning that the inventor did not intend. Using plain language will also reduce problems when the first application is translated for filing in other jurisdictions.

Unclaimed subject matter

The patent drafter must use their best judgement to balance the risks of too bare a description of embodiments section against those of disclosing too much unclaimed subject matter. Unclaimed subject matter cannot be conferred to a patent right and is considered to have been "dedicated to the public" by the inventor unless it will be claimed at a later stage. Drafting the claims *before* drafting the description of embodiments can help a patent drafter to ensure that they tailor the description to fit the content of the claims.

In drafting this section, the patent drafter will generally want to err on the side of inclusion. If sufficient details are not included in the description of embodiments section as of the filing date, it will not be possible to narrow the claims to overcome objection for lack of novelty or inventive step should an examiner find new prior art.

Most patent systems, including the PCT, have a "unity of invention" rule that permits only one invention, or more than one invention sharing a single "inventive concept," to appear within one patent application (see Module VI, section 11). Consequently, if the disclosure is found to include an unclaimed invention that lacks unity of invention with the original set of claims, the patent drafter cannot remedy this by introducing a new set of claims. In such a case, the problem may be solved only by filing a divisional or continuation application, as appropriate and with their client's approval, claiming any previously unclaimed invention.

Use of the term "invention"

Particularly in some jurisdictions, the patent drafter should avoid using in the description of embodiments phrases such as "the invention is …" and use instead phrases such as "an embodiment of the invention" or "an exemplification of the invention," or even "an embodiment/exemplification of the apparatus/method." This will ensure that patent claims receive the broadest interpretation possible. Without limiting words to the contrary, the description of embodiments section is generally presumed to disclose "an embodiment" of the invention rather than the invention itself – but if the patent drafter forecloses this broader reading by stating that "the invention is X" instead of "an embodiment of the invention is X," the scope of the claimed invention may be unnecessarily narrowed.

Professional tip

Remember to consult your client on every substantive matter pertaining to their pending application and to make no assumptions.

Known features

The patent drafter does not need to include, in the patent application, well-known material that would be necessary to make or use a product associated with the claimed invention. A patent application does not need to be a blueprint and at least one court has stated that a patent should preferably "omit" things that are well known in the art. For example, if every polymer X has to be cured for 5 hours at 200 degrees and this is well known in the art, this method of curing polymer X need not be included in the patent application – unless the invention modifies the method in some way.

Avoiding "limiting" the claims

In addition to describing the components used in an embodiment of the invention and the way in which those components operate, the patent drafter may also wish to include in the patent application one or more drawings and related disclosures that provide context for the invention and/or describe the invention in operation. In this case, it is advisable to condition those discussions so that the context does not necessarily become limiting – that is, part of the invention.

We have reiterated throughout this manual that the patent drafter must be very careful in their use of language in a patent application. Their language choices may have consequences not only during patent prosecution but also – and especially – should the patent be litigated. As in relation to the advantages of the invention described in the summary section, the patent drafter should be particularly careful in their use of words containing absolutes of any sort when preparing the description of embodiments. If a patent application uses words such as "must" or "always," those words should very precisely and accurately infer that the components or functions to which they refer are "essential" features of the claimed invention. In other words, if an invention disclosure says that a widget "always" does something, the patent drafter should make sure this is true (i.e., that the invention will not work otherwise).

Preferred/optional features

The subject matter or features in the dependent claims (also called *subsidiary claims* or *subclaims*) should be described as *preferred* or *optional* embodiments or features; otherwise, they may be regarded as "essential" features of the claimed invention (which features should be included in only the broadest claim). The section should also recite their advantages, which can be important if amendment becomes necessary during prosecution or opposition proceedings. If a claim sets out a preferred feature or range, it may also be useful to set out further characteristics of the feature or still narrower preferred ranges.

In the United States, practitioners avoid discussing "preferred" embodiments or features in this section, since case law has established that patent infringement will rarely be found where the accused infringer is not practicing the "preferred" features of the invention.

Incorporation by reference

In some jurisdictions, such as the United States, it is permissible to incorporate material by reference in a patent application, such as to a well-known chemical handbook. It is also permissible to incorporate in the patent application material from other sources, such as other patent publications. Such incorporation by reference should be used sparingly.

Number of embodiments or examples

The number of embodiments or examples required in a patent application will depend on the scope of the claims. For many inventions – in particular, mechanical

---

Professional tip

Because you will most likely be drafting applications using a computer, you can easily compile a list of absolute words to find and replace in the application when it is nearly complete.

and engineering inventions – a single embodiment including alternatives for important features will suffice. In chemical and biological inventions, meanwhile, many examples may be necessary, since these must be sufficient to provide supportive disclosure for broad claims.

4. Drafting drawings

The patent drafter is required to prepare good visual supporting materials that describe the claimed invention. Some patent drafters consider the *drawings* to be the most important part of the patent application after the claims, particularly in mechanical, electrical and electronic fields.

4.1 Types of drawing

In some jurisdictions, such as the United States, patent laws require every claimed element to be shown in the drawings. Where appropriate, the drawings should explain the invention in sufficient detail that reading the description of embodiments section merely confirms in words the information the drawings provide. This is, however, not always possible.

Sometimes, drawings are used to illustrate the principle of an invention rather than a specific embodiment. Sometimes, they present results obtained from using the invention, such as graphs relating to specific experiments in chemical cases, showing how the alteration of one reaction condition changes the results of the process.

4.2 Reference indicators

The elements shown in a patent's drawings are typically accompanied by a short description in words and a reference indicator (e.g., a reference numeral) such as "clock (102)." That indicator, "102," should be included in the description of embodiment section.

The patent drafter should use a consistent numbering scheme. In one such scheme, a reference number introduced for the first time is given a leading number that matches its figure number followed by, for example, two unique digits. For example, in "Figure 2" of a patent application, the patent drafter may already have labeled two previous elements. The third element, for example a computer memory, would then be numbered "203." All future reference to this computer memory in the patent application's drawings and specification will then state "computer memory (203)," or just "memory (203)." If another computer memory is discussed, it should be given another reference number; otherwise, the two will be assumed to be one and the same. One variation of this numbering scheme is to use only odd numbers (e.g., 101, 103, 105) in the early drafts. This simplifies the process of adding new elements when revising the application.

In another numbering scheme, a main component will be given a single-digit reference number and then any subcomponents will be given additional digits that lead with the main component's reference number. For example, "computer 8" may have a subcomponent "memory 82," in which the "8" in "82" refers to computer 8 and the "2" means that it is the second element to have been numbered.

Professional tip

When drafting the description of embodiment, give dictation a go. If you have prepared your draft drawings and an outline of the section, you may find that you can simply talk your way through the drawings. Many practitioners find that they can at least double their output using this approach.

Professional tip

Whatever reference scheme you choose, you must employ it consistently.

4.3 Level of detail

In preparing the drawings, the patent drafter should think of the story they want to tell and how they want to tell it. They should also think about the level of detail necessary to deliver supportive and enabling disclosure. For example, a black box labeled "widget engine" with no subcomponents will be insufficient explanation for a patent application that purports to disclose a "widget engine." Conversely, the patent drafter should avoid providing too much detail in the drawings, unless the accompanying explanation in the description of embodiments section explains that the additional detail pertains to only one specific embodiment of the invention. Should too much detail appear, there is a risk that someone may later argue – perhaps during litigation – that the detail illustrated is essential to the invention and hence narrows interpretation of the claims. This is especially true in those jurisdictions, such as the United States, where an application includes a means-plus-function claim (see Module IV, section 2.4), since defendants in a later patent infringement case will argue that all of the unnecessary details in the drawings are essential means of performing the recited function.

Drawings must be complete and omit no critical detail. If a drawing depicts a process flow, for example, then arrows must be appropriately depicted: if an arrow points in only one direction when it ought really to be double-ended, it may be difficult to convince the examiner that the flow between the two components is reversible. The patent drafter may provide sufficient written explanation in the description of embodiments to overcome any deficiencies in the drawings – but it would be poor practice to rely upon this as a remedy.

Professional tip

Your time and skill should be spent on creating clear and original drawings not on making them look attractive.

The patent drafter should remember, however, that they should not spend too much time perfecting drawings. A qualified draftsperson may help, but the patent drafter is not themselves expected to be such. Computer-aided design can be helpful in preparing drawings; sometimes, it is faster and cheaper to simply sketch on paper.

4.4 Drawings provided by the inventor

The client and/or the inventor may often offer the patent drafter their own drawings. These can be useful to the patent drafter in telling the story of the invention, but it is likely that they will include other features unnecessary for its disclosure. The patent drafter may therefore prefer to redraw or tailor the inventor's own drawings.

It is important to ensure that any detail on the drawings, including text, will remain legible when the drawings are scaled down to fit the published patent. For example, clients may provide screenshots to show the invention in operation, but such screenshots are rarely legible when scaled to fit on the printed page.

5. Drafting an abstract

The *abstract* is intended to summarize the essentials of the invention. In many cases, a version of the first paragraph of the summary of the invention section will be effective as the abstract, which itself may mirror the content of the main (independent) claim. The main purpose of an abstract is as an aid to searching. It is generally published on the front page in patent publications, entered into databases and commonly provides the keywords for automated searching tools. When several patent applications and patents appear as the result of a search, an individual will often check the abstract to determine whether they need to read further. For that reason, the abstract should be brief and it must be accurate.

Many jurisdictions require the abstract to be no longer than a certain word count. In many in which English is an official language, the abstract is limited to 150 words. In other jurisdictions, such as Japan, the Republic of Korea and China, the abstract is limited to a certain character count. The examiner may object to abstracts that exceed these limits.

In most countries, the abstract merely delivers technical information and cannot be taken into account for any other purpose, including to interpret the scope of the claims or to determine patentability. Even the courts in most jurisdictions will rarely look to the abstract as a source when interpreting the claimed invention. The United States is an exception, however, and abstracts for applications filed in that country should be drafted broadly, to avoid limitation.

As a consequence, in many jurisdictions, patent offices review the abstract only for its adherence to the word or character counts and conduct little substantive assessment – although that does not mean that the abstract may be misleading or poorly written.

It can be advisable to add to the abstract the reference indictors shown in the drawings (e.g., "clock (102)") if it will facilitate the audience's understanding of the invention. In the United States, however, such reference signs have been found to narrow claim interpretation by limiting the claimed feature to those disclosed in the drawings and hence they ought to be omitted or deleted from the abstract.

Novice patent drafters commonly make the mistake of preparing the abstract at an early stage – but the resulting risk is that it may disclose some patentable features of the invention not found in other parts of the patent application. Many patent drafters prefer to prepare the abstract at the very end of the drafting process, asking themselves as they do so: *Are all elements in the abstract disclosed in the description?* If the answer is not a resounding "yes," then they must add the missing element to the description or claims, or they must modify the abstract.

Key words

- Description
- Title
- Technical field
- Background art
- Summary of invention
- (Disclosure of invention or Detailed description)
- Brief description of the drawings
- Description of embodiments (Mode(s) for carrying out the invention)
- Order in which to draft a patent application
- Drafting drawings
- Drafting an abstract

Self-Test

- [ ] In your jurisdiction, how is the description part of the application divided?

- [ ] What kind of information should a "background art" section provide? What should a patent drafter avoid in preparing that section?

- [ ] What kind of information should be included in a "summary of invention" section?

- [ ] The description part of the application must describe at least one working embodiment of the invention. True or false?

- [ ] An embodiment disclosed in the description but not covered by the claims of the granted patent is dedicated to the public. True or false?

- [ ] Patent drafters are recommended to use absolute words, such as "must" and "always," in the description part of the application because it will facilitate clearer understanding of the invention. True or false?

- [ ] The "description of embodiments" section should describe not only the embodiments with essential features of the invention but also the embodiments with optional features. Why?

- [ ] Drawings that a client might offer to their patent drafter can be extremely useful when drafting drawings for inclusion in a patent application – but the patent drafter should use them with caution. What are the issues the patent drafter should consider?

Module VIII
Filing patent applications

1.	**Domestic/priority filings**	**110**
2.	**Foreign filings**	**110**
3.	**Patent office procedures and fees**	**112**
3.1	Patent office procedures	112
3.2	Fees and other cost considerations	112
4.	**Application filing procedures in specific jurisdictions**	**114**
4.1	Filing with the United States Patent and Trademark Office (USPTO)	114
4.2	Filing with the European Patent Office (EPO)	115
4.3	Filing under the Patent Cooperation Treaty (PCT)	115

Before filing, the patent drafter should make sure that their client reviews, understands and approves the patent application. Inventors rarely understand the relevant legal requirements and even fewer inventors understand and appreciate the customary language of patent applications (see Module IV, section 2), and hence it is the patent drafter's responsibility to explain to the client any parts of the application about which they have questions. The patent drafter should not change the patent application to make it more accessible to persons unfamiliar with patent drafting if doing so will compromise the scope or validity of the claimed patent, but they must make sure that the language they have used is correct and as plain as possible. Highly abstract claims can sometimes be opaque to anyone other than a patent specialist, but abstract language may sometimes be the most appropriate to ensure that the claims are as broad as legally permissible.

We have noted throughout this manual that the patent drafter must understand the requirements for filing patent applications in all countries of interest to their clients, including the rules related to formatting and drawings. A proactive patent drafter may prepare a checklist – for each of the various jurisdictions in which they may regularly file – of such items as the necessary parts of a patent application, then compare each application to the relevant checklist. Other useful checklists might relate to the review of an application before filing it with a given patent office (whether electronically or by mail) or issues to be addressed before responding to an office action. Such checklists can mitigate the risk of inadvertent omission(s) or error(s).

In many jurisdictions, the patent drafter will be required to accompany the filed patent application with a power of attorney and payment of various government filing fees. Depending on the legal requirements specific to the jurisdiction, they may also file a declaration of inventorship or a document confirming that the inventor has assigned the invention to the applicant or otherwise stating the patent applicant's entitlement. Some national patent offices will allow these formal papers to be filed after the patent application without jeopardizing its filing date.

In the United States, the *declaration of inventorship* is a statement whereby the inventor declares that they have read and understood the patent application and that they believe themselves to be the inventor (or an inventor, should there be more than one) of the invention it describes.

The *power of attorney* document bestows upon another person (typically a patent agent or a patent attorney who is entitled to practice before the patent office concerned) the authority to represent the applicant of the subject application in proceedings with the patent office.

The *assignment document* is a contract between the inventor and another party (typically their employer) indicating transfer of the inventor's patent rights to that party. (The patent drafter should check that their client has the right to pursue the patent before representing that party in proceedings.)

Among other formal papers that the patent drafter may need to file are papers related to national defense. Some countries, such as the United States, the United Kingdom, China, India and France, have specific requirements for the filing of patent applications that may be of interest for national security. In other countries, such as the United States, a resident inventor must obtain the government's permission to file any patent application abroad. Similarly, many countries have rules related to the export of technical data. At the very least, a patent drafter should familiarize

Professional tip

Do not let all your hard work go to waste because you missed a minor application requirement that could have been easily caught and dealt with.

themselves with any such rules in their own jurisdiction so that they do not inadvertently participate in the unlawful transmission of sensitive technical data across an international boundary.

1. Domestic/priority filings

Because inventors and their employers commonly want patent protection in the country in which the inventor works, a client will typically ask their patent drafter to make the first filing of a patent application in that country – that is, domestically. The inventor or their employer may also want to file patent applications in other countries under the Paris Convention (see the next section). Since the first filing of a patent application establishes the priority date for the family of foreign patent applications for the same invention that may be subsequently filed, the client will typically want to file as early as possible.

We have noted elsewhere that the precise filing requirements for patent applications can vary from jurisdiction to jurisdiction and that the patent drafter should be extremely well versed in the specific requirements of their own. This information is frequently available online[34] and from other publicly available resources.

2. Foreign filings

After asking their client in which countries they would like to file patent applications, the patent drafter should review the filing requirements in all jurisdictions of interest to the client and then provide them with an estimate of the costs. For example, the patent drafter must determine whether the countries of interest are Contracting States to the Paris Convention or members of the World Trade Organization (WTO).

The Paris Convention is an international treaty that provides, among other advantages, a right of priority among patent applications. The Convention allows a patent applicant from a Contracting State to enjoy a right of priority based on the first filing in any such state provided that a subsequent application claiming the same invention is filed within 12 months of the filing date of the first. The *right of priority* means that no subsequent application will be invalidated by an act that occurs between the priority date and the filing of that subsequent application. For example, if a patent application on the same invention is filed in Japan no later than 12 months after the initial patent application was filed in Canada, the Japanese application will not be invalidated by the publication of that invention in a journal within those 12 months. Thus, under the Paris Convention, the filing date of the first application made on that invention is known as the *priority date*. A certified copy of the initial application may also be required in each country in which priority is claimed to evidence the right.

In accordance with the Agreement on Trade-Related Aspects of Intellectual Property Rights (TRIPS), applicants may also enjoy the right of priority in members of the WTO that are not signatories of the Paris Convention.

Professional tip

Take care to check all of the dates by which foreign applications must have been filed and remind your client well in advance of those dates, so that they have time to make decisions.

The same right of priority under the Paris Convention can be claimed not only among Contracting States and members of the WTO but also when the applicant subsequently files an international application under the Patent Cooperation Treaty (PCT). The Treaty is a special agreement under Article 19 of the Paris Convention and we will look at it more closely in section 4.3 of this module.

Example

A patent drafter in Country A files a patent application on March 8, 2020. Country A is a party to the Paris Convention. The client would like counterpart applications filed in Countries B, C and D. Since these countries are also the parties to the Paris Convention, the patent drafter can wait until March 8, 2021 to file counterpart patent applications in Countries B, C and D that will enjoy the right of priority.

The inventor first publicly discloses the invention two weeks after filing the application in Country A – that is, on March 22, 2020. Thanks to the Paris Convention, the applications filed in Countries B, C and D retain March 8, 2020 as a priority date. Consequently, the public disclosure does not compromise the patentability of counterpart applications filed in Countries B, C and D.

If, however, an inventor were to have publicly disclosed their invention *before* the filing date of the first application (i.e., the priority date), the right of priority under the Paris Convention would be irrelevant to the question of patentability. To return to our example, if the inventor discloses every aspect of their invention to the public two weeks before filing the patent application in Country A (i.e., on February 17, 2020), then that disclosure may affect the patentability of the applications filed in Countries A, B, C and D. This will be a matter for the national patent law of each country – in this case, particularly any grace period provision (see Module II, section 2.1).

For every jurisdiction that is neither a Paris Convention Contracting State nor a WTO member and before filing the first (domestic) application, the patent drafter must determine the precise requirements for filing applications, which can vary widely. Given that, as of August 8, 2020, there are 177 Contracting States to the Paris Convention, however, such a situation may occur only rarely.

It is often the case that a client is unsure at the time of first filing whether they will want to file foreign patent applications and/or where. Based on their insight, the patent drafter can counsel their client appropriately, outlining the benefits of priority under the Paris Convention priority, the risks should the client decide to file in a country (or countries) that are not signatories to the Paris Convention countries or WTO members and the benefits of filing a PCT application within the 12-month Paris Convention priority period.

It is unlikely that a patent drafter will be allowed to represent their client before a foreign patent office directly; instead, a patent attorney licensed in that jurisdiction will need to be found. There are at least two models for working relationships between patent drafters with foreign patent attorneys and agents.

- In the *hands-off* model, the foreign attorney or agent sends official correspondence and provides information on local rules but takes little substantive action in the case. The patent drafter who filed the original priority application makes all of the major decisions.
- In the *hands-on* model, the foreign attorney or agent drafts proposed responses to office actions and forwards them to the patent drafter for approval.

The patent drafter may use different models for jurisdictions, for example hands-on in some and hands-off in others.

Professional tip

If you think that your work will regularly involve foreign filings, you should consider establishing ongoing working relationships with foreign associate attorneys in the relevant countries.

3. Patent office procedures and fees

3.1 Patent office procedures

Once a patent application is filed, the patent office checks the submitted application so that only those applications that comply with the requirements under the applicable law will lead to grant of a patent. The procedures vary significantly from one country to another, so it is impossible to provide an exhaustive step-by-step overview. The patent drafter should be familiar with at least the office procedure of their own country.

In general, the three main areas of office procedures are:

(i) examination of form;
(ii) prior art search; and
(iii) examination of substance.

In some offices, only step (i) is conducted; in some others, only steps (i) and (ii).

In each case, a patent examiner and the applicant (or their representative, who may be a patent drafter or another person) engage in a dialogue, largely in writing. The representative receives communications from the patent office, advises the applicant on the appropriate course of action, takes the applicant's instructions and responds accordingly to the patent office's communication.

Examination of form (step (i)) ensures that the application meets all formal requirements under law, such as that a request form is correctly filled in, that rules relating to the drafting of the description, claims, drawings and abstract have been fulfilled, and that other required documents, such as a power of attorney or a statement by the inventor, are submitted. The patent office will give the applicant an opportunity to remedy any defects identified during the examination of form; if the applicant does not do so within a given time period, the patent office will reject the application.

Depending on the examination procedure provided for in the relevant law, the prior art search (step (ii)) will be conducted either separately from and prior to the examination of substance or as part of the substantive examination process. If the search is conducted separately, a search report will be forwarded to the applicant setting out the relevant prior art documents identified.

The examination of substance (step (iii)) checks whether the application satisfies the patentability criteria and whether the invention is sufficiently disclosed, clearly and completely, in the application as filed. As in step (i), the patent office will give the applicant an opportunity to remove any objections raised during the substantive examination (typically by amending the claims and description); if the applicant fails to do so within a given time period, the patent office will refuse to grant the patent.

In many countries, patent applications are published 18 months after their filing (or priority) date.

If (or when) the examination process has reached a conclusion favorable to the applicant, the patent office will grant a patent. The details of the patent will be entered into the patent register and published in an official gazette. Many patent offices now publish patent applications and granted patents on their websites. The applicant will receive a *certificate of patent grant*, which is a legal document establishing their ownership of the patent.

Some national and regional laws provide for opposition and other administrative revocation and invalidation mechanisms that make it possible for third parties to intervene in the patent examination process before the grant of a patent or to challenge a patent after its grant. While the design of such mechanisms may differ across countries, the common objective is to provide a simple, quick and comparatively inexpensive means of raising the quality of patents by integrating additional contribution to the patent-granting process.

In some regions, there are regional patent offices that grant regional patents. These include the African Regional Intellectual Property Organization (ARIPO), Eurasian Patent Office (EAPO), European Patent Office (EPO), Gulf Cooperation Council Patent Office (GCCPO) and Organisation Africaine de la Propriété Intellectuelle (OAPI).

3.2 Fees and other cost considerations

The patent drafter should always aim to provide the client with sufficient information regarding fees and costs that the client can devise a meaningful patent strategy within their budgetary constraints. The patent drafter might also inform the client whether these fees and costs will need to be assessed at certain points in time. For example, it is important to tell a client that filing patent applications in five countries and maintaining the issued patents through to the end of their terms could cost in the region of EUR 150,000 – and it will be even more helpful to also tell them that only a portion of the total cost must be paid during the first five years after filing the initial local application, with the remaining cost comprising variable expenses that *might* arise over a 20-year period.

Some jurisdictions offer reductions in fees for applications filed by certain parties such as sole inventors, universities, research institutions and/or small companies. The United States, for example, provides for a 50 percent discount for most of the fees paid by sole inventors, nonprofits (including universities) and small companies. The patent drafter should investigate these options and act in their client's best interests accordingly.

Figure 9 provides an overview of the typical phases involved in patent prosecution from a cost perspective. The fees that may be associated with the steps taken include filing fees, publication fees, request for examination fees, search fees, prosecution-related fees, issue fees and maintenance fees. The patent grant procedure and associated fees do, however, vary among patent offices and according to the laws to which they are subject.

Not all offices require all of these fees and some offices may require other types of fee. Each of these fees may have an associated cost for professional services (e.g., fees to be paid to experts) and, in general, professional service fees will be higher than the government filing fees. Some of these fees, such as request for examination fees, are not charged in every jurisdiction, because not all offices have a "request for examination" system. In many jurisdictions, there are specific government fees for special procedures during the prosecution of an application. For example, some offices offer accelerated patent examination upon payment of a fee; others accept extension of a time limit under certain conditions, including payment of an additional fee. A significant amount of professional fees may be incurred at the substantive examination phase of the prosecution because this is the phase when the patent drafter performs tasks such as reviewing prior art cited by the patent examiner and amending the claims to overcome the objection. Most jurisdictions assess an issue fee to bring a patent into force and most charge some sort of maintenance fee to keep a patent in force.

If the client wishes to file patent applications in multiple national and regional patent offices, the cumulative government fees and professional service fees may become substantial. To file a patent application in a patent office abroad, the client may need to prepare a translation of the local application into the language accepted by that office. While the timeline for the preparation of such translation can vary from country to country, the professional translation of a complicated legal or technical document such as a patent application can be very costly. If the client is interested in filing counterpart applications in five further countries and none of those five countries accepts a language in common with another – including that of the initial application – the client will need to prepare translations in five additional languages: a significant expense.

Similarly, translation of a regional patent application may be required within the regional patent system itself. The EPO, for example, accepts applications in English, French or German and allows the prosecution of such applications to be completed in one of those three languages. However, once it has approved the application for grant, the EPO requires the patent applicant to choose in which EPO member countries they wish to validate the European patent and pay a validation fee to each office of these countries. This process may require translation of the application into a language other than that in which it was drafted.

Example

An application written in English has been filed with the EPO. The patent applicant has designated four countries on the EPO application: Spain, Italy, Austria and Portugal.

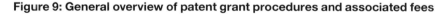

Figure 9: General overview of patent grant procedures and associated fees

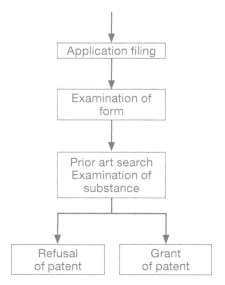

WIPO Patent Drafting Manual

After successful prosecution before the EPO, the patent applicant will need to pay the validation fee to the patent offices of these countries and provide a translation of the English application into Spanish, Italian, German and Portuguese.

While the validation fees and translation costs will vary from country to country, the total lifetime costs for protection in four European countries exceed EUR 200,000.

Professional tip

In addition to the country-specific reductions in fees for applications filed by certain parties, you should advise your client appropriately of international instruments that aim to reduce the costs of translating patents, such as the London Agreement,[48] which waives – either in large part or in full – the requirement for translations of European patents.

If the applicant is interested in filing a patent application in multiple countries, filing under the PCT may be a good option from a costs perspective. A PCT application can be filed in any language that is accepted by the receiving office. A translation of the PCT application may be necessary, however, if it is written in a language other than Arabic, Chinese, English, French, German, Japanese, Korean, Portuguese, Russian or Spanish. The PCT is nonetheless an effective mechanism for postponing the major costs associated with patent prosecution in foreign countries outlined earlier.

Since the costs of obtaining patents in foreign countries can be quite substantial, the patent applicant – the client – will need to make regular business judgements throughout the foreign filing process. Consequently, the patent drafter should provide sound advice about the costs of patent protection worldwide and offer ideas of how the client might limit its costs by filing a patent application in only those countries in which patent protection is business-critical. In other words, it is important to approach this decision strategically (see Module X).

4. Application filing procedures in specific jurisdictions

The procedures for filing an application vary from country to country. The following information is intended to be informative rather than to provide a step-by-step universal guide to filing. Many patent offices include information on their filing procedures, requirements and official forms on their websites.[35]

4.1 Filing with the United States Patent and Trademark Office (USPTO)

The United States Patent and Trademark Office (USPTO) is the agency responsible for receiving and examining patent applications in the United States. The USPTO ultimately decides whether a patent will be granted or rejected. Preparing a patent application and the accompanying documents for this jurisdiction may be challenging; the patent drafter should explore the USPTO's requirements before undertaking to do so.

In the United States, a nonprovisional patent application must include claims, an abstract, a description, an oath or declaration and, in most cases, drawings. A *nonprovisional* utility application is an application that includes claims, while a *provisional* application need not necessarily include claims and is primarily used to establish a priority date. A patent application must be in English or be accompanied by an English-language translation and a statement that the translation is accurate.

A *utility patent application transmittal form* (or *transmittal letter*) should be filed with every patent application. The purpose of this form or letter is to inform the USPTO

114

what types of paper are being filed (*e.g.,* description, claims, drawings, declaration and information disclosure statement). The transmittal also names the applicant and identifies the type of application, the title of the invention, the contents of the application and any accompanying enclosures.

A *fee transmittal form* may be used to calculate the prescribed filing fees and to indicate the method of payment, whether by check, credit card or electronic payment. The amount payable is dependent upon the number and type of claims presented and whether or not the client can provide a written assertion of small entity status, such as for individual inventors, which will typically reduce the government fees by half.

The filing, searching and examination fees for a patent application should be paid at the same time as the application is filed. If an application is filed without the required fees, the applicant will be notified and asked to submit the fees within a given time period. If the basic filing fee was not paid at the time of filing, a surcharge will be added for late acceptance.

An *application data sheet* will contain bibliographic data, such as applicant, correspondence, application, representative, domestic priority, foreign priority and assignment information.

The patent application should include an oath or declaration signed by the inventor(s) to affirm that they believe themselves to be the original inventor(s) of the subject matter of the application. The oath or declaration must be in a language that the inventor understands. If the oath or declaration is in a language other than English, an English translation and statement that the translation is accurate will be required.

4.2 Filing with the European Patent Office (EPO)

The EPO was created by the European Patent Convention (EPC). The EPC provides the framework for the granting of European patents via a single, harmonized procedure before the EPO – that is, the EPO functions as a common examining office for patent applications filed under the EPC. Once an application meets the requirements under the EPC – which include the use of specific forms, the payment of fees, and submission of various documents and their translation (if necessary) – the EPO grants a European patent for each of the Contracting States designated by the applicant. Grant of a European patent does not automatically mean patent protection in the designated Contracting States, however, and all Contracting States remain responsible for granting or rejecting national patents filed directly in their respective countries.

Because applications filed with the EPO are regional patent applications, they must include some indication of the Contracting States in which the applicant would like to receive patent protection. The applicant can designate one state, all

states or some states. Since April 2009, the EPO fee structure has been such that a single designation fee is charged regardless of how many countries are designated; hence a patent drafter might designate all of the states, so that the applicant can make a decision on the countries of interest once the European patent has been granted.

Once an application has successfully completed the EPO examination process and an European patent has been granted, the applicant must validate the European patent in each Contracting State in which it wishes to obtain patent protection. The validation process typically involves payment of further fees, as well as submission of certain documents and translation of the patent (if required) within a certain time limit from the date on which the European patent was granted.

Publication of the European patent also triggers the time limit for filing an opposition to it.

4.3 Filing under the Patent Cooperation Treaty (PCT)

General procedures

The PCT is a multilateral treaty administered by the World Intellectual Property Organization (WIPO), the headquarters of which are in Geneva, Switzerland. As of January 15, 2020, there were 153 Contracting States to the PCT.

The PCT enables a patent applicant to file a single "international" patent application and yet seek protection in any or all of the PCT Contracting States. The international patent application has the effect of filing a regular "national" patent application in each designated State. The term *designated States* refers to those countries that are members of the PCT at the time of filing. The term of patent protection available under the PCT is 20 years from the international filing (or priority) date.

It is important to understand that WIPO does not issue a "PCT patent" or "international patent" that provides protection in all of the Contracting States; each national or regional office can grant or reject the patent under its own patent law. An applicant must therefore still prosecute an international patent application in each country or region in which they seek protection and pay the appropriate national or regional fees.

The PCT procedure consists of two main phases: the international phase and the national phase.[36]

The *international phase* consists of the following steps.

(i) **Filing of the international application**   An applicant will often file their first patent application with a national patent office and file a subsequent PCT international application,

Figure 10: Overview of the Patent Cooperation Treaty (PCT) System

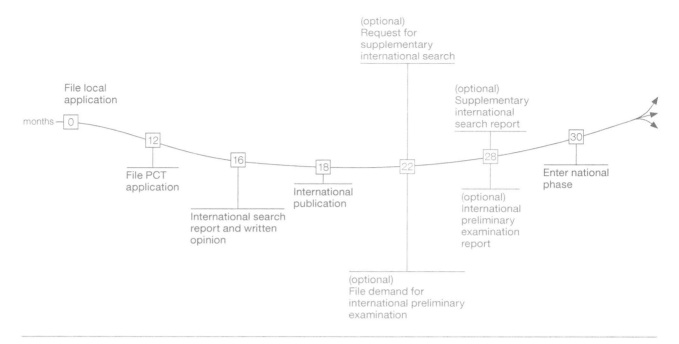

claiming priority based on the first. In principle, the filing of a PCT application designates all Contracting States that are bound by the Treaty on the international filing date.

(ii) **International search** The international search is carried out by one of the competent *international searching authorities (ISAs)* under the PCT[37] and results in an *international search report (ISR)* – that is, a list of published documents that might affect the patentability of, or be relevant to, the invention claimed in the international application. In addition, a preliminary and nonbinding written opinion is also issued on whether the invention appears to meet patentability criteria in light of the search report results. The ISR and written opinion are communicated to the applicant who, after evaluating their content, may decide to withdraw the application, particularly where that content indicates that the granting of patents is unlikely. Alternatively the applicant may decide to amend the claims in the application.

(iii) **Publication of the PCT application, ISR and written opinion** If the international application is not withdrawn within 18 months of the filing (or priority) date, WIPO's International Bureau publishes it, along with the ISR. The written opinion will also be made publicly available from that time.

(iv) [Optional] **Request for supplementary international search (SIS)** In addition to the international search (the "main international search"), the applicant has the option to request that a *supplementary international searching authority (SISA)* – that is, an ISA willing to offer this service – perform an additional search of relevant prior art specifically focusing on, for example, documents in the particular language in which that authority specializes. A SIS request must be made within 22 months of the priority date. The goal is to reduce the likelihood of further relevant prior art coming to light in the later national phase that puts grant of the patent at risk.

(v) [Optional] **Request for an international preliminary examination** If the applicant wishes to amend the international application to, for example, overcome prior art documents identified in the search report and conclusions set out in the written opinion – and to obtain another opinion on the potential patentability of the claimed invention "as amended" – they may request an optional international preliminary examination. The result of the preliminary examination is an *international preliminary examination report (IPER)* on patentability (IPRP Chapter I[38]), which one of the competent *international preliminary examining authorities (IPEAs)* under the PCT[39] will prepare, to include a preliminary and nonbinding opinion on the patentability of the claimed invention. It provides the applicant with an even stronger basis on which to evaluate the chances of obtaining a patent and, if the report is favorable, on which to continue with the application before national and regional patent offices. If no international preliminary examination has been requested, the International Bureau establishes an international preliminary report on patentability (IPRP Chapter I[40]) on the basis of the written opinion of the ISA and communicates this report to the designated offices.

After completing the international phase, the applicant must decide whether to pursue patent protection before specific national and regional patent offices. If so, the applicant should choose those designated offices in which to continue the processing of the international application before the expiration of the time limit, which is typically 30 months from the filing (or priority) date. This continued processing is known as the *national phase* and requirements at this stage include payment of national fees and, if necessary, translation of the application (as filed and/or amended).

If the applicant fails to meet these requirements before expiry of the time limit applicable to that country, the international application will lose its national effect. In other words, the procedure comes to an end in those Contracting States in which the international application did not enter the national phase.

Filing a PCT international application

An international application under the PCT must contain: a request; a description; one or more claims; one or more drawings, where drawings are necessary for the understanding of the invention; and an abstract. The request form is available in all PCT publication languages (i.e., Arabic, Chinese, English, French, German, Japanese, Korean, Portuguese, Russian and Spanish) and may be downloaded, free of charge, from the PCT website.[41] An online filing system, ePCT, is also available.

Any national or resident of one of the PCT Contracting States may file an international patent application. Where there are two or more applicants, at least one must be a national or resident of a Contracting State.[42] In principle, an international patent application may be filed with the applicant's national patent office or with WIPO in Geneva. In most cases, the national patent office will act as a *PCT receiving office*. If the applicant is a national or resident of a country that is a member of a regional patent organization (ARIPO, EAPO, EPO, GCCPO or OAPI), they may alternatively file the international patent application with the relevant regional patent office, if permitted under applicable national law. National security provisions may, however, oblige the applicant to file a national patent application or to request an authorization from their national patent office before filing abroad.

In general, an international patent application may be filed in any language that the receiving office is prepared to accept. At least one of the languages should also be acceptable to the ISA and a PCT publication language; otherwise, the applicant must supply a translation of the application.

When seeking patent protection through the PCT system, the applicant will potentially have to pay three sets of fees during the international phase. The first set of fees includes:

(i) a transmittal fee payable to the PCT receiving office for processing the international application;

(ii) a search fee payable to the ISA for carrying out the international search; and

(iii) an international filing fee payable to WIPO for various tasks including processing and publishing the international application, and transmitting documents to national offices.

These fees are all collected by the PCT receiving office, while WIPO collects any fees related to an optional supplementary international search. If the applicant opts for an international preliminary examination, the preliminary examination fee must be paid to the IPEA.

Another set of fees comprises those payable to the Contracting States in the national phase. Generally, this is the most expensive part of prosecuting a PCT application, because the costs include translation fees, official fees and payments for services to local patent drafters and/or patent attorneys. The official fees are paid directly to the offices concerned at the time of entering the national phase and payment of further fees may be required during the prosecution. Since the national fees vary from state to state, the patent drafter should consult the national chapters of the PCT Applicant's Guide for the exact amounts.[43] National fees must be paid in the currencies and within the time limits listed there. If any annual or renewal fees have fallen due on the international patent by the time the national phase starts, the applicant must pay these within the applicable time limit. The applicant should also consider, both now and from time to time, how the number of claims that they have presented in the patent application does and will continue to affect the fees they have to pay for annuities, examination, etc. The applicant may decide to cancel some rather than (continue to) pay a high price to maintain large claim sets with only limited strategic value.

The PCT offers some special reductions of fees for certain applicants at the international phase. A reduction of 90 percent on certain fees, including the international filing fee, is available to natural persons from certain countries filing in their own right. This same 90 percent reduction applies to any person, whether natural or not, who is a national of and resides in a state that is classed as a least-developed country by the United Nations. If there are several applicants, each applicant must satisfy those criteria. Some ISAs also provide for a reduction of the international search fee if the applicant is (or all of the applicants are) a national or resident of certain countries. In the national phase, various designated offices may grant exemptions, reductions and refunds of national fees for natural persons, universities, not-for-profit research institutes, and small and medium-sized enterprises (SMEs). The PCT Applicant's Guide contains information on fee reductions offered by ISAs and for entry into the national phase. In addition, PCT fee reductions are available to all applicants who file electronically, based on the type of filing and the format of the application submitted.

Advantages of the PCT

The main advantage of filing a PCT application is the additional time after the initial filing available to the applicant in which to decide whether or not to prosecute applications in other countries. Under the Paris Convention, the applicant generally has 12 months from the filing date of the initial application to decide in which other Convention countries they want to pursue protection for their invention; under the PCT, the applicant has at least 30 months (and more in many countries) from the date of initial filing to begin prosecuting their application elsewhere – effectively, a gain of 18 months in which the applicant can research the patentability and commercial prospects of its invention outside of the country of first filing. It also effectively postpones the costs of internationalizing a patent application, which we have already noted can be significant.

In addition to the time gained, the PCT adds value in the form of information on which applicants can base their patenting decisions. The international search report and the written opinion of the ISA give applicants a high-quality, realistic insight into their invention's likely patentability.

Another advantage of filing under the PCT is that it allows applicants to improve their applications in the international phase, for example by correcting formal defects before the receiving office, filing amendments to the claims after receiving the ISR and/or filing amendments to the entire application during the international preliminary examination procedure. Applicants may also request changes to the bibliographic data set out in the international application. All of this work will allow the applicant to submit stronger applications in the national phase before the designated atates. Moreover, the PCT has also built in a variety of safeguard measures to protect applicants from losing substantial rights as a result of procedural mistakes.

Professional tip

You can find complete information about filing a PCT application, including PCT procedures, timelines and fees, online at www.wipo.int/pct. In particular, the PCT Applicant's Guide, which is updated almost every week, contains comprehensive information on the international and national phases of the PCT procedures. You can also sign up to the monthly PCT Newsletter to keep up to date with PCT news.

Module VIII. Filing patent applications

Key words

- Power of attorney
- Declaration of inventorship
- Assignment
- Right of priority under the Paris Convention
- Priority date
- Examination of Form
- Examination of substance
- Fees
- Regional Patent Offices
- Patent Cooperation Treaty (PCT)
- International phase
- International Search
- International Publication
- International Preliminary Examination
- National phase

Self-Test

☐ What is a declaration of inventorship?

☐ An assignment document is a contract between the inventor and another party indicating that the inventor's rights have been transferred to the other party. True or false?

☐ When filing a subsequent application, what are the requirements for claiming priority of the earlier application?

☐ What is the effect, if any, of the priority date?

☐ The European Patent Office functions as a common examining office, with each Contracting State ultimately responsible for granting patents. True or false?

☐ Explain the difference between a nonprovisional utility application and a provisional utility application in the United States.

☐ What are the advantages of filing a PCT patent application?

☐ If a patent is granted under the PCT, WIPO will issue a PCT Patent that is effective in all PCT Contracting States. True or false?

☐ If a patent applicant uses the PCT, do they still need to prosecute the application in each country in which they seek protection? Why, or why not?

☐ What are receiving offices as defined in the PCT?

Module IX
Prosecuting patent applications

1.	**Responding to office actions**	**121**
2.	**Drafting responses**	**122**
3.	**Amendments**	**123**
3.1	Principle and basic requirement	123
3.2	Determining original disclosure and new matter	123
3.3	Broadening claims and adding claims	124
4.	**Getting claims allowed**	**125**
4.1	Interview	125
4.2	Responding to a second office action	125
4.3	Final office action	126
4.4	Deadlines	126
4.5	Appeal	126
4.6	Divisional applications, continuation applications and continuation-in-part applications	127
5.	**Opposition proceedings**	**127**
6.	**Issuance of the patent**	**127**

In addition to preparing and filing a high-quality patent application, a patent drafter filing in a country that requires substantive examination must skillfully and articulately advocate the patentability of their client's invention before the patent office reviewing the application.[44] This process of review is called *patent prosecution*. Should a patent examiner review the pending patent application and submit a negative office action, the patent drafter must prepare a respectful response to the patent examiner's objections and rejections in the office action. In the response, the patent drafter must explain the differences between the invention and the prior art cited by the examiner and demonstrate the patentability of the claimed invention.

The period between filing a patent application and receiving a first office action varies considerably among patent offices and from one application to another. For most patent applications in most patent offices, there is typically a long period of inactivity following the applicant's completion of the necessary filing formalities. Many patent offices have a backlog of patent applications waiting to be examined to various degrees; eventually, however, a patent examiner will review the pending application.

In some countries, an applicant must submit a separate request for examination to a patent office within several years of the filing date (typically, between three and five years). This deadline is important because if the application misses it, their application will be deemed to have been withdrawn.

As appropriate, the patent drafter may ask for an accelerated examination to obtain any official action much earlier than usual, if the patent office concerned offers such a service. The Patent Prosecution Highway (PPH) program also functions as an accelerated examination scheme.[45]

During substantive examination of patent applications, the patent examiner compares both the prior art cited by the applicant and the results of their own search of the prior art with the claims in the pending application. Most patent offices group examiners by specific technical subject. The examiners in these groups will review a vast number of patent applications for inventions that are technically closely related and so these examiners tend to become familiar with the prior art in their subject area. Some patent offices even supply their examiners with access to collections of prior art specially focused on their area of technical expertise. Of course, the patent examiners themselves typically hold science, technology or engineering degrees related to the field of the applications that they review. Many patent examiners hold advanced degrees and some even have legal training.

The prior art an examiner may cite does not necessarily constitute the earliest, best or even most original technical disclosure. They have no duty to find the earliest teaching on a given technical subject; all they have to do is to find prior art that discloses the applicant's claimed invention and which was made publicly available before the filing (or priority) date of the patent application. It is not uncommon for an examiner to find a particularly favored piece of prior art that they cite over and over again in the applications that they review.

Patent examiners often cite earlier patents and published applications as pertinent prior art, although they may also cite technical articles, books, treatises, etc.

1. Responding to office actions

After reviewing a pending application, if a patent examiner concludes that the claimed invention meets the patentability criteria, the invention is sufficiently disclosed in the pending application and the application meets all of the requirements under the law, they will proceed to grant the patent. Otherwise, a patent examiner will issue an *office action*, also known as an *official action*, *official communication* or *examination report*.

An office action represents the government's official position on the pending patent application. It may address almost any aspect of the application, from its title to the length of the abstract. The most important parts of the office action touch upon the basic questions related to the patentability of the pending claims. The patent drafter should inform their client immediately when an office action has arrived and explain the patent office's findings.

The examiner may question whether the description provides sufficient disclosure of the claimed invention for an ordinary person skilled in the art to understand and practice it: such questions are known as *enablement* rejections. The examiner may also question whether the description provides sufficient disclosure for a particular feature recited in the claims. The patent drafter can rebut these rejections by showing where the description actually discloses the allegedly missing subject matter or by arguing that the missing subject matter was sufficiently known in the prior art and hence its disclosure was not necessary for enablement. If necessary, the patent drafter may amend the pending claims so that they no longer recite this missing subject matter.

The examiner will almost always have conducted a review of the prior art and will typically find prior art that arguably *reads on* the claims – that is, prior art that is within the scope of the claims in the application as they are presently drafted. If the examiner finds even one piece of prior art that reads on one of the claims, they will reject the pending claim as having been *anticipated* by the prior art. If the examiner finds that a combination of the prior art discloses the claimed invention and that a person of ordinary skill in the art would have been

WIPO Patent Drafting Manual

Professional tip

Experience will teach you when to concede to a ruling and when to fight for better protection for your client. This is true of every patent application and every jurisdiction in the world – as is the fact that you should be similarly mindful of whether your foreign associates are working sufficiently hard on your client's behalf and when they may be toeing a line suggested (i.e., not required) for administrative efficiency.

motivated to combine the teaching from these prior art references, the examiner will reject the pending claim for obviousness. The patent drafter can rebut such a rejection by:

– arguing that the examiner has misunderstood the cited prior art reference(s);
– arguing that the examiner has misunderstood the applicant's invention and/or the pending claims;
– arguing that the lack of inventive step cannot be asserted by combining the prior art references cited by the examiner; and/or
– amending the pending claims so that they recite an invention not disclosed in, or obvious from, the cited prior art references.

The patent drafter must not be a passive actor in the patenting process. They may find, from time to time, that a patent examiner has misunderstood the claimed invention or misjudged the patentability of the claimed invention. The patent drafter should be ready to counsel their client on rebuttal in such instances, including the option of drawing the examiner's attention to additional information and documentation that offers evidence suggesting that the claims should be allowed.

2. Drafting responses

The patent drafter's reply to an office action is known as a *response*. In this reply, the patent drafter must fully answer (respond to) all of the examiner's comments on the application set out in the office action. If the patent drafter does not respond to all of the examiner's rejections and does not rebut all of the points raised, the response is likely to be considered *nonresponsive* and the patent examiner will reject the application. A patent drafter must always strive to file a complete response to an office action because not responding in full to the office action can seriously impair the client's rights.

Most of the world's patent offices impose time limits on the filing of responses to office actions. In some countries, the applicant will have a given number of months in which to respond to an office action without paying a fee, while an additional number of months may be available for responding to an office action with payment of an extension fee. In a typical office action in the United States, for example, the applicant has three months in the former instance and another three months in the latter (totaling six months). In some other countries, the applicant may be allowed to extend the period to respond to an office action only under certain limited circumstances.

The variety of time periods for response to an office action across world's patent offices is vast and hence it is essential that the patent drafter understands what is required in every country in which their client has pending patent applications. The patent drafter should also inquire whether the mailing date of the response or the date of office action is the date from which the time limit runs. Again, this may vary from country to country.

The patent drafter should explain their draft response to the office action to the client. The client may be extremely knowledgeable in the field of the invention and may be able to identify distinctions between the prior art cited by the examiner and the invention described in the pending patent application and/or the pending claims. Also, there are often choices to be made in amending a claim. Amendments that add elements that narrow the claims might overcome the cited prior art and render the claims patentable – but the patent protection conferred by the narrower claims might be no longer useful for the client's purposes, for example competitors may easily design around the narrower claims. The patent drafter should give their client the opportunity to make these choices, remembering that their client may know best which additional claim element will meet their business needs.

3. Amendments

3.1 Principle and basic requirement

In responding to the office action, when the patent drafter and applicant consider the examiner's argument to be reasoned and persuasive, they may amend the claims, typically adding limitations, and sometimes the description and drawings, if the applicant finds it worthwhile to pursue a patent with a narrower scope of protection. (See also Module VI, section 14, for more on the essential aspects of amending claims.)

When amending the application, a universal rule in most jurisdictions is that no new matter (new subject matter) beyond that originally disclosed as of the filing date may be added (except to remedy obvious mistakes, such as typographic errors). The same rule applies in principle to both the claims and the description and drawings.

The purpose of restricting amendments within the scope of the application as filed is to balance the interests of inventors and applicants and those of third parties. On the one hand, at the time of preparing a patent application, an applicant cannot possibly know all of the relevant prior art documents that the examiner might cite during the patent examination, which documents may have been published anywhere in the world in any language. It is consequently reasonable to provide the applicant with at least one opportunity to respond to the office action and, if necessary, to amend the application to comply with the patentability requirements. On the other hand, if the applicant could freely change and renew their invention to get a patent, the applicant could obtain the exclusive patent right on something that had not yet been "invented" by them as of the filing date and thus was not disclosed in the application as filed. This would run counter to the principle of the patent system, in which the exclusive patent right is granted in exchange for the disclosure of the invention to the public. It also contradicts the first-to-file principle whereby patentability is determined as of the filing date. In addition, third parties who may rely on the original disclosure as of the filing date would suffer from unpredictability and legal uncertainty if such unlimited subsequent amendments of the application were allowed.

This means that drafting a complete disclosure of the invention prior to the filing of the patent application is of paramount importance. If the examiner finds that broad claims are not fully supported by the disclosure of the invention in the description and the drawings, then that description and those drawings cannot be amended by adding "new matters" that have not been included in the original disclosure as of the filing date, for example new embodiments, to justify the broad scope of the claims. At the time when a patent drafter prepares a patent application, they cannot know what kind of rejection a patent examiner might deliver during the prosecution. Nevertheless, the patent drafter should prepare an application with sufficiently detailed disclosure of the invention and with a proper set of claims that are a solid foundation for possible amendments at the later stage.

3.2 Determining original disclosure and new matter

Examiners generally raise no objection if an applicant introduces, by amendment, further information regarding prior art, straightforwardly clarifies obscure expressions or resolves an inconsistency. When the applicant seeks to amend the description (beyond references to the prior art), drawing or claims, most of the jurisdictions share the same rule prohibiting introduction of a new matter into the description, drawing or claims after filing.

In general, the original disclosure on the filing date covers not only those matters explicitly described as of the filing date but also those matters that a person skilled in the art would recognize as inherent to or self-evident from the original disclosure *as a whole*. In other words, matters that are inherent or self-evident to a person skilled in the art from the original disclosure may be introduced in the application through an amendment even if these matters were not explicitly mentioned in the application as filed. Demonstrating that certain information is "inherently" disclosed in the application as filed typically requires more than a mere possibility or probability that a person skilled in the art *might* be able to deduce that information from the explicit disclosure; rather, it requires that the information be necessarily present in the disclosure and that the person skilled in the art would readily recognize that information from the disclosure.

Example

An application as filed describes and claims an apparatus mounted on resilient supports, without disclosing any particular kind of resilient supports.

In response to the office action, the applicant seeks to add specific information that the resilient supports could be, for example, helical springs. In the absence of explicit disclosure of the helical springs in the original application, such amendment may be regarded as introducing new matter.

If the applicant can convincingly show that, in the technical field and the particular circumstances of the claimed invention, the person skilled in the art would naturally use helical springs in mounting the apparatus on resilient supports, the inclusion of a specific reference to the helical springs may be permissible.

Similarly, if a technical feature X were clearly disclosed in the original application but its specific effect not mentioned or not mentioned fully, it may not be regarded as new matter to clarify that effect if a person skilled in the art could deduce the effect from the application as filed.

While many jurisdictions share common principles regarding permissible amendments to the description, drawings and claims, there are certain variations in what is the scope of the original disclosure as of the filing date and what constitutes impermissible new matter. In Europe, matters that are not "directly and unambiguously derivable by those skilled in the art from the original disclosure" are assumed to be new matters that cannot be introduced in the application once it is filed. Consequently, when filing a patent application before the European Patent Office (EPO), patent drafters often use extensive multiple dependent claims and explain all possible combinations of elements and features in the description as filed.

In the United States, where a reference to another patent literature is found in the description, such cross-referencing by "incorporation by reference" could be part of the original disclosure and thus could be the basis for the amendment.

When amending the claims substantially and limiting their scope, examiners may pay particular attention to the following questions.

(i)   Do the amended claims satisfy the requirement of unity of invention (see Module VI, section 11)?
(ii) Will the amended claims be seriously inconsistent with the description, meaning that the description requires corresponding amendment?
(iii) Conversely, are all amended claims supported by the description as filed?

On receipt of an office action raising lack of inventive step of the claimed invention, a patent drafter may seek to restrict the claims and revise the stated problem to emphasize a particular effect obtainable by the claimed invention, as restricted, that the prior art cited by the examiner does not achieve. Again, such modification of the "problem to be solved" by the claimed invention is permissible only if that emphasized

effect is something that is deducible from the application as filed by a person skilled in the art.

Similarly, sometimes, a patent drafter will amend the claims by introducing a negative limitation (e.g., "excluding X" or "without performing Y"), so that they can exclude some aspect of the prior art cited by the examiner. While use of such negative limitations, exclusions or disclaimer requires various special considerations, a patent drafter may approach it through the lens of new matter. In some jurisdictions, a negative limitation added by means of a new claim or by amendment will raise the issue of new matter if the subject matter being excluded does not have support in the application as filed. For example, if the original disclosure describes a genus of compounds but does not provide support for any particular species within that genus, a negative limitation excluding a particular species would raise the issue of new matter. In some other jurisdictions, a negative limitation or disclaimer with no basis in the application as filed is permissible if, for example, it is added to overcome accidental anticipation by a reference – that is, an anticipation so unrelated to and remote from the claimed invention that the person skilled in the art would never have taken it into consideration when making the invention – or to exclude parts of a claim that might exclude it as patentable subject matter (such as the word "nonhuman").

3.3 Broadening claims and adding claims

In many jurisdictions, broadening the claim by removing claimed features is permissible during the prosecution of the patent as long as no new matter is introduced. In Japan, amendment to claim a broader (generic) concept or to remove claimed features is not allowed unless such amendments do not add any new technical significance to the claims and hence do not introduce any new technical matter. In some jurisdictions, such as the EPO and China, it is not permissible to delete from an independent claim a feature that the application, as originally filed, consistently presented as being "essential" to the invention, since this amendment is regarded as introducing new matter. The patent drafter should therefore be careful about including any statement in the description asserting that feature X of embodiments is "essential" or "indispensable" for a claimed invention unless they have a particular need to do so.

Likewise, in many jurisdictions, adding a new claim during the prosecution is not prohibited as such as long as no new matter is introduced. Some jurisdictions, however, have special rules. In Japan, once a first office action is received, amendment to the claims that change the special technical feature of the invention is prohibited. Moreover, in some jurisdictions, applicants are not allowed to add a new claim after receiving a final office action. In the United States, substantial amendments to the claims cannot be made after the final office action unless the claim amendments can be characterized as:

(i) deletion of a claim;
(ii) amendments as requested or suggested by the examiner; or
(iii) amendments that raise no new issue (i.e., impose no further burden of prior art search).

Similarly, in Japan, after receiving the final office action, amendments to the claims are limited to those made for:

(i) deletion of a claim;
(ii) narrowing the already claimed feature;
(iii) correction of errors; or
(iv) clarification of an ambiguous term in response to the examiner's findings, as stated in the office action.

4. Getting claims allowed

The next step in the patent prosecution is the examiner's review of the patent drafter's response to the office action and their amendments. If they consider it necessary, the patent examiner may conduct a supplemental search for pertinent prior art, particularly where the applicant amended the claims, taking into account the prior art reference cited in the first office action. The patent examiner may consider the patent drafter's response not to be persuasive either in light of newly found prior art or in view of the prior art originally cited. If the examiner is not persuaded that the claims are patentable – giving the claims their broadest reasonable interpretation in view of the prior art – then they may issue another office action that explains the reasons they cannot allow the application and/or the claims in their present form.

4.1 Interview

Many patent offices allow patent drafters and inventors to speak with the patent examiner about the pending application. This process is known as an *interview* with the examiner. Because official business will be discussed, both parties may be required to submit complete and accurate written descriptions of the interview, these records typically becoming part of the file history for the patent application.

In preparing for the interview with the patent examiner, the patent drafter should thoroughly review the office action and the prior art cited, and be ready to explain to the patent examiner in clear, concise and persuasive language why the pending claims are patentable over the prior art. The patent drafter may want to prepare some possible additional claim amendments and share these with the patent examiner. For example, if the patent examiner and the patent drafter can work out a set of acceptable claim amendments during the interview, the review process can be successfully concluded.

During the interview, the patent drafter may learn that the examiner has been interpreting the cited prior art in a different way, or with a different nuance, from the patent drafter and their client. Once the patent drafter fully understands how the examiner sees the prior art, the patent drafter may be in a better position to:

(i) explain the prior art to the examiner (if the examiner has misinterpreted it); or
(ii) see more clearly what range of claim amendments would remedy the application.

In some countries, the patent drafter is permitted to bring the inventor to the interview, and many patent examiners find inventors' own comments and explanations to be very persuasive. Of course, the patent drafter should counsel the inventor and their client before the interview.

Patent examiners are not typically allowed to conduct interviews before issuing the first office action, but they may conduct interviews thereafter.

4.2 Responding to a second office action

If the patent examiner issues a second office action, the patent drafter will need to prepare and file another response. Any second and subsequent office actions should, hopefully, involve a narrower set of issues than the first. Additionally, if the second office action involves some of the prior art cited in the first office action, the patent drafter should be able to respond to the second office action much more quickly than they did the first.

The process of office actions and responses may be repeated until the patent examiner agrees to allow the applicant's pending claims or comes to the conclusion that the application should be rejected, or until the applicant abandons the application, perhaps because the narrowing of the claims mean that they can no longer achieve a meaningful scope of protection. For financial or administrative reasons, many patent offices do not allow the office action/response cycle to continue indefinitely, however, and progressing an application beyond second or subsequent actions may be subject to payment of additional fees.

4.3 Final office action

The potential for additional fees is sometimes signaled by a "final" office action. As already noted, the specific procedural aspects of patent prosecution vary widely across patent offices. In the United States, a final office action will require that the application be remedied to the examiner's satisfaction, appealed or abandoned. Patent examiners will not typically entertain the applicant's further arguments regarding the prior art in a response to a final office action. At this stage, the pending claims need to be amended to reflect the patent examiner's comments – and if the applicant disagrees with the patent examiner's characterization of the prior art or interpretation of the patent claims, the applicant may appeal the patent examiner's decision.

The patent examiner will sometimes allow some claims while rejecting others. They may also merely object to some claims as depending on a rejected base claim. In such situations, the patent drafter can obtain a patent for their client by canceling the rejected claims so that a patent will be issued on the remaining claims that have not been rejected. The patent drafter could even file a continuation (or divisional application) containing the rejected claims and continue to argue for their patentability in a subsequent case (see section 4.6).

Whether to accept the claims as allowed by the examiner rather than continuing to fight is a strategic decision that only the client can make – after appropriate counseling from the patent drafter.

4.4 Deadlines

The final office action will include a deadline for response. While the specific procedural requirements of the world's patent offices vary, this deadline is six months in the United States, with the first three months not requiring payment of an extension fee. The patent drafter may file a response to the final office action. The patent examiner will review the response and issue either a *notice of allowance* or an *advisory action*, which is typically a short one-page form in which the examiner states their objections to the application. The patent drafter may even prepare and submit one or more supplemental responses to the patent examiner in view of the advisory action – but, in doing so, the patent drafter must understand that the application will be abandoned on a certain date and that all prosecution must be completed by that date, unless (in the United States) the applicant files a request for continued examination and makes payment of the requisite fee to reopen examination.

If, for example, a patent drafter in the United States were to submit their reply to a *final* office action extremely close to the six-month deadline date (e.g., on the last day), then it is highly unlikely that the examiner will even review the response before the six-month deadline arises, in which case the patent application will simply go abandoned. This is because, unlike filing a response in a nonfinal office action, the filing of a response in a final office action does not itself satisfy the deadline requirements. The only actions that actually suspend the deadline are:

(i)   the examiner issuing a notice of allowance;
(ii) the examiner issuing a new, nonfinal office action;
(iii) abandoning the application;
(iv) filing a request for continued examination; or
(v)   filing a notice of appeal.

Consequently, the patent drafter must closely watch the dates related to final office actions. Even when the patent drafter files a timely response (e.g., within three months), the application can still go abandoned if one of these actions has not been taken.

4.5 Appeal

In the United States, if the examiner does not find the response to a final office action persuasive, the patent drafter can file an appeal or a request for continued examination. Many patent offices provide some form of administrative appeal for decisions made by individual patent examiners. In some jurisdictions, in cases in which the applicant wishes to challenge the decision of the patent office that rejected their application, they have the option to appeal to an administrative body (rather than a court) within a certain time limit. Such an appeal typically involves review of the patent application by a board, often a quasi-judicial body, comprising several administrative judges or senior officials who are familiar with patent examination and practices. The decisions of that body can be further appealed to a court, in accordance with the law of the country concerned. In those countries in which administrative appeal bodies do not exist, decisions of the patent office can be challenged directly before a competent court.

The specific procedures followed in appeals vary from country to country. In the United States, the patent drafter first submits a document known as an *appeal brief* and they may request an oral hearing for the appeal. Again, of course, the appeal procedure will typically involve the payment of various fees and hence the client will want to weight up the business benefit.

4.6 Divisional applications, continuation applications and continuation-in-part applications

In many jurisdictions, an alternative to appeal is the filing of some form of divisional application or a continuation application. In general, a *divisional application* is a type of a patent application that is "divided" from the previously filed application (the so-called *parent application*); thus it claims only part of the invention set out in the parent application. While a divisional application is filed later than the parent application, it may retain its parent's filing date and, in general, its priority date. In some jurisdictions, where an application is refused, the applicant has the option to file a divisional application within a certain time limit. In other jurisdictions, if an application has been refused, a divisional application may be filed at any time until expiry of the appeal period.

In the United States, a patent drafter may also or alternatively file a continuation application or a continuation-in-part application. The *continuation application* discloses and claims only subject matter disclosed in a parent application. In general, the applicant is entitled to the benefits of the filing date of the parent application. The continuation application is typically used when the applicant wants to pursue the patentability of claims that differ from those in a parent application – sometimes with only a slight change in language but in ways the applicant deems important. The *continuation-in-part application* repeats some substantial portion of the parent application and adds matter not disclosed in the parent application. It may be a convenient way of claiming enhancements developed after the parent application was filed. For a continuation-in-part application, claims to subject matter that was also disclosed in the parent application are entitled to the parent's priority date, while claims to the additional subject matter are entitled only to the filing date of the continuation-in-part application.

By comparison, divisional applications in the United States are appropriate for pursuing claims that are withdrawn in a parent application following a restriction requirement, which is akin (but not identical) to the unity of invention requirement under many national laws and the Patent Cooperation Treaty (PCT).

5. Opposition proceedings

Third parties may challenge the decision of a patent office to grant a patent and request a revocation of a patent before a court. In addition, many countries' patent systems integrate an administrative mechanism that provides third parties the opportunity to oppose the issuance of a patent. Depending on the applicable law of the country, the opposition may be conducted before the examiner reviews the patent application or after the examiner intends to grant a patent (*pre-grant opposition*) or after the patent is granted (*post-grant opposition*), or both.

In a country with a pre-grant opposition procedure, the patent examiner will send the applicant a notice that they intend to grant a patent as drafted and then publish the final, approved claim set for public opposition. If no one files an opposition to the application within the time period, a patent will be issued. If someone does file an opposition, this party must convincingly argue why the patent should not be granted, for example because the examiner has not considered a key piece of prior art, in which case they must explain why the claims lack inventive step in view of this prior art. The patent applicant is typically allowed to rebut the opponent's arguments. The opposition may be heard either by the patent examiner in charge of the application or by a special panel of examiners. The opposition results may typically be appealed by the losing party and, in many instances, the appeals can ultimately be heard by a court of law.

The patent drafter should be aware that some companies may routinely use oppositions as a mechanism to delay issuance of their competitors' patents (in jurisdictions that facilitate pre-grant opposition, after a positive determination on patentability by an examiner) and/or to reduce the scope of the claims issued to their competitors. In addition to competitors, some public interest groups may routinely oppose the issuance of patents in particular technical fields.

Requests for opposition and other necessary documents are typically prepared by patent drafters. For many, opposition practice is simply a normal part of their regular work. Consequently – and particularly in those countries that provide for opposition systems – the patent drafter should counsel their client that receipt from a patent office of notice that the office intends to grant a patent does not necessarily mean that the client will receive their patent without further delay.

6. Issuance of the patent

Once the patent examiner issues a *notice of allowance* or similar paperwork, the patent drafter will need to complete various formalities related to issuance of a patent. The patent drafter may wish to ask their client if they would like to file any form of continuation application (see section 4.6). Since a continuation application will retain the filing date of its parent application, the client might be inclined – for strategic reasons – to have a pending application in which the patent drafter can add new claims specifically tailored to counter a particular infringer.

In many jurisdictions, a patent is issued many months after the patent drafter has paid all of the necessary government fees (the time period until patent issuance may be even longer if the jurisdiction provides for an opposition process.) Unfortunately, there is not usually a way of speeding up the printing and issuance of a given patent. Once the patent is issued, the patent drafter will not typically need to take any action to maintain the patent (i.e., to keep the patent alive) beyond payment of any required periodic maintenance or annuity fees. The patent drafter should docket the dates on which they pay such fees as a service to their client; alternatively, the patent drafter must ensure that the client has acknowledged that they will manage and take responsibility for the payments or that they have arranged for a third-party payment service to do so.

Key words

- Patent prosecution
- Office action
- Amendment
- New matter
- Interview with an examiner
- Appeal
- Divisional application
- Continuation application
- Continuation-in-part application
- Opposition
- Issuance of a patent

Self-Test

☐ What is patent prosecution?

☐ What is an office action?

☐ What does it mean when claims "read on" the prior art?

☐ When drafting a response to an office action, the patent drafter needs only to respond to the most important rejections, not all of them. True or false?

☐ An examiner states, in their first office action, that the claimed invention lacks inventive step on the basis of the two prior art references, X and Y. What are the possible actions that a patent drafter could take on receipt of the action?

☐ The patent drafter should explain the office action to the inventor/applicant. True or false? Why?

☐ What is meant by adding "new matter" in the context of amendments of the description, drawings and claims?

☐ During patent prosecution, can the patent drafter speak with the patent examiner? If so, what is this process usually called?

☐ When should a patent drafter file a divisional application or continuation application? When might a patent drafter need to file a continuation-in-part application in the United States, instead of a continuation application?

☐ After a patent has been issued, the patent owner may still need to pay periodic maintenance or annuity fees to keep it in force. True or false?

Module X
Patent strategy

1.	Offensive blocking patenting to mount attacks on competitors	131
2.	Defensive patenting to protect against infringement actions	132
3.	Design-around techniques	132

Once a government patent office has granted a patent, what next? *What can its owner do with that patent?*

In a few rare instances, a single patent will be so revolutionary and pioneering that its owner can control a particular industry or a given industry segment throughout the life of the patent – but this rarely happens.

The common reasons for the failure of a patent are that they are often poorly claimed and too close to prior art. In fact, some "famous" patents were not nearly as successful at cornering a market as is commonly believed. For example, Thomas Edison received several patents related to light bulbs – but an English inventor named Joseph Swan obtained the first patent on the light bulb and, over the years, Edison had to pay royalties to Swan for the rights to use the patent. Remember from Module I that patents do not give the patent owner the right to practice the invention; rather, they grant the right to exclude others from making, using, offering for sale or selling the invention claimed in the patent without permission of the patent owner. Thus Edison had to seek permission from Swan to use the claimed invention.

As an aside, a common misconception about patents is that the patent office considers infringement issues when awarding patents. In reality, patent offices look only at prior art pertinent to the pending patent application; they do not review whether making or using the claimed invention would infringe another patent. The patent drafter will likely have to remind their clients of this fact from time to time.

Patent strategy also becomes more complicated, and typically more lucrative, as the number of patents in a portfolio increases. Holding a single patent rarely provides the same power and flexibility that holding a dozen or 100 patents provides.

Example

Company A holds a single Patent Y related to Product X. If Patent Y has been well drafted, it will likely cover several embodiments of Product X and several of its key features or components, including the use of these features and components in different/unrelated products.

Product X is highly useful but not the first product of its kind: Product X is not the very first automobile or the very first telephone or the very first computer.

If this is the case, Competitor B can make a product very similar to Product X that does not infringe Patent Y. In other words, Competitor B can "design around" Patent Y to produce its own noninfringing Product X (although this does not necessarily mean that Competitor B's design-around would be commercially viable).

What if Company A holds 10 patents related to variations of Product X in addition to Patent Y?

The other patents could provide claim coverage for additional features or components of Product X beyond those covered by Patent Y. In addition, the other patents owned by Company A might provide coverage related to the use of Product X in various commercial environments related to Product X and/or alternative variations of Product X, etc.

Competitor B will now have a much more difficult time in designing around Company A's patent portfolio to produce a noninfringing Product X. Indeed, the legal expenses related simply to studying Company A's portfolio sufficiently to understand the coverage provided by Company A's patent claims may eventually become prohibitively expensive for many competitors.

In our example, Company A's patent portfolio may eventually become large enough that it can either force its competitors to take royalty-bearing licenses to its patents or force competitors out of the market by suing them for patent infringement. If Company A's competitors have large patent portfolios of their own, Company A and these competitors can cross-license each other's patents. Such cross-licenses may either be free of charge or royalty-bearing, depending on the patents and the competitive market. A cross-license with its competitors will allow Company A to manufacture its products without fear of a lawsuit. Of course, Company A could still seek patent infringement litigation against a new competitor in the market who had no pertinent patents to cross-license.

As noted, Company A's patents are likely to provide coverage for key features or components of Product X even when they are not used in Product X. This situation can arise when a key feature or component is particularly novel and has been claimed so as not to limit the scope of coverage to only Product X. In addition to using its patents against competitors, Company A could also consider using its patents against other parties who make products that include the key features or components protected by its patents.

Company A's licensing of patents outside its own "field of use" could be quite lucrative. Typically, Company A's only costs for licensing its patents in new fields of use will be a small amount of time from one or more licensing attorneys or licensing executives, as well as – potentially, but not certainly – occasional patent litigation. Company A may, however, hesitate to litigate its patents against third parties because of concerns that the patent in suit may be declared invalid (e.g., "revoked"). Once the patent has been invalidated, Company A will no longer be able to enforce it against anyone, including its competitors.

Patent valuation is a complicated topic that relates to patent strategy. A thorough discussion of patent valuation is outside the scope of this manual, but what is known as the *real property* metaphor may be useful.

Intellectual property bears many similarities to real property. Prior art is analogous to public lands (nonpatented prior art) and/or lands already claimed by others (issued patents that are still in force). The real estate catchphrase "location, location, location" applies equally to patents: a patent whose claims fall squarely on top of a valuable invention is worth much more than a patent whose claims map to a less lucrative space. A patent as a legal instrument is analogous to the quality of a home's construction: a patent located on top of a valuable invention can still be worthless if the patent has not been properly constructed. The legal remedies associated with patent infringement are similar to the legal remedies associated with encroachment on another's real property.

1. Offensive blocking patenting to mount attacks on competitors

A patentee may employ their patents directly against any and all infringers. A patent typically does not give its owner any rights to make, use or sell the invention covered by the patent. In fact, it is quite possible to obtain a patent for an invention that might *not* be made, used or sold because doing so would infringe someone else's patent or need approval from a government regulatory agency.

If a company has manufacturing capacity, manufacturing and selling a product covered by patents is often (although not always) more lucrative than licensing the patents necessary to manufacture the product. Consequently, many patent owners who also manufacture products use their patents to force competitors either to design around their patents (and produce, hopefully, an inferior product) or to license their patents.

Some companies disburse their patent royalties to their research and development (R&D) departments as a matter of policy. This makes some sense in that the department probably created the invention that resulted in the patent by which the royalties are generated and, by channeling money from the patent licensing to the R&D department, the company may facilitate its creating more new products and services.

When a company aggressively licenses its patents to competitors, it takes from competitors the money that they could have spent on their own R&D efforts. This is sometimes known as the *$2 swing* – in the sense that every inbound licensing USD 1 from a competitor takes USD 1 away from the competitor's programs and adds USD 1 to the licensing company's programs, creating a relative USD 2 difference between the two companies.

In developing an offensive patent strategy, the patent owner should continually consider the nature of the infringement by potential licensees. The infringer could be guilty of direct infringement, contributory infringement and/or inducement of infringement. The nature of the damages may also vary based on the use of the infringing technology. Direct infringers do not necessarily incur greater damages than contributory infringers. Some country's patent laws also recognize infringement under the doctrine of equivalents. Thus a defendant who is not directly infringing a patent claim might still be considered an infringer by virtue of their use of a substantially similar component in a substantially similar manner. Analysis

Professional tip

In any licensing campaign, it is rarely a good idea to first pursue the biggest player in any given industry. Licensing campaigns are typically more successful when they start with small-to-medium-sized players in a given industry and build momentum by working toward larger ones.

under the doctrine of equivalents is quite complicated, but one key factor is whether the patent's prosecution history includes statements indicating that the patentee surrendered claim coverage for the substantially similar component during patent prosecution (another reason why responses to office actions need to be carefully worded and concise).

2. Defensive patenting to protect against infringement actions

Patents are "swords" and not "shields" in the sense that a patent does not give its owner the right to manufacture a product protected by the patent. A patent provides a negative right that allows the owner to say who *cannot* practice the invention protected by the patent. Holding a patent will provide its owner with little assurance that their manufacture of a product covered by the patent will not infringe another patent owned by someone else. Patents can, however, effectively operate as shields should patent-holding competitors refrain from suing for infringement out of fear that the new patent owner will counter-sue. When facing allegations of patent infringement, it is frequently of little help for the defendant to say that they have a patent and that their own products fall within the scope of protection accorded by that patent – unless the defendant's product is so different from the plaintiff's patent that a legal factfinder (e.g., a judge or jury) could readily see the differences between the two inventions. Even in such situations, however, it is often easier for the defendant simply to explain why they do not infringe the claims in suit.

In certain circumstances, a patent or group of patents may provide a defensive shield for a patentee against their own competitors. If Company A were to hold 5,000 patents related to Product X and its top three competitors each hold 1,500 patents, the competitors might consider suing Company A to achieve some business objective, but they would most likely refrain for fear that Company A would counter-sue for patent infringement, using its much weightier patent portfolio. Certainly, whether a given company will benefit from having more patents depends on the scope of protection covered by the company's patents, its industry segment, and its particular technical characteristics and business strategy. There is typically little reason for a company to acquire patents without a specific business purpose.

In many industries in which the major players each hold substantial numbers of patents, it is quite common for them to cross-license their patent portfolios to each other. Such cross-licenses may include some royalty formula or they may be completely free based on mutual benefit. Additionally, the cross-licenses may include a major limitation such as a field-of-use limitation, which would still permit infringement litigation should the licensee stray outside the field of use.

Example

Company A and its major competitors cross-license their patent portfolios in a nonroyalty-bearing license pertaining to the manufacture and sale of Product X. While Company A cannot sue its competitors for manufacturing and selling Product X, if one of the competitors were to produce a new Product Z by using Product X, Company A would sue the competitor for infringement related to Product Z, which uses Product X.

If Company A's patents were particularly strong and Product Z were particularly lucrative, Company A could use its patents to force the competitor to stop the continued manufacture and use of Product Z. Alternatively, Company A could grant a royalty-bearing license to the competitor for the manufacture and use of Product Z.

A patent owner can employ many tools in their efforts to determine how best to use the patents. They should probably model various economic scenarios before deciding how to exploit the patents. A simple matrix may be helpful in some situations, whereby the company can list its products and decide on a per product basis how to exploit the intellectual property related to the product. For some products, the company may decide to use the related patents in a purely defensive manner to block out all competitors; for other products, the company may decide to follow a licensing strategy.

At a high level, the company can provide estimates of its likelihood of success following each path and/or the likelihood of senior management agreeing to follow a particular approach. The options that receive the highest ratings for a given product can then be analyzed further to arrive at the company's ultimate intellectual property strategy for the product. This analysis will also likely require analysis of the strength and weaknesses of the patents involved, as well as the values of the relative markets.

Ultimately, a well-developed patent portfolio focuses on the company's core businesses and protects particular features and functions that transcend the company's specific product offerings. Also, a well-developed patent portfolio will likely create barriers to market entry and hence minimize competition.

3. Design-around techniques

Designing around one or more patents involves determining the scope of claim coverage provided by each patent. Designing around also typically involves detailed review of the patent, taking into account the prior art cited during the prosecution. Close analysis of the prosecution history of the patent application can also expose whether the applicant made any damaging admissions about the invention during prosecution (e.g., "This invention pertains to improved buggy whips and absolutely nothing else!").

The attorney performing the design-around analysis may wish to determine the precise meanings of the terms used in the patent claims by applying rules regarding patent claim construction or claim interpretation. The rules for determining the scope of claim coverage vary from jurisdiction to jurisdiction. In many, claim elements will initially receive the "plain meaning" (or ordinary meaning) of the terms recited but may be further interpreted in light of their use in the patent's description and/or in the prosecution history. If "means-plus-function" claim language is used, the attorney will need to consider how such claims are interpreted in the jurisdiction concerned.

The attorney will likely prepare their analysis in the form of an *opinion*. In some cases, the opinion may be fairly short; in other cases, it may be extremely detailed. *Opinion letters* may be quite helpful in jurisdictions in which willful infringement is severely punished. *Willful infringement* arises when an infringer knows of another party's patent and deliberately infringes it and/or when the infringer makes no effort to determine whether or not they infringe the patent. Obtaining a noninfringement or invalidity opinion from a neutral attorney may provide a defense to willful infringement in many of the jurisdictions that recognize it. The damages associated with willful infringement are typically a multiple of the actual or direct damages for patent infringement. Obtaining a noninfringement or invalidity opinion may be helpful even in a jurisdiction that does not recognize willful infringement, since such opinions can provide valuable guidance to a company on whether a competitor's patent might be an infringement problem.

Patent opinions are typically written by an attorney – usually by a patent attorney. Many law firms and attorneys will not prepare opinions because of the high possibility of a malpractice suit should the opinion turn out to be inadequately prepared. Of course, an attorney will not typically write an opinion for a client if, in the attorney's opinion, the client really *is* infringing a valid patent. In such situations, the attorney typically expresses their concerns in a nonpermanent medium (e.g., verbally). Because a patent drafter has in-depth knowledge of a particular technology, they may assist the attorney in preparation of an opinion.

Opinions of attorneys in many countries are typically protected by attorney–client privilege and do not need to be disclosed to adverse parties during litigation. A plaintiff typically must seek special permission from the court to compel a defendant to produce an opinion. Accordingly, whenever a company has an opinion prepared by its attorney, the appropriate persons in the company should make sure that the opinion is retained by the company in strictest confidence and not shared with anyone other than the company's key executives, if and as necessary. Additionally, the opinion should not be provided to the company's customers.

Note that reliance on an opinion of an attorney may result in a waiver of attorney–client privilege for all opinions relating to the same subject matter. In some circumstances, the company may share its opinions with other parties using a vehicle known as either a *common interest agreement* or a *joint defense agreement*. The preparation of such agreements is beyond the scope of this manual.

Key words

- Design-around
- Infringement
- Offensive patent strategy
- Defensive patent strategy

Self-Test

☐ The patent office considers infringement issues when awarding patents. True or false?

☐ What is offensive blocking patenting?

☐ A patent gives the owner the right to practice the invention. True or false?

☐ Explain how a patent can effectively operate as a "shield."

☐ What is meant by the term "design around" with respect to patents?

Module XI
Organizing, educating and motivating the technical team

1. Training management personnel and marketing personnel to understand the significance of patents and portfolio building   135

2. Training scientists/technologists to understand what might be patentable and who might be a co-inventor, and to prepare invention disclosures   137

3. Setting up an in-house patent review committee to periodically review invention disclosures and make patenting recommendations   138

4. Inventor incentive programs to encourage inventors to invent and report   138

5. Professional ethics   139

A patent drafter will probably find that no two of their clients are alike. Some clients will simply want to obtain one or two patent applications, while others will want to establish patenting as a routine, ongoing program. The patent drafter should always be willing to raise their clients' awareness about the benefits of obtaining patents and they can help clients to develop a *patent culture*.

Once a patent culture has been established within an organization or company, its scientists, engineers and managers will routinely consider patents and other intellectual property rights in the company's decision-making process. Intellectual property will no longer be an "occasional" endeavor but a routine part of its business.

The patent drafter will likely want to identify certain key members of their client's organization. In addition to the key decision-makers, the patent drafter should also identify the organization's technical "gatekeepers" – that is, those within the organization who are highly adept at introducing new technologies to the company. They are likely to be key inventors of new products and services, and are also typically those with whom the other scientists and engineers discuss and brainstorm their own ideas.

The patent drafter can help clients to establish internal patent program infrastructure. A major component of such infrastructure is some form of a *patent review committee*, which oversees development of the organization's patent portfolio. Another key component is some form of incentive program to encourage inventors to report their inventions to the patent drafter.

The patent drafter can also assist clients in developing internal procedures for handling patent-related documents, such as invention disclosure forms, patent applications, prior art collections and issued patents. The patent drafter can help clients to establish patent docketing systems and procedures, so that critical dates are not missed – while the patent drafter must take care to put such a system in place for their own purposes. A *docketing system* is basically a diary program that feeds through patent information such as when responses to office actions must be filed, when foreign filing decisions must be made, when annuities must be paid, etc.

While the patent drafter should not themselves seek to create inventions for their clients (this can present a conflict of interests), they can certainly help their clients to establish an enabling environment within which creativity is likely to flourish. Important to this mission is educating and motivating the client's prospective inventors on the use and value of the patent system, as well as making sure that the client has the appropriate infrastructure in place to organize and control the organization's invention-reporting mechanisms, so that patent applications can be filed before critical deadlines.

1. Training management personnel and marketing personnel to understand the significance of patents and portfolio building

The patent drafter may find it helpful to offer learning opportunities to their clients' senior management team. If their offer is accepted, the patent drafter will have a perfect opportunity to raise awareness within the client organization about the benefits of patenting and to dispel any lingering misunderstandings. Many management teams are, however, extremely busy and may not be easily able to take advantage of the offer.

In the alternative, the patent drafter can take the initiative to discuss the benefits of patenting with individual managers in the organization on an ad hoc basis, whenever the opportunity (or need) arises. The patent drafter may also seek out opportunities to address larger audiences to generate interest in patents.

The patent drafter should seek out opportunities to raise awareness among their client's engineering, scientific and management teams, as well as marketing staff, of the benefits of patenting. Engineers and scientists often do not know the proper procedures to follow in reporting their inventions, and many engineers and scientists do not fully understand the strategic and business value of patents to their organization or research institute. The same is true of marketing staff, whose expertise and input are frequently overlooked in decisions about what should be patented. Often, companies lack sufficient resources to exploit the full benefits of inventions that have patenting potential.

Unfortunately, many patent drafters will find that there are key managers within their client's organization who are either ignorant of the value of patenting or hostile to the notion. Admittedly, not every organization can benefit from patents and some managers may have experienced them negatively. Their hostility may be underpinned not by resistance in the abstract but by experience of a patenting program that has, or they believe to have, harmed the company (or another company for which they formerly worked) in some way. The sensitive patent drafter will come to understand this experience and develop ways of diminishing that resistance. And they can usefully highlight that even companies in the beverage industry, such as Coca Cola®, which cannot patent their primary products, hold fairly substantial patent portfolios.

One useful tool with which the patent drafter can supply their clients is the *invention disclosure form* (see Annex B for an example). Researchers or engineers can fill out this form to describe in brief a potentially patentable invention. Over time and with experience, the patent drafter may arrive at other questions that will add value to the invention disclosure form for specific clients or clients in particular industries. They may also want to tailor their invention disclosure form template to specific clients by including the company's logo or other company-specific information, such as its internal docketing numbers for patents and patent applications.

The patent drafter will also learn over time how to process invention disclosure forms for particular clients. Because of potential time bars to patent filing (e.g., after a public disclosure of the invention), the patent drafter should accept the invention disclosure form whatever its condition on arrival. They then need to determine whether the time bar has arisen or is about to arise and take action accordingly. Processing of the form will follow.

If the form is brought before a patent review committee, the inventor should be encouraged to join the meeting and inform discussion of their invention. If they cannot do so, they should arrange for someone else to advocate the invention on their behalf, because the patent review committee may not understand its significance or may have questions about it.

Organizations with fairly sophisticated patenting programs may have strategic maps characterizing and identifying inventions specific to a product, a product category or an entire industry segment. If the client has developed such a tool, any invention disclosed should be positioned on that map. Of course, many small clients will not have such a strategic map.

Another benefit of the invention disclosure form is that it will provide evidence of inventorship, especially when co-signed by a noninventor, the rules of which may vary from country to country. Under the first-to-file principle, determining who invented the invention first is generally irrelevant to patentability, but issues arise in relation to who is the inventor and thus entitled to a patent in the first place. Similarly, invention disclosure forms may also offer secondary evidence in the event that the inventor has assigned their rights to an invention to a third party, such as their employer.

Some patent systems require that patent applications disclose the best mode known to the inventors for carrying out the invention. Invention disclosure forms may be helpful here as well.

Conversely, invention disclosure forms can pose risk to the company. Consider, for example, how a defendant might use a patent holder's invention disclosure form during infringement litigation. The defendant might use the form as evidence in arguing for a particular construction of the patented claims based on some limiting language that appears in the invention disclosure form. Similarly, a defendant might argue that the inventor engaged in inequitable conduct by pursuing their patent without disclosing known prior art if the original invention disclosure form mentions that prior art. To mitigate this risk, a patent drafter should offer training to ensure that their client's staff know how to complete an invention disclosure form properly. Similarly, the patent drafter should help their client to ensure that information disclosure issues are properly and professionally handled.

The company should select for patenting those inventions that will result in the highest return on investment to the organization – either through direct licensing of the patent or through higher sales of a product protected by a patent.

Professional tip

Always try to understand how the patent application you are preparing will serve your client's needs. This will guide you in drafting the claims and in making decisions on additional claim limitations during patent prosecution.

Remember too that effectively selecting the best inventions for patenting may mean consulting people with a wider cross-section of skills than those of the team of scientists and engineers who created the invention.

Example

Engineer Y has created two inventions, A and B. Invention A is an extremely brilliant solution for a minor problem related to the company's least successful product. Invention B is a fairly mundane, but still probably patentable, enhancement to the company's most successful product. The company can afford to patent only one invention at this time.

Because Invention A is so technically brilliant, Engineer Y advocates that it be patented. The patent drafter discusses the invention with Marketing Manager Z, who informs the patent drafter that the enhancement provided by Invention B would boost the company's product sales by 75 percent.

Taking into consideration the important information provided by the marketing department, the company's management opts to file a patent on Invention B.

In reality, the scenario set out in our example is likely to present other complicating factors, such as the ease with which a competitor could design around a patent on Invention B, as well as how broadly Invention B could be patented. If Invention B were not to appear to be patentable in a meaningful way, the company would be better served by patenting Invention A.

2. Training scientists/technologists to understand what might be patentable and who might be a co-inventor, and to prepare invention disclosures

In addition to raising awareness of the value of patents, the patent drafter should ensure that key engineers and scientists within the organization understand certain key points about the patent process. Identifying and empowering a *patent advocate* within the client's organization can be invaluable – likely to be a key inventor who is well respected by their peers (i.e., a technical gatekeeper), who can share with both those peers and the patent drafter observations about opportunities emerging in the engineering laboratory.

We have noted too that invention disclosure forms involve time-critical decisions. The patent drafter must either ensure that someone within the client organization not only provides forms to the scientists and engineers but also can support them with the forms' completion. Alternatively, the patent drafter may agree with the client simply to conduct an interview with the inventor(s) to obtain all the information contained on a typical invention disclosure form.

Example

The client wants to obtain a patent on an invention pertaining to Product W, which it will be displaying at a trade show within two weeks. Unless a patent application is filed within the next two weeks, the client will lose all rights to patent the product in most countries that provide a grace period of only very narrow scope.

This is an important piece of information that the patent drafter needs to know immediately.

Fortunately, they have established a patent advocate within the company, who learns of the forthcoming product disclosure and informs the patent drafter well

Professional tip

You may need to enlist the support of managers in investigating and enforcing inventorship requirements. Moreover, it should be apparent that you must decline to prepare a patent application for someone whom you know does not own the subject invention.

ahead of the two-week deadline. The patent drafter gets to work immediately, aiming to file a patent application for their client before the critical date.

Had there been no advocate in place, the patent drafter would have had the difficult task of explaining that patenting of Product W is no longer possible in some of the jurisdictions of interest to the client.

A patent drafter may find that their clients pay significantly more attention to patents either when they realize that they have missed the opportunity to patent a key invention or when a competitor sues – or threatens to sue – them for patent infringement. As difficult as this situation may be, it can raise awareness in the long term, helping the patent drafter to protect their client's own valuable inventions.

Whether they gather it with an invention disclosure form or by interview, the patent drafter will need access to key basic information about an invention before preparing the patent application. Certain key dates related to the invention are necessary to verify that the invention is still patentable; likewise information on the inventor(s), so that the patent drafter can identify the possible universe of inventorship for that application. The patent drafter may need to be firm and direct when exploring inventorship: it is not uncommon for senior managers to insist that they have provided an inventive contribution merely by sponsoring or supervising work, but few of the world's patent laws would recognize them as such (meaning that practice in relation to patent applications is very different from that when attributing authorship of scientific papers). Conversely and for diverse reasons, some of those who provided an inventive contribution may not to want to be named as (one of) its inventor(s). Under the Paris Convention, inventors have the right to be mentioned as such in the patent; in many countries, inventors are permitted to waive this right.

Should the patent drafter file a patent application that fails to accurately identify the inventors, that application may be held to be invalid. In the worst case, should they do so knowingly, the application may be considered fraudulent and the patent drafter may expose themselves to malpractice suits. Consequently, they may frequently find themselves conducting inventorship investigations, aiming to remove from the list of inventors those who did not provide an inventive contribution.

3. Setting up an in-house patent review committee to periodically review invention disclosures and make patenting recommendations

As noted at the start of this module, some clients may valuably establish a patent review committee that periodically assesses invention disclosures and makes recommendations on what the organization should be patenting. The patent drafter may sit on the committee and provide advice regarding patentability and other related matters, but they must not drive the client's patenting decisions. Other members of the patent review committee will include the client's key scientists, engineers and inventors, as well as a member of the client's marketing staff. A key member of the client's senior management team may also offer valuable insight and build buy-in at the top.

The committee should meet regularly if it is to be effective, helping the company to sustain a dynamic patent strategy that reflects the marketplace and business environment.

4. Inventor incentive programs to encourage inventors to invent and report

A creative person who conceives patentable inventions that are ignored and unrecognized may either stop inventing or stop reporting their inventions – and the organization will lose a precious opportunity to benefit from the inventor's talent. To maintain motivation and morale among the inventive team, many companies offer some sort of reward to their inventors for patentable contributions.

The nature of the reward will vary. Some companies include specific incentives in their employment contracts with particularly important inventors. Compensation schemes can involve:

(i) the payment of a small sum for completing an invention disclosure;
(ii) the payment of a slightly larger sum when a patent application is filed with the patent office; or
(iii) the payment of a larger sum when the patent is issued.

Few companies reward inventors at all of these junctures, with most companies offering either (i) and (iii) or (ii) and (iii).

Some organizations compensate their inventors whenever the patent on their invention is successfully licensed. This approach is common among universities. For example, a university might offer its inventors either a small fixed percentage of the royalties from their inventions or a larger percentage of the royalties on condition that these funds will be invested in the inventor's laboratory. Alternatively, a university may divide and disburse the proceeds from licensing as both a monetary reward to the inventors and a contribution to the inventors' laboratory or department. Some particularly significant inventors have been known to have staff whose salary is paid entirely by the inventor's patent royalties. This type of licensing compensation is usually paid in addition to any other incentives that an inventor might receive, such as those set out above.

In addition to such reward schemes, many organizations often provide other, more personal, recognition programs. Some will give an inventor a framed copy of their patent or a special plaque bearing information about the patent. Others might offer quirkier recognition, such as a jacket on which the patent's number is embroidered above the breast pocket. Many organizations hold an annual inventor recognition dinner, usually attended by significant members of the organization's senior management team, such as the president or chief executive officer, who will thank the inventors for their creations and express sincere gratitude for their efforts. These programs add an emotional element to the compensation scheme that some inventors may deeply appreciate and which can have a keenly positive impact on motivation and incentive.

If a client asks the patent drafter for advice on compensation programs for inventors, however, it is important also to mention to the client that inventor compensation programs can intersect with other areas of the law, such as securities law and employment law. For example, the company will likely be required to publish its inventor compensation policy and follow it rigorously, and if the program effectively amounts to an ad hoc gift from the company to an inventor, this may be difficult to explain to government securities regulators. As is the case in so many areas of patent drafting, these rules and requirements vary across jurisdictions and the patent drafter should understand the laws around ownership of inventions in their own jurisdiction and those of interest to their clients. For example, in the United States, an inventor owns their creations as a matter of law, but U.S. employment law typically allows employment contracts to force inventors to assign all rights to work created in the course of employment to their employer without any additional compensation. In contrast, in Germany, companies must provide their inventors with additional compensation for the patentable inventions that they create in the course of their employment. While the patent drafter is not expect to counsel their clients on matters of employment law, the patent drafter will need to know who owns the inventions for which patent protection is sought.

5. Professional ethics

In many countries, only regulated professionals can represent applicants and prosecute patent applications before the patent office. Known as *patent attorneys* or *patent agents*, they are required to abide by the professional ethics and rules of the relevant jurisdiction(s). This section primarily applies to patent drafters who hold such a title, but any patent drafter should be mindful of professional ethics and hence what follows has wide application.

Many jurisdictions maintain a code of ethics to which all patent attorneys and patent agents must subscribe to continue their professional practice. The ethics codes for patent professionals in some jurisdictions have been modeled on that jurisdiction's code of ethics for *all* legal professionals. Some jurisdictions also track complaints sent to the patent office either by clients or by legal organizations such as bar associations: a patent attorney who loses their license to practice law also typically loses their license to represent clients before the patent office.

The patent drafter must familiarize themselves with the relevant code of ethics for their own jurisdiction and the jurisdictions of interest to their clients. Ethics codes typically model common sense. If a patent drafter asks themselves, *Does this seem proper or fair?* and answers "No," then they should think again about taking the action, whatever it is (not least because ethics codes are not exhaustive and even if a situation is not covered by an ethical rule, it may still be considered malpractice).

The following are some of the rules likely to be common among national or regional codes of ethics.

(i) **A patent drafter should never knowingly file an invalid patent application (a time-barred invention, a nonenabling description, etc.).**
From time to time, a patent drafter may need to file an application that will provoke a challenge from the government, the result of which may be that the application will not be patented. For instance, in the United States, many early biotech inventions were of questionable patentability at the time they were filed. In fact, the question of patentability of biotech inventions was decided ultimately not by the USPTO but by the U.S. Supreme Court. It was entirely ethical for the patent drafter to file the application that led to the challenge; however, it might have been of questionable ethics for the patent drafter not to advise their client beforehand that the application may well provoke a challenge.

(ii) **The patent drafter must keep their client informed of developments in their applications and patents.**
For example, a patent drafter should notify their client, well before the due date for response, that an office action has been received from the patent office. The patent drafter should ask their client to review the draft response to the office action before filing it with the patent office.

(iii) **The patent drafter must keep abreast of changes in the rules and procedures applicable to their area of practice.**

The patent drafter should also notify their client(s) of these rule changes when they could impact a pending case.

(iv) **The patent drafter must always be honest in their communications with the patent office and with their clients.**

In practice, this means that a patent drafter cannot advocate the patentability of an invention even when they personally have doubts. Compare the following two situations.

(a) The patent examiner says that the client's pending claims are shown completely in Figure 1 of a prior art reference. The patent drafter agrees with the examiner but files a response intentionally mischaracterizing the reference and arguing that the pending claims are *not* shown in the prior art reference.

(b) The patent examiner says that the client's pending claims are shown completely in Figure 1 of a prior art reference. The patent drafter finds the language used in the reference to be ambiguous and believes the patent examiner to have construed the reference with hindsight, in light of the client's pending application. They frame their response accordingly.

Situation (a) is probably unethical in most jurisdictions; situation (b) is likely to be ethical.

(v) **The patent drafter should always perform the work they have agreed to perform and perform it on time.**
A patent drafter cannot tell a client that they will prepare a patent application and then fail to deliver. If the patent drafter knows that they will not be able to prepare the application in time, they should not accept the work. If the patent drafter has already accepted the work, they should notify the client as soon as they know that they will not be able to complete it, so that the client can urgently find another patent drafter to do so. A patent drafter should never be the primary cause of a client's failure to obtain patent protection for their valuable invention.

(vi) **The patent drafter must be an advocate for their client.**
Initial responses from the patent office to many patent applications are commonly negative. The patent drafter cannot simply report to their client that the application has been rejected and not inform the client that a response to this first office action is possible. There are certainly times when the prior art cited by the patent office is so compelling that the client would be unlikely to obtain meaningful protection and so will abandon the application, but this is not the typical situation.

The patent drafter should not draft only narrow patent claims unless their client has requested only narrow claims. A patent application with narrow claims is more likely to obtain patent protection than a patent application with broad claims, but the narrow claims will likely deprive the client of the full scope of protection to which they are entitled. As noted elsewhere in this manual, the patent office has no duty to tell the patent drafter or the inventor that broader claims are possible; the patent office awards only those claims it receives. It will not object to claims as being too narrow.

Similarly, the patent drafter should not indulge the whims of the patent examiner simply to expedite allowance of a case unless they have informed the client and received the client's explicit permission to accept a narrower scope than that to which they may properly be entitled. In short, the patent drafter must always be ready to argue on their client's behalf.

Being a patent drafter is more than a matter of completing forms and drafting technical documents; it includes a duty to prosecute their client's applications with all the care that the patent drafter would take if they were themselves the inventor. A client places an enormous amount of trust in their patent drafter – and the patent drafter must prove themselves worthy of that trust.

(vii) **The patent drafter must be mindful of conflicts of interest.**
A patent drafter cannot position the interests of one client over the interests of another. If a patent drafter were to file two applications disclosing similar claims for two different clients and both applications were pending at the same time such that the patent examiner cites one application as prior art over the other, the patent drafter will need either to amend the claims of one application to become patentable over the other or argue that one application is not pertinent to the other – *but how can they do so while vigorously advocating the best interests of each client?*
Many ethics codes recognize that a patent drafter in such circumstances cannot appropriately perform this task under *any* circumstances. Consequently, the patent drafter must carefully screen the work they accept from their clients to avoid possible conflicts of interest. If a conflict of interest arises despite the patent drafter's best efforts, many jurisdictions require the ethical patent drafter to transfer both of the conflicting applications to new counsel. The patent drafter must steadfastly avoid situations in which they will have to choose sides between their own clients.

Key words

- Patent docketing system
- Incentive program
- Technical gatekeeper
- Patent review committee
- Professional ethics
- Conflict of interest

Self-Test

☐ What is a "technical gatekeeper" and how might they play an important role in establishing a patent culture within an organization?

☐ List several people who should be on an organization's patent review committee.

☐ How can a patent drafter create an environment that values patents in an organization?

☐ How should an invention disclosure form be used?

☐ What is a code of ethics for patent attorneys or patent agents? Provide three examples of ethics rules.

Annexes

Annex A	**Examples of databases**	**143**
Annex B	**Example of an invention disclosure form**	**144**
Annex C	**WIPO resources and tools**	**147**

Annex A
Examples of databases

PATENTSCOPE (www.wipo.int/patentscope)

PATENTSCOPE is a database maintained by the World Intellectual Property Organization (WIPO). It provides access to international Patent Cooperation Treaty (PCT)[46] applications in full-text format on the day of publication, as well as to patent documents published by national and regional patent offices that are collaborating with WIPO.[47]

Information may be searched by entering keywords, the names of applicants, International Patent Classifications (IPCs) and many other criteria in multiple languages. As of June 2020, the search interface is available in 10 languages (Arabic, Chinese, English, French, German, Japanese, Korean, Portuguese, Russian and Spanish).

Note that PCT international applications are published 18 months from their filing (or priority) date. Similarly, pending patent applications in most countries are published only 18 months after filing (or 18 months from the priority date).

Patent databases of national/regional patent offices

Many national and regional patent offices publish patent applications and granted patents on their own websites. Some offices also publish applications or granted patents in hard copy (e.g., in the Official Gazette). In some countries, only bibliographic information is published online or in hard copy. In those countries, those who wish to access full contents of published applications or patents may need to visit the patent office and inspect the file held there.

Examples of online databases maintained by national and regional patent offices can be found at www.wipo.int/patentscope/en/national_databases.html

Contact information for the national and regional patent offices, including the URLs of their websites, is available at www.wipo.int/members.

Patent databases may also be found by visiting a national or regional office's own website.

Scientific databases

There are different scientific and technical databases that are specific to various fields of technology. It is helpful for a patent drafter to become familiar with these databases, since they contain articles that discuss technological advances in the field. Because prior art encompasses more than only patent documents, screening these scientific databases is important when conducting a thorough patentability (prior art) search.

Annex B
Example of an invention disclosure form

Confidential
Disclosure No.: _____
Status: _____

Invention Disclosure Form

Name: _____
Work phone number: _____
Email address: _____

1. PROPOSED TITLE: _____

2. FIELD OF INVENTION _____

A. This invention relates primarily to:

_____

3. BACKGROUND AND RELATED ART

A. The technical problem addressed by the invention is as follows:

_____

B. The closest related art is described as follows:

_____

C. The advantages presented by the invention are as follows:

_____

4. DRAWING(S)

Drawings for this invention are available/not available. If available, please attach.
COMMENTS about drawings provided:

_____

5. WRITTEN DESCRIPTION

The invention is described as follows:

_____

Note 1: Please attach additional pages as necessary.
Note 2: If you have other documents and/or drawings related to the invention, please attach copies to this form.

6. INVENTOR(S) (this section must be completed)

INVENTOR 1: _____

Name: _____

Residence address: _____

Citizenship: _____

INVENTOR 2: _____

Name: _____

Residence address: _____

Citizenship:

COMMENTS on inventors or inventorship (please make a note if any of the inventors reside out of the country).

_____

7. DATES OR PRODUCT TESTING AND RELEASE

Alpha testing: _____

Beta testing: _____

General release or sale: _____

Offers for sale: _____

COMMENTS on product testing and release:

_____

8. DISCLOSURE OF INVENTION

Has there been any disclosure to or use of the invention by the public? Any expected future disclosure of the invention? When and to whom? Under a non-disclosure agreement?

_____

Please attach a copy of any disclosure and/or nondisclosure agreement.

9. INTERNAL DISCLOSURE(S)

First internal disclosure date: _____

Name of first person to whom invention was disclosed: _____

COMMENTS about first internal disclosure: _____

10. ARTICLE(S)

Have any articles been published?

_____

DETAILS about publication of articles(s):

_____

Please attach a copy of any published article(s).

11. ADVERTISEMENTS, PRESS RELEASES AND PRODUCT ANNOUNCEMENTS

Any advertisements, press releases or product announcements?

_____

DETAILS about any advertisements, press releases and product announcements:

_____

Please attach copies of any advertisements, press releases and/or product announcements.

12. OUTSIDE DISCLOSURE(S)

Have there been any disclosures outside the company?

_____

Were all outside disclosures under a nondisclosure agreement?

_____

DETAILS about any disclosures outside the company:

_____

Please attach copies of any information disclosed and/or any nondisclosure agreement.

13. TRADE SHOWS AND CONFERENCES

Are there any upcoming trade shows or conferences?

_____

DETAILS about upcoming trade shows and/or conferences:

_____

ADDITIONAL COMMENTS BY INVENTOR:

_____
_____
_____

Signed: Witnessed and understood by:

_____   _____

Date: _____   Date: _____

Annex C
WIPO resources and tools

Guides and other publications

Certain Aspects of National/Regional Patent Laws, Revised Annex II of Document SCP/12/3 Rev.2: Report on the International Patent System (2020): www.wipo.int/scp/en/annex_ii.html
Finding Technology Using Patents: An Introduction (2015): www.wipo.int/publications/en/details.jsp?id=173&plang=EN
Guide to Technology Databases (2012): www.wipo.int/publications/en/details.jsp?id=249&plang=EN
Guide to Using Patent Information (2015): www.wipo.int/publications/en/details.jsp?id=180&plang=EN
Identifying Inventions in the Public Domain: A Guide for Inventors and Entrepreneurs (2020): www.wipo.int/publications/en/details.jsp?id=4501
Inventing the Future: An Introduction to Patents for Small and Medium-Sized Enterprises, Intellectual Property for Business Series No. 3 (2018): www.wipo.int/edocs/pubdocs/en/wipo_pub_917_1.pdf

Tools and web pages

Directory of Intellectual Property Offices: www.wipo.int/directory/en/urls.jsp
International Patent Classifications (IPC): www.wipo.int/classifications/ipc
Opposition and Administrative Revocation Mechanisms: www.wipo.int/scp/en/revocation_mechanisms
Patents: What Is a Patent? www.wipo.int/patents
PATENTSCOPE database and user guides: www.wipo.int/patentscope
PCT: The International Patent System: www.wipo.int/pct
PCT Applicant's Guide, The: www.wipo.int/pct/en/guide/index.html
PCT FAQs: www.wipo.int/pct/en/faqs/faqs.html
PCT Newsletter: www.wipo.int/pct/en/newslett
Utility Models: www.wipo.int/patents/en/topics/utility_models.html
What Is Intellectual Property? www.wipo.int/about-ip
WIPO Academy, Distance Learning Advanced Course, 'Patents', DL301: https://welc.wipo.int/acc/index.jsf?page=courseCatalog.xhtml&lang=en
WIPO Lex Database Search: https://wipolex.wipo.int/en/main/legislation
WIPO Pearl: WIPO's Multilingual Terminology Portal: www.wipo.int/reference/en/wipopearl

Endnotes

Endnotes

1 Article 1(2) of the Paris Convention for the Protection of Industrial Property (Stockholm Act 1967) reads as follows: "The protection of industrial property has as its object patents, utility models, industrial designs, trademarks, service marks, trade names, indications of source or appellations of origin and the repression of unfair competition."

2 This definition is found in Article 27.1 of the Agreement on Trade-Related Aspects of Intellectual Property Rights (TRIPS). Some countries replace "involve an inventive step" with "are non obvious" and "capable of industrial application" with "useful-" These terms are synonymous, but they are not identical, as we will discuss.

3 In some countries, designs may be protected as "design patents" (e.g., China and the United States). In the United States, "plant patents" may be obtained on "any distinct and new variety of plant, including cultivated sports, mutants, hybrids and newly found seedlings, other than a tuber propagated plant or a plant found in an uncultivated state."

4 The *priority date* may be relevant if a patent application claims priority of an earlier application on the same invention that was filed in another jurisdiction. The priority date is the filing date of that earlier application. See Module VIII, section 2.

5 *Merck & Co., Inc.* v. *TEVA PHARMACEUTICALS USA*, 288 F. Supp. 2d 601 (D. Del. 2003).

6 Article 27.1 of the TRIPS Agreement treats these terms as synonymous. However, they are not exactly so.

7 35 U.S. Code § 101 ("Inventions patentable").

8 Article 2(1) of the Patent Act (Act No. 121 of 1959).

9 Article 52(2) EPC.

10 Article 52(3) EPC.

11 The administrative rules for filing a patent application are described in Module VIII.

12 As in Article 5 PCT, the term "description" is used in this manual. In some countries, the terms "description" and "specification" are used interchangeably; in other countries, the term "specification" embraces both the description and the claims.

13 See www.fiveipoffices.org/activities/globaldossier/CAF

14 Giles S. Rich, "The Extent of the Protection and Interpretation of Claims: American Perspectives" (1990) 21 Int'l Rev. Indus. Prop. & Copyright L. 497, 499.

15 EPO Guidelines for Examination, Chapter IV, paragraph 1 ("General"), available at www.epo.org/law-practice/legal-texts/html/guidelines /e/f_iv_1.htm

16 EPO Guidelines for Examination, Chapter IV, paragraph 2.11 ("Technical features"), available at www.epo.org/law-practice/legal-texts/html/ guidelines/e/f_iv_2_1.htm

17 One possible way of avoiding the transitional phrase "comprising" being interpreted as a closed phrase is to include a sentence in the description along the following lines: "Throughout the description and claims, the word 'comprise' and variations of the word are not intended to exclude other elements, technical features, limitations, additives, components or steps."

18 Claim sets and independent/dependent claims are explained in section 3.

19 Note that this is different from adding text for clarity where there are multiple labeled drawings, e.g. "(13 – Figure 3; 14 – Figure 4)." This type of approach is unobjectionable in many jurisdictions.

20 In a few countries, "omnibus claims," which include a general reference to the description or drawings without providing any specific limitations, are allowed. Examples of omnibus claims are "1. An apparatus for harvesting corn as described in the description," or "1. A juice machine as shown in Figure 4."

21 Named for the case *Ex parte Jepson*, 243 Off. Gaz. Pat. Off. 525 (Ass't Comm'r Pat. 1917).

22 EPO Guidelines for Examination, Chapter IV, paragraph 2.2 ("Two-part form"), available at www.epo.org/law-practice/legal-texts/html/ guidelines/e/f_iv_2_2.htm

23 Based on EP 463,756 B1.

24 EPO Guidelines for Examination, Chapter IV, paragraph 3.2 ("Number of independent claims"), available at www.epo.org/law-practice/legal-texts/html/guidelines/ e/f_iv_3_2.htm

25 All issued patents begin with Claim 1.

26 Based on EP 463,756 B1.

27 See Article 26 PCT, "Opportunity to correct before Designated Offices."

28 For the text of the Treaty, see www.wipo.int/treaties/en/registration/budapest

29 Taking its name from the case *In re Beauregard*, 53 F.3d 1583 (Fed. Cir. 1995).

30 Taking its name from the case *In re Lowry*, 32 F.3d 1579 (Fed. Cir. 1994).

31 It is said that a defendant accused of infringing a claim for two "perfectly aligned" elements argued that while it did indeed align its own elements, it did not do so "perfectly."

32 PCT International Search and Preliminary Examination Guidelines, Part III ("Examiner considerations common to both the international searching authority and the international preliminary searching authority"), Chapter 10 ("Unity of invention"), Rule 10.17, available at www.wipo.int/pct/en/texts/ispe/10_11_19.html

33 In this example, the reference number "102" indicates that the number "102" is allocated to the warning device on one or more of the drawings contained in the application. Reference number schemes for drawings will be discussed in section IV.

34 The World Intellectual Property Organization (WIPO) hosts databases of national/regional/international intellectual property laws (see https://wipolex.wipo.int/en/main/legislation) and lists the contact details of national/regional IP authorities (see www.wipo.int/members).

35 Contact information for the patent offices and links to their websites is available at www.wipo.int/directory

36 The expressions "national phase" and "international phase" do not appear in the PCT but are convenient shorthand customarily used.

37 As at June 1, 2020, the following national and regional patent offices were considered competent ISAs under the PCT: Australia, Austria, Brazil, Canada, Chile, China, Egypt, Finland, India, Israel, Japan, the Philippines, the Republic of Korea, the Russian Federation, Singapore, Spain, Sweden, Turkey, Ukraine, the United States, the European Patent Office, the Nordic Patent Institute and the Visegrad Patent Institute.

38 For an explanation, see www.epo.org/law-practice/legal-texts/html/guidelinespct/e/c_i_3.htm

39 See n. 38 for a list of competent IPEAs under the PCT (as at June 1, 2020).

40 For an explanation, see www.epo.org/applying/international/guide-for-applicants/html/e/ga_c3_2_11.html

41 See www.wipo.int/pct/en/forms/index.htm

42 An up-to-date list of Contracting States is available at www.wipo.int/export/sites/www/treaties/en/documents/pdf/pct.pdf

43 See www.wipo.int/pct/en/guide/index.html

44 In some countries, anyone may represent a patent applicant before their respective patent office. In other countries, only certain qualified professionals, e.g., patent agents or patent attorneys registered with the respective patent office, may represent applicants, particularly where the applicants resides abroad. In this manual, we use the term *patent drafter* to mean anyone entitled to represent applicants under the applicable law.

45 For explanation of the PPH, see www.wipo.int/pct/en/filing/pct_pph.html

46 See Module VIII, section 4.3, for more on the Patent Cooperation Treaty (PCT).

47 For an up-to-date summary of data coverage, see https://patentscope.wipo.int/search/en/help/data_coverage.jsf

48 More formally, the Agreement on the application of Article 65 of the Convention on the Grant of European Patents. See www.epo.org/law-practice/legal-texts/london-agreement.html